Why do adolescents kill? Can they ever be trusted to live safely in the community again? How does the experience of adult prison help or hurt them in reaching that goal? Simone Deegan takes on these tough questions in her book and has done an excellent job of shedding light on these issues.

James Garbarino, *PhD Emeritus Professor of Human Development, Cornell University*

From her meticulous case studies and exhaustive examination of the literature, Simone Deegan demonstrates why there are no real winners, neither society or the offender, nor the victim's or offender's family when juveniles are sentenced to life imprisonment for murder. During her riveting discussion of the tortuous prison adjustment problems that such juvenile offenders experience, she reveals the heart-wrenching dilemmas that both they and their parents undergo for which there does not presently exist any possible means of either one of them escaping. Deegan makes the strongest case that I am aware of for the need of reforming the juvenile justice system's treatment of violent juvenile offenders.

Lonnie Athens, *Professor of Criminal Justice, Seton Hall University*

This book is an important, timely, and much needed contribution to the literature. The author illuminates the diverse pathways that lead juveniles to kill and provides a compassionate account of these individuals and the significant others in their lives. She shines an intense spotlight on sentencing policies and correctional environments that, all too often, ignore the juvenile's immaturity and impede rehabilitation and a successful transition to society.

Kathleen M. Heide, *Distinguished University Professor, University of South Florida*

Juvenile Lifers

This book is the first Australian study, based on extensive fieldwork, of the personal backgrounds and processes by which juveniles get drawn into risky and violent situations that culminate in murder. Drawing on interviews with *every* juvenile under sanction of life imprisonment in the State of South Australia (2015–2019), it investigates links in the chain of events that led to the lethal violence that probably would have been broken had there been appropriate intervention.

Specifically, the book asks whether the existing criminal justice frame is the appropriate way to deal with children who commit grave acts. The extent to which prison facilitates and/or inhibits the mental, emotional, and social development of juvenile 'lifers' is a critical issue. Most – if not all – will be released at some point, with key issues of risk (public protection) and rehabilitation (probability of desistance) coming sharply to the fore. In addition, this book is also the first to capture how significant others, including mothers, fathers, grandparents, and siblings, are affected when children kill and the level of commitment these relatives have towards supporting the prisoner in his or her quest to build a positive future.

Written in a clear and direct style, this book will appeal to students and scholars of criminology, sociology, and penology; practitioners working in social policy; and all those interested in the lives and backgrounds of juvenile offenders.

Simone Jessica Deegan is Lecturer and Research Associate at the Flinders University Centre for Crime Policy and Research and also Principal Training Centre Advocate at the Office of the Guardian for Children and Young People. She has also worked as a criminal defence solicitor in the South Australian justice system. Her research interests include homicide, serious repeat offending, and life sentences.

Routledge Studies in Crime, Justice and the Family
Edited by Rachel Condry, The University of Oxford, UK

This series is the first series of its kind for Criminology. It offers a space to capture work on a range of topics that share the common theme of the relationship between crime, justice and the family, and aims to interrogate common-sense understandings of this relationship to explore just who is affected by crime and how they are affected, whether as victims of crime within the family, as secondary victims, or as parents, children, spouses, or other kin of offenders.

Families, Imprisonment and Legitimacy
The Cost of Custodial Penalties
Cara Jardine

Generations Through Prison
Experiences of Intergenerational Incarceration
Mark Halsey & Melissa del Vel-Palumbo

Juvenile Lifers
(Lethal) Violence, Incarceration and Rehabilitation
Simone Jessica Deegan

Juvenile Lifers

(Lethal) Violence, Incarceration and Rehabilitation

Simone Jessica Deegan

Routledge
Taylor & Francis Group
LONDON AND NEW YORK

First published 2021
by Routledge
2 Park Square, Milton Park, Abingdon, Oxon OX14 4RN

and by Routledge
52 Vanderbilt Avenue, New York, NY 10017

Routledge is an imprint of the Taylor & Francis Group, an informa business

British Library Cataloguing-in-Publication Data
A catalogue record for this book is available from the British Library

Library of Congress Cataloging-in-Publication Data
A catalog record for this book has been requested

ISBN: 978-0-367-67702-2(hbk)
ISBN: 978-1-003-13243-1 (ebk)

Typeset in Times New Roman
by Apex CoVantage, LLC

Contents

Acknowledgements

There are many people who contributed to the production of this book, and I am pleased to publicly thank them here.

This book would not have been possible without the contribution of an Australian Government Research Training Program Scholarship (Joyner Law).

The book would also not have happened without the cooperation and support of the South Australian Department for Correctional Services and the correctional institutions where the study was conducted. Particular thanks are due to Kevin Harkin, who assisted with access to prisoners in the initial stages.

To my colleagues, Professors Mark Halsey and Andrew Goldsmith, I express my gratitude for your support and valuable advice through the years this work has taken. The various opportunities you have given me are very much appreciated.

Thanks to Michael Savvas for your editing and also for your encouragement and understanding of the 'essence' of the work: know when to hold 'em and all that.

To Mark Alessandrini, I literally couldn't have done it without you. Through your own personal qualities, experience, and insight, you managed to keep my arguments on an even keel. To Elton and Evana, you remind us what it's all about.

The struggle to combine a family and an academic career is real. A special shout out to Yvonne Deegan and Dani Alessandrini for supporting me and always getting me where I needed to go. You ladies are just incredible.

To my wider family, thank you.

Natalie Diestel-Feddersen, Jan Harry, Phillip Brook, Dixie Southby, John Briggs, Howard Rigney, Stephen De Villiers, Michael O'Connell, Anton Stavreas, Belinda Lorek, Alan Fairley, Penny Wright, Rhys Aston, David Pope, Luke Broomhall, Dr Jeremy Ryder, Dr Esther Erlings, and the Flinders University Students Association (FUSA), thank you for your help along the way. The end result is much improved because of you.

My deepest gratitude, however, is reserved for the participants of this study who risked much to open their lives up to a complete stranger. To the 19 individuals who generously and graciously revisited an incredibly painful chapter of the past (and present), you have taught me much about understanding youth violence, the impact of sentencing decisions, and various prison regimes. I have tried to write this book in a way that does justice to who you are and/or who you might wish to 'become'. I dedicate this book to you.

Introduction

The lives and adjustment patterns of juvenile lifers

> *I have a question that I have been asking everyone and no-one's given me an answer for it yet. My question is this: After a man has done something horrible, after he has killed or after he's done something that he can never take back, is there anything he can ever do to make up for it? No-one's been able to give me an answer to that yet. I would really like to have an answer before I die.*
>
> Sean Sellers, executed for crimes committed at age 16 (ABC Television, 1999)

This observation captures something of the philosophical and existential crisis to envelop offenders, prison administrators, and the wider community across a life (and, indeed, death) sentence. Unfortunately, intense media coverage and social commentary relating to juvenile homicide offending have failed to translate into a sizeable body of research on how these individuals fare post-conviction. Certainly, very little is known about their adjustment to prison life and success in obtaining parole and in reintegrating into the general community (Ruddell & Gileno, 2013). Here, importantly, and I think correctly, Russell (2013, p. 498) identifies how 'judges, legislators, and the public have little sense of the actual consequences of sentencing decisions because there is no occasion to examine the circumstances of a prisoner who has spent many years behind bars'. This failure presents me with my primary objective, namely to critically examine and offer possible ways of overcoming this situation.

I do not pretend that the content of this research, 'particularly in the most violent cases where the convicted are viewed as less than human' (Russell, 2013, p. 492), will not present a troubling picture for many. Perhaps it is unrealistic to ask readers to put aside the strong feelings they may have about some of the young people in this book while assessing these offenders. Certainly, there are many questions raised when children act in violent and even gratuitously violent ways, not the least of which is how a young person could be so cruel to another human being. Accordingly, I do not suggest that we as a community should be at ease with what such children have done. We *ought* to feel very distressed and concerned. At the same time, this unease points starkly and directly to the importance of coming to terms with features of these offenders' childhoods that may explain – though not justify – their subsequent criminal actions. In this way, more effective intervention strategies can be developed for other young people who may be at risk of serious violent offending.

Beyond their deleterious social backgrounds, there is also widespread empirical recognition that the management of offenders with complex needs – particularly prisoners serving long or indeterminate sentences – is both a challenge and an area of focus for correctional agencies the world over. In South Australia, the ultimate objective of the Department for Correctional Services (DCS) is to 'improve outcomes for offenders through measures to reduce recidivism and provide for successful reintegration back into the community' (Department for Correctional Services, 2017, p. 4). Clearly, the realization of such an objective can be problematic, especially where people (such as those sentenced to life in their juvenile years) have essentially grown up in gaol. By virtue of their brain development, children (as distinct from adults) are recognized as immature, impulsive, less future-oriented, susceptible to peer pressure, prone to engage in risky behaviour, and lacking in sound decision-making skills (Ruddell & Gileno, 2013, p. 235). The extent to which prison facilitates and/or inhibits the mental, emotional, and social development of juvenile 'lifers' is a critical issue. Most – if not all – will be released at some point, with key issues of risk (public protection) and rehabilitation (probability of desistance) coming sharply to the fore. As Russell (2013, p. 492) continues, 'coming face to face with someone after he or she has served a lengthy period of time in prison might begin to make more tangible the real meaning of prison time'. Thus, this project aims to broaden understanding of the challenges faced by juveniles who are processed by the adult system for the offence of murder. While these individuals may initially serve time in a youth facility, this arrangement is destined to be (comparatively) short-lived. As Singer notes, 'juveniles are no longer juveniles by the time they serve their minimum sentences. They have graduated into adulthood while in prison. Their adult status is their current status' (Singer, 2003, p. 120).

The chief concept underpinning this research is *change*: specifically, the capacity and proclivity of young (ex-)prisoners to meaningfully attenuate the pains of imprisonment and spoiled identity that are inextricably linked to a life sentence in order to plan positively for their futures. Throughout, a major focal point is the various patterns emerging from young people taking others' lives. At issue here is how this research might connect to and impact on what is appropriate treatment for those who commit homicide or other serious crimes.

Interviews with nominated significant others (i.e. parent, grandparent, sibling, friend, teacher) will provide an appropriately calibrated realism about the circumstances associated with each young person's involvement in a serious crime. These interviews will also identify the commitment significant others have towards supporting the prisoner's quest to build a positive future and how this may fluctuate over a long or indeterminate sentence. Effects of the political dimension on the scope of penal and parole board decisions will also be discussed.

Study location

In the main, the juvenile lifers at the centre of this research were interviewed within six facilities (including one privately owned prison) for low- to high-security adult males under sentence in South Australia (Yatala Labour Prison, Mobilong Prison, Port Augusta Prison, Mount Gambier Prison, Cadell Training Centre, and the Adelaide Pre-release Centre). Two other men's prisons are located across South Australia, but no juvenile lifers were incarcerated at the Adelaide Remand Centre or Port Lincoln Prison during the study period. The sole female prisoner participant was interviewed at the Adelaide Women's Prison. In rare instances, (ex-)prisoners were interviewed in community settings across the State, as they were completing mandatory periods of 10–99 years post-release parole supervision. In demographic terms, the population of South Australia edges towards 1.7 million, with the vast majority (over 75%) residing in the capital city, Adelaide (Population Australia, 2018). As with many domestic and international prison systems, a key issue confronting the South Australian prison estate is a surge in prisoner numbers, which has, since 2004, increased by around 7% per annum (compared to just over 1% growth for the overall population of the State) (Halsey, 2015). In fact, 'between the 2013 and 2014 December quarters, South Australia recorded the largest increase in the average daily imprisonment rate, from 181 to 200 prisoners per 100 000 adult population' (ABS, 2015a). In these circumstances, it is difficult to avoid the conclusion that 'we are putting more people in prison (irrespective, say, of improvements in policing or changes in sentencing guidelines) than might "reasonably" be expected' (Halsey, 2015, para. 9). Figures from the *DCS 2013–2014Annual Report* show an average daily number of 2,409 prisoners, 35% of whom were on remand. With an approved capacity of 2,448 for all facilities, South Australia hovered dangerously close to the brink (with 98% capacity) at all material times throughout the year. For prisoners, the upshot was that 'doubling' or 'tripling-up' in cells was common practice, with DCS also managing emergency beds at the City Watch House and a number of suburban police cells to accommodate prison overflow as needed.

For South Australia, the implication beyond the numbers game extends much further than a maligned double bunk. It was recently revealed to the Budget and Finance Committee of the SA Parliament that unprecedented growth in the prisoner population saw the DCS record a $9 million budget blowout for the 2014–2015 financial year (ABC News Online, 2015). At the same time, an impressive array of literature (de Viggiani, 2007; Salins & Simpson, 2013) is dedicated to the adverse effects of overcrowding (increased risk of riots, assaults on prisoners and staff, staff burnout, etc.). Of course, even a cursory examination of available statistics indicates that juvenile (or indeed, adult) homicide offenders account for negligible fluctuations in daily admission or release figures. Of the 6,544 homicide incidents that occurred in Australia between 1989 and 2014, 6% (410) of these involved an offender aged between 10 and 17 years. This equates to an average of 23 offenders aged 10–17 years charged with homicide each year during this period (Bricknell & Bryant, as cited in Australian Institute of Criminology,

2018, p. 3). Put differently, Australian Bureau of Statistics data shows that *nationally*, only 0.5 young offenders committed homicide per 100,000 relevant population after 2008–2009, down from a peak of 2.1 per 100,000 in 1993–1994 (ABS, 2015b). However, it makes intuitive sense that life-sentence prisoners will, by virtue of their extremely long sentences, reside in adult correctional settings. Such persons, as a group, make up 14% and 17.6% of, respectively, male and female custodial numbers in South Australia (*DCS Annual Report, 2015–2016*). The vital statistic here is that, in June 2015, investment in rehabilitation accounted for only 11% of the total correctional budget spend (*DCS Annual Report, 2015–2016*). High demand means that prisoners face significant barriers to accessing prison programmes, and, with eligibility often based around earliest release date and lowest security classification, those serving life sentences for violent crimes are clearly disadvantaged. There is a certain dissonance, therefore, between the State's condemnation of each juvenile lifer as a 'monster child' – 'a damaging and inappropriate trope typically invoked by a perplexed and/or outraged public to explain away heinous offending' (Halsey & Deegan, 2014, p. 7) – and the priority ascribed to juvenile lifers' rehabilitation, development, and opportunity for successful reintegration into the community upon release from custody.

Conceptualizing adolescence

Although this study is about the adults that life-sentenced juveniles *become* from within the deep end of the criminal justice system, it is in equal measure about the children they *were* before their incarceration for murder. Terms such as *youth*, *adolescent*, *juvenile*, and *minor* are commonly and interchangeably used to describe those who have not yet achieved adult status. Despite a large body of literature on adolescent development, the American Psychological Association (2002) notes that no consensus regarding an operational definition of adolescence currently exists. For some, it is an empirical variable, expressed as a chronological age range that ends abruptly with the attainment of legal adult status at 18 years. However, the way in which this construct fails to reflect other factors such as physical, social, and cognitive development during this period (and beyond) has been subject to growing scrutiny. It is well-documented that around puberty, which typically commences by age 12 or 13, large-scale structural changes in the central nervous system support a variety of outcomes related to adrenaline flow, emotion processing, cognition, motivation, memory, forward-planning, impulse control, and the evaluation of risk and reward (see Boyer, 2006; Buchen, 2012; Dahl, 2001; Furby & Beyth-Marom, 1992; Halpern-Felsher & Cauffman, 2001; Keating, 1990; Reyna & Rivers, 2008; Siegler, 1997; Spear, 2000; Steinberg, 2013; Steinberg & Morris, 2001; Steinberg & Scott, 2003; Vinokur, 1971). At the same time, it is recognized that a key development task, the process of identity formation (Erikson, 1968), encourages young people to seek higher levels of novelty and experimentation with risky, illegal, or dangerous activities (Dahl, 2001).

The tendency to make ill-considered decisions is not necessarily synonymous with age, psychological, or biological factors. Studies of large-scale adolescent and adult cohorts clearly illustrate the weight of group processes on individual and group decisions involving risk, a phenomenon known as the *risky shift* (Vinokur, 1971; see also Gardner & Steinberg, 2005). In other words, people who are incredibly smart on their own can do some surprisingly dumb things in groups. However, during the period of adolescence, it is especially evident that reliance on the peer group is 'most intense, [with] conformity and concerns about acceptance . . . at their peak' (American Psychological Association, 2002, p. 21; see also Gatti, Tremblay, & Vitaro, 2009; Hay, Payne, & Chadwick, 2004; Steinberg, 2005).

Some researchers even draw parallels between the developing competencies of teenagers and the capabilities of high-performance vehicles without sufficient braking systems, noting that 'with powerful impulses under poor control, the likely result is a crash' (Buchen, 2012, p. 305; see also Romer & Hennessy, 2007; Steinberg, 2005, p. 70).

As Dahl (2004, p. 3) rightfully observes, difficulties in controlling behaviour and emotion are implicated in disproportionately high rates of death and disability from the period of early school age into adolescence and early adulthood – through accidents, suicide, homicide, depression, alcohol and substance abuse, violence, reckless behaviours, eating disorders, and health problems related to unsafe sexual activity. The link between age and criminal behaviour is similarly noted as 'one of the most generally accepted tenets of criminology' (Fagan & Western, 2005, p. 59) and is explored in greater detail in Section ' Trajectories of Juvenile Offending'. Fortunately, for most young people, these behaviours will be 'tentative and exploratory expressions rather than enduring representations of personhood' (Steinberg & Scott, 2003, p. 1015), with few individuals developing entrenched patterns of antisocial behaviour (Farrington, 1986; Moffitt, 1993).

To this extent, *maturational reform* (or 'ontogenic theories') is a leading explanation for crime cessation and revolves around the idea that individuals 'grow up' and desist from offending behaviour (Glueck & Glueck, 1968; Gottfredson & Hirschi, 1990; Moffit, 1993). Indeed, studies of large-scale offender cohorts routinely demonstrate the impact of aging as a distinct pathway leading away from undesirable destinations. However, increasing capabilities of neurological investigation continue to challenge long-standing assumptions about the exact timing of brain maturation (U.S. National Institute of Mental Health, 2015). In short, 'important changes in brain anatomy and activity take place far longer into development than previously thought' (Steinberg, 2013, p. 259), leading psychologists to conclude that 'there is no simple answer to when an adolescent brain becomes an adult brain' (Steinberg, 2009, pp. 743–744). Capturing the nature of adolescence has, therefore, been a somewhat easier task than attempting to define strict boundaries around it. The latter, as shall become clear in the stories presented in this book, 'involves the timely convergence of personal, social, as well as symbolic factors' (Halsey & Deegan, 2015, p. 21). However, the focus of this research is on the 19 South Australians serving sentences of life imprisonment for their involvement in crimes that occurred prior to their 18th birthdays.

Overview of chapters

The book evolves in the following way:

Chapter 1 ('Do the crime, do the time: responding to kids who kill') outlines the sentencing principles that surround the offence of murder in South Australia, as well as the social and economic consequences of incarcerating youth into adulthood from local and international perspectives. I visit the existing literature on (violent) young offenders and draw attention to the difficulties in distinguishing the impulsive and foolish actions of individuals who should know better from the 'rare juvenile offender' whose offending represents 'irreparable corruption' (*Roper v. Simmons* 543 US 551 at 560). The signature qualities of youth, I argue, orbit around a transient but no less spectacular inability to evaluate competing demands. This chapter (as well as the book more broadly) affirms the harsh, long-standing, and profound effects of a life sentence for crimes (most often) appropriately framed as tragic and aberrant events.

Chapter 2 ('Approach to the field: data') details the impetus for this study, as well as the methodologies employed for the collection and analysis of data. It also speaks to the emotional toll from conducting sensitive research, along with the idea of reciprocity between researcher and participants in the course of such endeavours.

In Chapter 3 ('Accepting the challenge: male-on-male confrontational violence'), I focus on those scenarios of lethal violence that, by their very nature, typically involve (groups of) young men. These are the cases that, to some extent, revolve around not so much what people did but concepts crucially related to awareness and foresight. Through interview excerpts, I examine the social and psychological dimensions of the mindset where young men just do not back down from fights: rather, they go headlong back into them to prove their mettle. At the same time, I raise questions about the scope and breadth of that awareness and foresight.

Chapter 4 ('Misfits, murder, and the "monster child"') provides an in-depth account of the circumstances associated with particularly heinous offending by young people. The reading is shocking, the reality is worse, and, in my experience, the central theme uniting these teenagers is the sheer misery of their daily existence. I have attempted to show a variety of circumstances inclined to promote a lack of empathy and/or a callous indifference regarding the lives of others and to situate these stories against the backdrop of a prolonged period in adult custodial facilities, further marked by the deprivation of normal love and affection.

Chapter 5 ('Making sense of murder: significant others in the lives of young homicide offenders') addresses in detail some of the personal, situational, and structural factors that characterize the lives of juveniles' nominated significant others (NSOs). Understandably, relatives remain deeply disturbed by the events surrounding the victim's death, their child's role in it, and their resulting incarceration. Here, I describe the range of pre- and post-homicide experiences extolled by each NSO whose motivation to support their young person is routinely undermined by a lack of institutional and public support.

Chapter 6 ('Killing time: life as a career prisoner') draws heavily upon the accounts of the longest-serving participants to relay how the realities of life sentences have uniquely converged and compounded the emotional and developmental difficulties that these young people suffer. Crucially, I open up some interesting lines of enquiry regarding the extent to which modern penal practices actively work against wider aims to promote the rehabilitation of 'serious' young offenders and to give them some hope and encouragement in becoming productive members of society.

In Chapter 7 ('Going straight . . . or straight back inside?'), I focus on the young people who were released on parole during the later stages of the study period. I examine in detail the factors that have underpinned (or derailed) the fledgling success of each individual: chiefly their capacity to transition from adolescent offender and 'professional' prisoner to responsible adult and law-abiding citizen.

The final chapter rounds off the discussions by drawing together the key features that stand out in these case studies and highlights a number of areas related to youth homicide that I have identified for future research. My suggestions are based on the idea that making genuine attempts to improve the social circumstances of juveniles only after they have committed a serious crime is woefully inadequate, not to mention totally offensive for victims and the community alike. Again and again, there were links in the chain of events that led to the offending that probably would have been broken had there been appropriate intervention to 'prevent the accumulation of damaging experiences and negative labeling so vividly exemplified in [the] participants' narratives' (Robinson, 2015, p. 158). The reality, of course, is that young people will, from time to time, engage in a wide array of risky behaviours leading to injury and, unfortunately, death. Failure to seriously wrestle with how to provide a regime that is therapeutic, constructive, and safe for those sentenced to life has serious implications when they are ultimately released from prison. This book aims to do just that.

References

ABC Television. (Producer) (1999). *Dead kid walking* [Television series episode]. *Dateline*. Retrieved from http://www.abc.net.au/4corners/stories/s50027.htm

Australian Bureau of Statistics (ABS). (2015a). *4512.0 corrective services, Australia, December Quarter 2014*. Retrieved from www.abs.gov.au/ausstats/abs@.nsf/mf/4512.0

Australian Bureau of Statistics (ABS). (2015b). *4519.0 recorded crime- offenders, 2013–2014*. Retrieved from www.abs.gov.au/ausstats/abs@.nsf/Lookup/by%20Subject/4519.0~2013-14~Main%20Features~Youth%20Offenders~5

American Psychological Association. (2002). *Developing adolescents: A reference for professionals*. Retrieved from www.apa.org/pi/families/resources/develop.pdf

Boyer, T. (2006). The development of risk-taking: A multi-perspective review. *Developmental Review*, *26*(3), 291–345. DOI:10.1016/j.dr.2006.05.002

Bricknell, S., & Bryant, W. (2018). *Co-offending among young homicide offenders in Australia* (Australian Institute of Criminology: Statistical Bulletin 12). Retrieved from https://aic.gov.au/publications/sb/sb12

Buchen, L. (2012). Science in court: Arrested development. *Nature*, *484*(7394), 304–306. Retrieved from www.nature.com

Dahl, R. (2001). Affect regulation, brain development, and behavioral/emotional health in adolescence. *CNS Spectrums*, *6*(1), 60–72. DOI:10.1017/S1092852900022884

Dahl, R. (2004). Adolescent Brain development: A period of vulnerabilities and opportunities. *Annals of the New York Academy of Sciences, 1021*(1), 1–22. DOI:10.1196/annals.1308.001

Department for Correctional Services SA (DCS). (2014). *Annual report 2013–2014.* Retrieved from www.corrections.sa.gov.au/_data/assets/pdf_file/0007/27979/DCS20Annual20Report202013-141.pdf

Department for Correctional Services SA (DCS). (2016). *Annual report 2015–2016.* Retrieved from www.corrections.sa.gov.au/_data/assets/pdf_file/0009/27972/AR202015-1620FINAL1/pdf

Department for Correctional Services SA (DCS). (2017). *Annual report 2016–2017.* Retrieved from www.corrections.sa.gov.au/_data/assets/pdf_file/0011/29936/2016-17-DCS-Annual-Report.pdf

de Viggiani, N. (2007). Unhealthy prisons: Exploring structural determinants of prison health. *Sociology of Health and Illness, 29*(1), 115–135. DOI:10.1111/j.1467-9566.2007.00474.x

Erikson, E. (1968). *Identity, youth and crisis*. New York: W.W. Norton.

Fagan, A. A., & Western, J. (2005). Escalation and deceleration of offending behaviours from adolescence to early adulthood. *Australian and New Zealand Journal of Criminology, 38*(1), 59–76. DOI:10.1375/acri.38.1.59

Farrington, D. P. (1986). Age and crime. *Crime and Justice: An Annual Review of Research, 7*, 189–250. DOI:10.1086/449114

Furby, L., & Beyth-Marom, R. (1992). Risk-taking in adolescence: A decision-making perspective. *Developmental Review, 12*(1), 1–44. DOI:10.1016/0273-2297(92)90002-J

Gardner, M., & Steinberg, L. (2005). Peer influence on risk taking, risk preference, and risky decision making in adolescence and adulthood: An experimental study. *Developmental Psychology, 41*(4), 625–635. DOI:10.1037/0012-1649.41.4.625

Gatti, U., Tremblay, R., & Vitaro, F. (2009). Latrogenic effect of juvenile justice. *Journal of Child Psychology and Psychiatry, 50*(8), 991–998. DOI:10.1111/j.1469- 7610.2008.02057.x

Glueck, S., & Glueck, E. (1968). *Delinquents and nondelinquents in perspective*. Cambridge, MA: Harvard University Press.

Gottfredson, M. R., & Hirschi, T. (1990). *A general theory of crime*. Stanford: Stanford University Press.

Halpern-Felsher, B., & Cauffman, E. (2001). Costs and benefits of a decision: Decision-making competence in adolescents and adults. *Journal of Applied Developmental Psychology, 22*(3), 257–273. DOI:10.1016/S0193-3973(01)00083-1

Halsey, M. (2015, April 14). State of imprisonment: South Australia's prisoner numbers soar, with just 10% of budget for rehab. *The Conversation*. Retrieved from http://theconversation.com/state-of-imprisonment-south-australias-prisoner-numbers-soar-with-just-10-of-budget-for-rehab-38906

Halsey, M., & Deegan, S. (2014). "Picking up the pieces": Female significant others in the lives of young (ex) incarcerated males. *Criminology and Criminal Justice*. Retrieved from http://crj.sagepub.com/content/early/2014/03/12/1748895814526725.ref.html. DOI:10.1177/1748895814526725

Halsey, M., & Deegan, S. (2015). *Young offenders: Crime, prison and struggles for desistance*. London: Palgrave Macmillan.

Hay, D., Payne, A., & Chadwick, A. (2004). Peer relations in childhood. *Journal of Child Psychology and Psychiatry, 45*(1), 84–108. DOI:10.1046/j.0021-9630.2003.00308.x

Keating, D. (1990). Adolescent thinking. In S. S. Feldman & G. R. Elliot (Eds.), *At the threshold: The developing adolescent* (pp. 54–89). Cambridge, MA: Harvard University Press.

Moffitt, T. (1993). Adolescence-limited and life-course persistent antisocial behaviour: A developmental taxonomy. *Psychological Review, 100*(4), 674–701. DOI:10.1037/0033-295X.100.4.674

National Institute of Mental Health, U.S. Department of Health and Human Services. (2015). *The teen brain: Still under construction.* Retrieved from www.nimh.nih.gov/health/publications/the-teen-brain-still-under-construction/index.shtml

Population Australia. (2018). *Adelaide.* Retrieved from www.population.net.au/adelaide-population Prison overcrowding causes SA budget blowout for Correctional Services. (2015, May 18). *ABC News Online.* Retrieved from www.abc.net.au/news/2015-05-18/prisons-overcrowding-budget-blowout-correctional-services/6477572

Reyna, V., & Rivers, S. (2008). Current theories of risk and rational decision making. *Developmental Review, 28*(1), 1–11. DOI:10.1016/j.dr.2008.01.002

Robinson, A. (2015). Young offenders: Crime, prison and struggles for desistance review (book review). *British Journal of Community Justice, 13*(2), 157–158.

Romer, D., & Hennessy, M. (2007). A biosocial-affect model of adolescent sensation seeking: The role of affect evaluation and peer-group influence in adolescent drug use. *Prevention Science, 8*(2), 89–101. DOI:10.1007/S11121-007-0064-7

Roper v Simmons, 543 U.S. 551 (2005). Retrieved from www.courts.ca.gov/documents/BTB_23_THURSDAY_LUNCH_PLENARY_3.pdf

Ruddell, R., & Gileno, J. (2013). Lifers admitted as juveniles in the Canadian prison population. *Youth Justice, 13*(3), 234–248. DOI:10.1177/1473225413505386

Russell, S. (2013). A "second look" at lifetime incarceration: Narratives of rehabilitation and Juvenile offenders. *Quinnipiac Law Review, 31*(3), 489–521. Retrieved from www.quinnipiaclawjournals.com/quinnipiac-law-review.html

Salins, L., & Simpson, S. (2013). Efforts to fix a broken system: Brown v. Plata and the prison overcrowding epidemic. *Loyola University Chicago Law Journal, 44*(4), 1153–1200. Retrieved from http://lawcommons.luc.edu/luclj/vol44/iss4/6

Siegler, R. S. (1997). *Emerging minds: The process of change in children's thinking.* New York: Oxford University Press.

Singer, S. (2003). Incarcerating juveniles into adulthood: Organizational fields of knowledge and the back end of waiver. *Youth Violence and Juvenile Justice, 1*(2), 115–127. DOI:10.1177/1541204002250871

Spear, P. (2000). The adolescent brain and age-related behavioral manifestations. *Neuroscience and Biobehavioural Reviews, 24*(4), 417–463. DOI:10.1016/S0149-7634(00)00014-2

Steinberg, L. (2005). Cognitive and affective development in adolescence. *Trends in Cognitive Sciences, 9*(2), 69–74. DOI:10.1016/J.TICS.2004.12.005

Steinberg, L. (2009). Should the science of adolescent brain development inform public policy? *American Psychologist, 64*(8), 739–750. DOI:10.1037/a0016610

Steinberg, L. (2013). Does recent research on adolescent brain development inform the mature minor doctrine? *The Journal of Medicine and Philosophy of Medicine, 38*(3), 256–267. DOI:10.1093/jmp/jht017

Steinberg, L., & Morris, A. (2001). Adolescent development. *Annual Review of Psychology, 52*, 83–110. DOI:10.1891/194589501787383444

Steinberg, L., & Scott, E. S. (2003). Less guilty by reason of adolescence: Developmental immaturity, diminished responsibility and the juvenile death penalty. *American Psychologist, 58*(12), 1009–1018. DOI:10.1037/0003-066X.58.12.1009

Vinokur, A. (1971). Review and theoretical analysis of the effects of group processes upon individual and group decisions involving risk. *Psychological Bulletin, 76*(4), 231–250. DOI:10.1037/h0031568

1 Do the crime, do the time

Responding to kids who kill

Young people can do terrible things. Indeed, from October 2010 to January 2011, five South Australians were killed by juveniles in a series of 'ghastly and senseless knife attacks' which 'elicited months of media coverage and soul-searching' (Guilliatt, 2013). In the case of *R v. Omonte-Extrada* (2013, No. SCCRM-13–263), the Honourable Justice Kelly remarked that 'it is a disturbing fact that in the past five years some of the most callous and brutal murders committed in this State have been committed by teenagers'. She went on to find that, by his actions, Mr Omonte-Extrada, 19, had 'most surely included himself in that group'. The cases to which Justice Kelly refers are notable not only for their extreme violence but for reigniting intense public debate about what should be done with the State's most notorious young offenders. In these moments, we are reminded of CCTV footage from the UK showing two 10-year-old boys leading 2-year-old James Bulger to a death so violent that it left indelible marks on the psyche of an entire nation (Young, 1996).

Courtrooms, in particular, are recognized as a 'haven for extreme emotional turbulence' (Halsey & Deegan, 2015, p. 9; see also Freiberg, 2001). In the Bulger case, near riot scenes erupted outside the court, as Robert Thompson and Jon Venables appeared as the youngest murder accused of the twentieth century. As May (2000, p. 205) observes, 'to be a murderer obliterated all other dimensions of the person; all that was left was an evil master status'. At this juncture, irreconcilable conflict between states of childhood and adulthood impress most heavily. As an explanatory construct, *distancing* 'normal' or 'regular' juveniles from homicide offenders allows cherished views about the innocence and immaturity of childhood to be maintained (see Applegate & Davis, 2006; Steinberg & Schwartz, 2000). Accordingly, accepting the homicide offender as a psychopath 'whose behavior has the added edge of unpredictability' (Loeber & Farrington, 2011, p. 21) is an easier pill to swallow than the anomalous act committed by a normal child. Under these circumstances, labels such as *super-predators* are 'meant to suggest that we share no shred of humanity with these youth and to justify our simple punitive response' (Merlo, 2000, p. 642). Such was the animosity directed at Thompson and Venables that *The Daily Star* newspaper (25 November 1993) headline accompanying photographs of their smiling faces read, 'How do you feel now, you little bastards?', as each boy was sentenced to life imprisonment with a minimum term of eight years (McNutt, 2010). Upon release, each offender was granted a new identity out of (seemingly well-placed) fears for their personal safety. It has taken considerable time to reconcile the horror of this killing with the youth and apparent ordinariness of the two boys. I suspect that we will never truly arrive at a satisfactory explanation for how things could go so catastrophically off-course. Fortunately, very few juveniles (comparatively speaking) end up taking another person's life. Fewer still can lay claim to orchestrating a crime so immense that it continues to capture public imagination decades after its commission. Nevertheless, juvenile homicide remains a stable fixture on snapshot data from across the world. In more pointed fashion, the Bulger case gets to the heart of how we approach the notion of justice for serious young offenders in regard to philosophy, policy, and practice.

In his article, 'When children kill children: the search for justice', Asquith (1996, p. 104) implores that 'a balance has to be struck somehow in achieving justice for the death of [the victim] . . . and with the justice of the treatment meted out to the children who committed the murder'. It makes sense then to propose that 'while conventional views of murder hold the individual as the locus of the act [more useful approaches] implicate the wider social system as important in considering any understanding of the act' (Lennings, unpublished, p. 8). If so, this would, at minimum, 'mean thinking about social obligation as well as individual responsibility' (Halsey & Deegan, 2015, p. 2). If the combination of personal and social factors underpinning normative childhood development is reasonably clear (secure attachment to parents; engagement in prosocial networks; positive experience of school; limited exposure to violence, firearms, and substance abuse in the home and community; physical and mental health; appropriate strategies to manage anger and conflict; etc.), the actual convergence of any or all of these elements in the lives of juvenile homicide offenders is less common than it should be.

Unsurprisingly, young children and adolescents who kill frequently share 'a constellation of psychological, cognitive, neuropsychiatric, educational, and family system disturbances' (Myers, 1992, p. 47). Put simply, these individuals are often victims *before* they are offenders. Some have appalling personal backgrounds, marked by physical and/or sexual abuse and/or chronically inconsistent or indifferent parenting. Others have crafted aggressive or 'gangsta' identities out of a misplaced sense of juvenile bravado 'due to the presence of extreme environmental stressors [that seem] unlikely to be repeated regardless of sentence or treatment' (Bailey, 1996, p. 35). This is to say nothing of the scenarios that arise when incarceration comes at a critical time in juveniles' maturation; in many ways, such timing augments and reinforces the problems that have produced the admission to the setting in the first place. Each of these circumstances will be plain from the juveniles' accounts in the current research. And each life discussed will highlight just how difficult it is to successfully balance rehabilitation and ongoing personal development against the realities of growing up in prison with little, if any, assistance from a wider prosocial network of parents, teachers, employers, and the like. If these arguments are accepted, the evidence in this book justifies a second look at whether the criminal justice frame is the most appropriate way to deal with children who commit grave acts. I should make it clear that I am not advocating for nothing to be done regarding the child who kills. But, as will become apparent, a child welfare approach with a focus on treatment, monitoring, and reintegration is where the rubber of empathy and forgiveness meets the road of rehabilitation. In this, our criminal justice policy in South Australia can claim no great success.

Inevitably, many will ask why we should continue to care about those who show such disregard – even contempt – for the lives of others. To this end, Green (2008) observes how those who try to understand children who kill are often perceived as condoning their violence, thereby 'not only dishonoring victims in the process but also displaying intolerable weakness in the face of moral crisis' (p. 202). To respond to these concerns, we must first understand the factors relating to the creation of serious and violent young offenders – particularly those convicted of murder. In addition, and perhaps more than any other juvenile justice population, the nexus between competing sentencing considerations and the potential impacts on post-release outcomes for juvenile lifers also needs explication. As I have argued previously, 'unless we know of and account for these subtle differences, we risk misunderstanding how each person could, or otherwise would' ultimately emerge from institutional settings (Halsey & Deegan, 2015, p. 18).

(Juvenile) life sentences in South Australia

A good place to start looking at how prison impacts on the mental, emotional, and social development of young people serving long sentences is within the sentencing principles that surround the crime of murder. Intentionally and unlawfully taking the life of another person is acknowledged as the most serious offence in the criminal calendar. Not only is the victim robbed of a future, profound trauma and suffering are also inflicted upon the family and friends the victim leaves behind. Victim impact statements tendered to the court at sentence graphically set out the consequences of murder and make for highly emotional reading. In each case, the sense of grief and loss is all too clear and is almost impossible to put into words. Not surprisingly, the impact on the community is also considerable. In line with this, the Supreme Court remarked as follows in the 2013 case of *R v. Ormonte-Extrada* (No. SSCRM-13–263: 8):

> [T]here is a need for this court to recognise the longstanding obligation of the State to vindicate the dignity of each victim of violence, to express the community's disapproval of that offending and to afford such protection as can be afforded by the State to the vulnerable against the repetition of violence.

As such, regardless of an offender's age at the relevant time, there is only one penalty for the crime of murder in South Australia and that is imprisonment for life (see *Criminal Law Consolidation Act*, 1935 [SA] s11; *Criminal Law [Sentencing] Act* 1988 [SA] s5(ab); *Young Offenders Act*, 1993 [SA] s29(4)(a)(b)). In addition to a mandatory life term (the 'head sentence'), a sentencing judge must also fix a non-parole period (NPP), which is the minimum period of time an offender will be kept in custody before being eligible for release back into the community. It is only in extremely rare cases, where it is evident that a person is unlikely to respond to parole in a positive way or that the offending and circumstances surrounding the case are of such gravity, that a court will determine that a person should not be released and decline to set an NPP (see s47(5)(e) *Sentencing Act* [SA] 2017). Generally speaking, however, adjudicating an NPP requires the court to maintain a fair balance between punishment and deterrence on the one hand and between punishment and rehabilitation on the other. However, in this State at least, Parliament has determined that for adults, the mandatory minimum NPP for murder is 20 years' imprisonment (see s47(5)(b) *Sentencing Act* [SA] 2017, formerly s32A(5) *Criminal Law [Sentencing] Act* [SA] 1988). This represents a baseline for offending categorized as at the lower end of objective seriousness for a crime of murder. Under s48(3) of the *Act*, limited scope exists for the court to depart from the mandatory minimum NPP if satisfied that 'special reasons' exist (i.e. if the offence was committed in circumstances in which the victim's conduct substantially mitigated the offender's conduct, and/or in light of the circumstances/consequences of their guilty plea and cooperation with the police investigation). However, the gravity of the offence of murder will generally render the mandatory minimum sentence inevitable in order to achieve the objects prescribed by statute.

Prior to 12 December 2017, if a person under the age of 18 was found guilty of murder, the purpose of sentencing was 'to seek to secure such care, correction and guidance as is necessary for the development of that youth into a responsible and useful member of the community and to have regard to the proper realisation of that youth's potential' (*Young Offenders Act* [SA] 1993, s3(1)). Judges were therefore obliged to craft an NPP with the assumption that the youth had potential for rehabilitation that could be realized despite the fact that he or she was to be sentenced as an adult. Put differently, retribution had a lesser place in the sentencing of young offenders. At the same time, the community was entitled to protection against the violent conduct or wrongful acts in which the youth had engaged (s3(2a)(b)(ii)(A)). In these cases, the Supreme Court often said that when judges are ordering a penalty for a youth being punished as an adult, the gravity of the offending, the safety of the community, and the need to deter the individual and other like-minded youths from similar conduct could, and should, be afforded considerable weight. Sometimes, the result was irreconcilable conflict between the various considerations a judge was required to take into account. Nevertheless, the *Young Offenders Act* made it clear that justice must be tempered with mercy, so as to leave scope for young offenders to re-establish themselves and make a new life after their release (s3(2a)(ii)(B)). This approach appeared to endorse a view of the adolescent brain as 'plastic and open to influence by experience' (Posner & Rothbart, 2000, p. 428).

However, following two fatal hit-and-run accidents committed by youths driving dangerously (i.e. 'hoon' driving) on our roads in 2016 and 2017, respectively, the Statues Amendment (Youths Sentenced as Adults) Bill 2017 was passed on 12 December 2017 (see the *Statutes Amendment [Youths Sentenced as Adults]*

Act 2017). The new formulation removed the requirement (under s3(2a)(b)(ii) of the *Young Offenders Act*, 1993) to achieve *balance* between (A) the protection of the community and (B) the need to rehabilitate the youth, by making community safety the 'paramount' sentencing consideration (see s3(2a)(c)). The Attorney-General spoke to Section 3(1) of the *Young Offenders Act*, 1993 when announcing the amendments, observing that the rationale behind this reform would be

> to displace the principle that primacy is to be given to the object of the Act and the statutory principles, and to rehabilitation, when sentencing a youth who is being dealt with as an adult. Rather, the paramount consideration of the court when determining sentence for a youth who is being dealt with as an adult must be to protect the safety of the community. The amendment provides that the paramount consideration outweighs any other consideration, object or statutory principle, including the need to rehabilitate the youth.
>
> (Parliament of South Australia, House of Assembly, July 5 2017, p. 10435, John Rau, Attorney-General)

The Attorney-General also remarked the following in his second reading speech:

> [R]egard must also be had to the deterrent effect any proposed sanction may have on other youths. The new provision also outweighs the usual statutory object in sentencing young offenders to 'secure for youths who offend against the criminal law the care, correction and guidance necessary for their development into responsible and useful members of the community and the proper realisation of their potential'.
>
> (Parliament of South Australia, House of Assembly, July 5 2017, p. 10434, John Rau, Attorney-General)

Given that murder committed by young people is a rare event, as at the study period, no youth has yet come before the court for sentence under the new Act. However, the upshot for young people found guilty of murder *after* 12 December 2017 is that they *will* be dealt with as if they are adults (s29(4)(a)(b) *Young Offenders Act* [SA] 1993). To that end, they will be subject to the imposition of the same 20-year mandatory minimum NPP regardless of whether their involvement resides at the more moderate end of seriousness. An interesting comment by the Guardian for Children and Young People and Training Centre Visitor, Penny Wright, was noted in the South Australian media. Wright said that the Bill 'flies against everything we know about young people and their behaviour' and ignores rights protected by the United Nations *Convention on the Rights of the Child* (especially Article 3) and other instruments that Australia has signed (Wright, 2017, para. 3). To set the context, as Wright emphasized in her response to the Bill, we have to understand two things. The first is as follows:

> [H]arsher sanctions will apply more to offenders from social groups that carry the weight of current and historic as well as personal disadvantage and

> therefore may become more engaged in the youth justice system. Young people from Aboriginal and Torres Strait Islander communities and those who have been or are under the guardianship of the Minister are notable here, as are those suffering from the impact of trauma or experiencing various psychosocial difficulties.
>
> (Guardian for Children and Young People, 2017, p. 7)

The second thing that should be understood is that

> [the Bill] incorrectly assumes that the offender is the sole beneficiary of rehabilitation (whereas the community clearly stands to benefit equally where young offenders have the opportunity to learn, mature and grow into constructive members of society) and discards the need to balance factors such as developmental (im)maturity with the gravity of an offence.
>
> (Guardian for Children and Young People, 2017, p. 7)

Economics of a life sentence

Beyond the fact that murder is an irreversible and particularly frightening crime, there are other good reasons to be intensely interested in juveniles who commit this offence. The best reason, of course, is to help preserve human life and prevent the immense cycles of grief, hardship, and trauma that are inextricably linked to a violent and premature death. But it is not only the deceased and their families who will suffer and who are the victims of murder. Those killed by juveniles often belong (whether intentionally or co-incidentally) to a category of vulnerable persons, including the very old, the very young, defenceless women, other teenagers, or those providing a valuable service to the general population (i.e. those making house calls or 'good Samaritans' attempting to intervene in a dispute in which they have no stake). The circumstances of each of the deaths in this book speak volumes as to the vulnerable nature of many people killed by juveniles.

The way other vulnerable individuals function in the aftermath of a murder is forever altered. So too are the lives of individuals who witness the event or attend the scene. In a real sense, the community is a victim of the crime. But as Halsey and Deegan (2015, p. 16) contend, there is another reason to be concerned with serious young offenders, 'and it is one that avoids tedious debate around whether [they] "deserve" a second . . . chance to "make good"'. Sensing the signs of high-risk youth and positively intervening in the latter's lives *before* they commit a serious violent crime is important because it makes economic sense. As previously mentioned, the *Young Offenders Act*, 1993 (SA) holds juvenile offenders responsible for their actions so that like-minded young people receive a strong message about the costs of crime and to protect the community and the individual members of it from further violent behaviour or wrongful acts (see also Bennett, DiIulio, & Walters, 1996). In most cases, this calls for a longer rather than shorter NPP. In the current research, the median NPP for all participants was 12 years and 6 months, with the longest sentence being 20 years. As highlighted, recent changes to legislation will only compound the punitive impact of s29(4) of the *Young Offenders Act*, 1993, ensuring much longer sentences for future youth found guilty of murder. Irrespective of these changes, however, many life sentence juveniles serve well in excess of their minimum tariff before any indication of making parole. As Justice Nyland stressed to the youth in *R v. T, J* (SCCRM-11–175), release on parole at the expiration of an NPP for murder 'will not be automatic. . . . Your release, and the conditions of such release, will very much depend on how you behave and respond to treatment while you are in custody.' But perhaps even this explanation is unduly optimistic. In reality, South Australian prisoners convicted of murder (as at 2014) could 'expect to spend more time in prison than anywhere else in the country', with 'the average time spent in jail from arrest to release [being] 21.6 years' (Keller, 2014, para. 20). This is mostly due to an ideological shift dominated by a 'get tough' approach to crime and criminal offenders seen over the past few decades in South Australia.

While the electorate may have varying interpretations of justice and accountability, the political value of proper punishment as a key campaign promise leads some to observe that the criminal justice system is 'beholden to all manner of political forces and is always one step away from being judged in the court of public opinion about how it manages the "dangerous" among us' (Halsey & Deegan, 2015, p. 189). Indeed, from 2005 to 2016, the ultimate power to grant parole to life-sentence prisoners resided with the Governor in Executive Council, as opposed to the South Australian Parole Board. This arrangement has been widely criticized as politicizing the parole process. From January 2014 to June 2015, 10 out of 14 life-sentence prisoners that the Parole Board had recommended for release were denied by Cabinet, while another 15 lifers were also eligible for parole. No reasons were given (Donnellan, 2015, para. 7). In fact, during the research period, ten juvenile lifer participants had served over their NPP by two to seven years despite receiving endorsement by the Board for parole.

Of course, it goes without saying that managing prisoners is a very expensive business. This point is made forcefully by a recent news report detailing the immense cost of incarcerating the five men who had brutally gang-raped and murdered Sydney nurse Anita Cobby in 1987:

> It costs $108, 000 a year to house a maximum security prisoner. According to research from 7 News, over 32 years and adjusted to CPI, the Cobby killers have cost NSW taxpayers $17.28 million. That is about the same as if they had stayed in a five-star hotel for 30 years.
>
> (Graham, 2018, para. 7–8)

In the context of a 12.5-year NPP, this equates to a cost of around A$1.4 million for each juvenile convicted of murder in South Australia (or a combined cost of around A$26 million for the entire cohort of this study). However, the true costs associated with the offending of the young men and women in this study are likely to be much higher in light of the significant police investigations, prosecution/court costs, compensation of victims, and indefinite periods of community-based parole supervision to which lifers are subject following their release from custody.

Statistics often tend to become more alarming through the lens of the US homicide experience. Recent examinations suggest that while 'homicide offending by juveniles is relatively rare, approximately 7–8% of all murders between 2010 and 2014 in the United States involved a juvenile perpetrator' (Baglivio & Wolff, 2017, p. 197). Across the United States in 2016, 10 offenders aged 9–12, 374 offenders aged 13–16, and another 1,413 aged 17–19 committed murder (Statista, Crime and Law Enforcement). Accordingly, homicide remains the third leading cause of death for young people aged 10–24 years and is the leading cause of death for African American youth (National Center for Injury Prevention and Control, Division of Violence Prevention, 2016). As Baglivio and Wolff (2017, p. 197) argue, 'the "all in" average cost to society of a single murder is estimated to exceed $17 million'. Indeed, an earlier study found that the average murderer 'posed costs approaching $24 million' and that 'the most violent and prolific offenders singly produced costs greater than $150–160 million in terms of victim costs, criminal justice costs, lost offender productivity, and public willingness-to-pay costs' (DeLisi et al., 2010, p. 501).

Trajectories of juvenile offending

As mentioned, a disproportionately strong relationship exists between age and illegal activity. Certainly, the age–crime curve supports the observation that crime (and street violence in particular) is a 'young person's game' (McNeill & Maruna, 2008, p. 227), with offender rates 'consistently highest among persons aged 15 to 19 years and lowest among those aged 25 and over' (Richards, 2011, p. 2; see also Blumstein & Cohen, 1987; Fagan & Western, 2005; Farrington, 1986; Hirschi & Gottfredson, 1983; Moffitt, 1993). Taken together, juveniles' situational (un)awareness, susceptibility to peer influence, perception of and attitude towards risk, short-term future orientation, and impulsivity demonstrably increase their risk of contact with the criminal justice system. In the case of 'normal' mature individuals, there is an understanding of an act but with an ability to view and appreciate other factors: 'If I do this, how is it going to impact on the victim, his/her family, my family?'

Due to the difficulties elaborated previously, many youthful offenders are unable to see, evaluate, or appreciate that element of empathy during critical moments. It is overruled by their single-minded determination to undertake the task that they have committed themselves to do. Similarly, Zimring (2000) casts doubt on the cognitive capabilities of youthful offenders to comprehend the morality of rules or to apply the social controls necessary to avoid punishment. It has also been argued that juveniles, as legal minors, 'have limited control over their own environment and lack the ability to extricate themselves from horrific, crime-producing settings' (*Miller v Alabama*, 2012, 132 S. Ct at 2464). Consistent with juveniles' youth and inexperience, the crimes juveniles commit tend to be episodic, unplanned, and opportunistic (Cunneen & White, 2007). It comes as little surprise then that theft, offences against public order, and acts likely to cause harm (e.g. assaults) hold steady as the principal offences committed by juveniles (ABS, 2015). A good many of these individuals will be diverted from formal court processes and have no further contact with the criminal justice system. In the case of murder, it becomes all the more unfortunate when a juvenile appears for sentence as a first-time offender. The correspondence between a moment of madness and a lifetime of regret is especially salient for the young people who make up the vast majority of the juvenile lifer population. These are the stories of teenagers who portray themselves and are portrayed by others (post-sentencing) as the freaks, the rebellious, and the dispossessed, but who were rarely thought of as dangerous prior to their crime. We know that a lot of marginal adolescents engage in types of behaviour that are, in some respects at least, capable of causing death or serious harm, even if they do not actually end up taking a life. Central to this book is the notion that what separates many violent boys from their counterparts serving life is that, 'legally, there is a world of difference between violent assaults that end in death and violent assaults that fail to produce a dead body' (Garbarino, 2000, p. 25).

Teen killers: a review of the literature

In spite of sustained scholarly and popular interest in juvenile-led homicide, knowledge regarding this particular population is still relatively limited. Certainly, the visibility of Australian juveniles in the context of murder offending, long-term imprisonment, and post-release support remains low (but see Carcach, 1997; Lennings, 2002, 2004; Wekinson, 1995). The experiences of juvenile murderers' significant others (parents, siblings, grandparents, partners, and the like) in the aftermath of this most serious violent crime also form an important yet under-researched dimension of the Australian criminal justice landscape. Instead, and somewhat predictably, the overwhelming majority of research on juvenile homicide offending is situated in the United States. Without doubt, a host of factors, irrespective of geographic and demographic variables, are recognized as motivating young people to engage in lethal violence. A key aim of this research is to explicate some of these factors. However, Australia also evinces some stark disparities from the United States in relation to urbanization, gang culture, and gun control policies, which are all commonly implicated in homicide rates and characteristics (see also Cubbin, Pickle, & Fingerhut, 2000; Sloan et al., 1988; Weisheit & Wells, 2005; Woodworth, Agar, & Coupland, 2013). To this extent, some international researchers question the generalizability of US research findings (Woodworth et al., 2013). Indeed, clinical and forensic psychologist Dr Christopher Lennings (2002) confirms the need to establish local portraits of juvenile homicide offenders for greater utility within the Australian context.

Nevertheless, the merits of US data as a source of direction and comparison for other countries investigating youth-perpetrated homicide are difficult to deny. As such, there is no reason to automatically discount any of the following perspectives as possible explanations for juvenile homicide offending. In a sense, this book tests elements from the international literature and supports previous observations that the involvement of Australian youth in homicide is, among other factors, the result of lifestyle and routine activity patterns (Carcach, 1997; Cohen &

Felson, 1979). Certainly, it is difficult to find fault with the conclusion 'that most criminal acts require the convergence in space and time of likely offenders, suitable targets and the absence of capable guardians against crime' (Cohen & Felson, 1979, p. 589). The reality, of course, remains that the pains of imprisonment (Sykes, 1999 [1958]), particularly those concomitant on a life sentence, and the 'burdens of caring for prisoners from the outside' (Codd, 2007, p. 260) are a universal experience.

Antecedents of juvenile murder

Responding to the incidence of lethal youth violence, Garbarino and Haslam (2005, p. 448) pose the visceral question, 'What is the cause for this tragedy?' Their response was as follows:

> There's no cause, there's only an accumulation of risk. . . . [I]t's as if a boy is building a tower of blocks, block after block and finally puts one more block on the tower and it falls over. You can't really say that the last block was the cause of the fall because if that block was there by itself, it wouldn't fall over.

Perhaps this type of explanation, which suggests that if juveniles have enough risk factors, they are 'doomed to deviance' (Maruna, 2001), overlooks complex and specific circumstances that combine to create a 'perfect storm' of never-to-be-repeated violence in some juvenile homicide cases involving 'normal' or 'typical' teenagers. For example, Steinberg and Scott (2003, p. 1014) find that 'because of their developmental immaturity, normative (i.e. 'ordinary') adolescents may respond adversely to external pressures that adults are able to resist', provoking a particularly impulsive, aggressive response under duress. In fact, very few juvenile (or indeed, adult) murderers reoffend by committing another homicide when they return, presumably, to the same (impoverished) families and communities (Broadhurst, Maller, Maller, & Bouhours, 2018; Eronen, Hakola, & Tiihonen, 1996; Hagan, 1997; Liem, Zahn, & Tichavsky, 2014; Trulson, Caudill, Haerle, & DeLisi, 2012). Some large-scale studies have even found that homicide offenders, collectively, exhibit the lowest re-arrest rate of any violent offender group (Langan & Levin, 2002; Sheppard, 1971). Of course, not all juveniles who commit murder are raised in violent or aversive families (Langevin, Paitich, Orchard, Handy, & Russon, 1983) or exhibit warning signs or symptoms of impending disaster (Adams, 1974). By the same token, many individuals who tick all the right boxes in terms of predicted dangerousness never go on to engage in violent criminal acts, giving rise to stereotyping and potential injustices (Athens, 1997, p. 5; Farrington, 1997; Huizinga, Loeber, Thornberry, & Cothern, 2000; Loeber et al., 2005; Loeber & Farrington, 2011; Malmquist, 1971). As Athens (1985, p. 428) rightly points out, possessing 'low stakes' in the conventional world is not enough to foreshadow violent behaviour; otherwise, 'there would probably be very few persons with low stakes alive, since they would soon annihilate each other'.

Nevertheless, it is impossible to deny the merits of the view that an 'accumulation of risk' (as opposed to an 'accumulation of opportunity' or 'assets') (Garbarino & Haslam, 2005; see also Loeber et al., 2005; Loeber & Farrington, 2011; Muftić & Moreno, 2010) plays a critical role in setting youth on a path to serious violent crime. Just *how* serious may be influenced by factors including the availability of a firearm (Bingenheimer, Brennan, & Earls, 2005; Blumstein, 1995; Cook & Moore, 1999; Cornell, 1993; Fagan & Wilkinson, 1998; Fox, 1996; Hagan & Foster, 2001; Heide, 1999; Webster & Wilson, 1994; Zimring, 1998, 2005); the marksmanship of the perpetrator and timeliness of medical response (Block, 1977); the number of offenders involved (Fiddes, 1981, p. 52; Shumaker & McKee, 2001); the presence of an audience (Luckenbill, 1977; Polk, 1994, 1999; Felson & Steadman, 1983); alcohol and/or drug intoxication levels (Corder, Ball, Haizlip, Rollins, & Beaumont, 1976; Cornell, Benedek, & Benedek, 1987a; DiCataldo & Everett, 2008; Dolan & Smith, 2001; Labelle, Bradford, Bourget, Jones, & Carmichael, 1991; Myers, Scott, Burgess, & Burgess, 1995); or gang status (Block & Block, 1993; Busch, Zagar, Hughes, Arbit, & Bussell, 1990; Darby, Allan, Kashani, Hartke, & Reid, 1998; Ewing, 1990; Rogers, 1993; Trulson et al., 2012). Factors that do not tend to feature prominently in juvenile homicide offending, however, include psychosis (American Psychiatric Association, 1994; Busch et al., 1990; Zagar, Arbit, Sylvies, Busch, & Hughes, 1990) or mental retardation (Heide, 2003). In short, the degree of separation between an aggravated assault, an assault causing actual serious harm with intent, an attempted murder, and a completed murder can be frightfully narrow. For instance, as Wolfgang (1958) puts it, 'quick communication, rapid transportation, and medical technological advances . . . may mean that many cases of physical assault are kept in the column of aggravated assault statistics and are thereby prevented from being listed as criminal homicide' (p. 119). Certainly, we know that a great number of killings commissioned by young people occur in the course of another major indictable or 'felony' offence such as rape, robbery, arson, and so on (Cornell, 1990; Cornell, Benedek, & Benedek, 1987b, 1989; Darby et al., 1998; Irwin, 2009; Myers et al., 1995). In one influential study on youth homicide, the number of youths involved in a criminal enterprise that resulted in the victim's death was as high as 51% (Cornell et al., 1987b, 1989). The remaining deaths were found to occur in the context of interpersonal tension, such as an argument or a dispute with the victim (42%), and, to a much lesser extent, where the juvenile offender suffered symptoms of severe mental illness, including hallucinations and delusions (7%). Not surprisingly, psychotic killers have been observed with 'lower levels of criminal history but higher levels of psychiatric referral prior to the murder' (Lennings, unpublished, p. 7).

Against this backdrop, it seems no mere coincidence that striking similarities appear in the personal circumstances of juvenile homicide offenders and those young offenders who have committed serious, but not lethal, acts of violence (DeLisi, Piquero, & Cardwell, 2016; DiCataldo & Everett, 2008; Farrington, Loeber, & Berg, 2012; Lewis et al., 1988; Shumaker & McKee, 2001; Toupin & Morissette, 1990; Zagar, Grove, Busch, Hughes, & Arbit, 2009). Indeed, DiCataldo and Everett (2008) found that non-homicidal, violent youth can actually present *more* problematic profiles in terms of family history, delinquency history, mental health, and other developmental factors than their homicidal counterparts. With few notable exceptions, a collection of features routinely differentiates serious violent youth from their non-violent peers. These features include the violent youths' criminally violent family members (Busch et al., 1990; Cornell, 1990; Heide, 1992; Hill-Smith, Hugo, Hughes, Fonagy, & Hartman, 2002; Lewis et al., 1988; Lewis, 1992); familial abuse and neglect, 'including rejection and discontinuity of care' (Hardwick & Rowton-Lee, 1996, p. 265; see also Corder et al., 1976; Cornell et al., 1989; Ewing, 1990; Lewis et al., 1985; Myers et al., 1995; Post, 1982; Russell, 1979, 1984, 1985; Widom, 1989); low educational attainment regardless of intelligence potential (Bernstein, 1979; Ewing, 1990; Sendi & Blomgren, 1975); and alcohol and substance abuse (Bradford, Greenberg, & Motayne, 1992; Dolan & Smith, 2001; Labelle et al., 1991).

A causal link between screen violence and very violent behaviour in young people, while controversial, has also been found in a growing body of research (Newson, 1994; Myers, 1992; Sege & Dietz, 1994; Wheeler, 1993; see also Donnerstein, 1984; Donnerstein, Linz, & Penrod, 1987). The key point of difference for DiCataldo and Everett (2008) is that juvenile murderers demonstrated greater access to firearms and a greater incidence of substance abuse contemporaneous with the offence in question. Similar results have been observed elsewhere (Sorrells, 1977; Bailey, 1996; Corder et al., 1976; Cornell et al., 1987a; Malmquist, 1971; Myers & Kemph, 1990; Myers & Scott, 1998; Zagar et al., 1990). Recent work by DeLisi et al. (2016; see also Hardwick & Rowton-Lee, 1996) confirms the difficulties in distinguishing youth charged with homicide from those youth charged with other violent offending. If such difficulties are valid, popular portrayals of the juvenile murderer as a clinically identifiable 'super-predator' or 'cold remorseless psychopath' (Bennett et al., 1996) are most surely outmoded and/or plainly incorrect. Meanwhile, these findings should have a major impact on our thinking in relation to how we attempt to sanction and rehabilitate these particular individuals. As Busch et al. (1990, p. 484) remind us, adolescents who murder 'are not exotic individuals, but, rather, persons with violent, abusive, inconsistent, and aggressive environments'. I certainly believe this best describes the situations of the young people in my study.

Steps to murder

Clearly, much foundational work on violent crime references the impact of an offender's personal circumstances (i.e. neurological, psychological, behavioural, sociological, structural, and environmental circumstances, along with situational risk factors) on the violent event. These are certainly apparent in the present study cohort. However, some commentators have challenged the utility of relying solely on antecedent factors or conditions in the pursuit of a 'complete explanation of the violent crime problem' (Athens, 2005, p. 632). Instead, such commentators suggest a more pressing need to explain the escalating set of steps that take place between two or more individuals, and possibly an audience, that culminate in the death of the victim (Athens, 2005; Luckenbill, 1977; Polk, 1994, 1999; Wilson and Daly, 1985; Wolfgang, 1958). To wit, the idea of asking how 'senseless' violence can erupt over seemingly nothing – an insult, a spilled drink, a dirty look – can evince some of the most powerful lessons to inform our understanding of antisocial (criminal) behaviour. As Griffiths, Yule, and Gartner (2011, p. 62) remind us, 'senseless violence, it turns out, is not senseless. Nor is it random. People commonly quarrel, disagree, or have words with others, but they do not customarily resort to violence during the course of those exchanges' (Griffiths et al., 2011, p. 88). Therefore, unless we know about and account for what takes place during (lethal) assaultive encounters, we risk missing opportunities to effectively direct legal and social welfare strategies and to prevent future loss of life.

With this in mind, three perspectives dominate thinking about the interplay between victim and offender during a violent event. These include symbolic interaction: namely, 'character' or 'honor' contest violence; instrumental theories of aggression; and 'doing gender' (for a detailed overview, see Athens, 1997).

Symbolic interaction (or 'interpretive') theories recognize violence as situated, collective transactions that occur as individuals, in physical proximity and confronted with social conflict, form (and re-form) plans of action based on their definition of the unfolding scenario (Blumer, 1962; Felson & Tedeschi, 1993; Goffman, 1963; Luckenbill, 1977). Pioneering work by Athens (1985, 1992, 1997, 2005, 2009) suggests that resorting to violence is contingent not only upon the actors' definitions of the situation but also their internalization of *the generalized other* or *phantom community*. Here, importantly, and I think correctly, differential interpretation of the same event is explained by an individual's concept of self, identity, and role, a concept which is liable to change over time (Athens, 1997). Accordingly, 'as it changes, the individual will begin to judge both situations and himself differently, then engage in new forms of conduct' (Athens, 1997, p. 30). This observation appears compatible with the general idea that (even serious) young offenders can 'grow up' and desist from further offending (Glueck & Glueck, 1968; Gottfredson & Hirschi, 1990; Moffitt, 1993).

First described by Goffman (1967), '*character*' or '*honor contest*' *perspectives* emphasize the distinctive proclivity of some males, largely from lower socioeconomic ranks, to violently escalate real or imagined threats to their reputation or status, sometimes resulting in death (Polk, 1999, p. 6). Goffman (1967, pp. 211–212) claims the following in relation to such behaviour:

> [T]o find those who indulge in this sport we are likely to look to 'outsiders'; who, like adolescents, have not been tightly woven into organizational structures. . . . [A]mong them these fateful activities will be least disruptive and the most tolerable; it is a case of having little to lose, or little to lose yet; a case of being well organized for disorganization.

In fact, so pronounced are the specific themes or patterns whereby individuals become involved in this form of violence that Wilson and Daly (1985, 1993) describe the latter as 'young male syndrome'. For Luckenbill (1977, p. 177), the character contest 'is a confrontation in which one, but usually both, attempts to establish or save face at the other's expense by standing steady in the face of adversity' (see also Goffman, 1967). Such work attests to the active role victims can play in their own demise, as willing combatants in or instigators of the physical attack that provokes the lethal response (Wolfgang, 1958; see also Felson & Messner, 1998; Luckenbill, 1977; Muftić & Hunt, 2012; Polk, 1999; Toch, 1969). Again, I find this to be broadly the case in my study. To this end, Polk (1994, 1999) and others (see Block & Block, 1993; Luckenbill, 1977; Wolfgang, 1958) categorize this form of homicide as 'fundamentally nothing more than a fatal assault – that is, a physical assault that escalated beyond the projected course of action' (Warley, 2011, p. 6).

The second explanatory construct, the *instrumental theory of aggression*, postulates violent criminal conduct as deliberate, cognitively mediated, goal-oriented behaviour requiring 'a string of decisions' made on behalf of the offender (Felson, 2002, p. 17; see also Felson & Tedeschi, 1993). For example, individuals must consider, in turn, critical issues, including *if*, *when*, and *how much* physical force will be necessary to achieve their readily identifiable objectives (Felson, 2002). Presumably, additional decision-making will be triggered by victims' compliance or lack thereof. According to Richard Felson (2009, p. 28), conventional wisdom around human behaviour is likely to explain such aggressive behaviour as underscoring rewards and costs. Specifically, he suggests that people harm others for the following reason:

> [I]t gets them something they want at not too great a cost. Aggression can be a method of getting retribution when one has a grievance, a method of impressing others, a method of getting others to comply, and a form of thrill-seeking. By forcing others to comply, the actor can get money, sex, and other rewards.

Ipso facto, this theory posits that every violent act has an identifiable goal or motive as *distinct* from the goal of harm, which rides alongside as more of a tacit means to an end (Tedeschi & Felson, 1994; see also Bushman & Anderson, 2001; Fontaine, 2007; Vitaro, Barker, Boivin, Brendgen, & Tremblay, 2006). However, this perspective holds less weight for defensive or retaliatory violence, which is perceived primarily as a hostile response to a perceived attack (Berkowitz, 1989, 1993; Bushman & Anderson, 2001; Vitaro et al., 2006). The instrumental theory of aggression has also been criticized on grounds that it overlooks the victim's perspective during violent interactions (Athens, 2005, p. 639) and oversimplifies highly complex behaviour that has multiple motivations (Bushman & Anderson, 2001, p. 278). In fact, some commentators go as far as to suggest that instrumental aggression has such limited practicality that it is 'now time to pull the life-support plug on this dichotomy' (Bushman & Anderson, 2001, p. 278).

Finally, *doing gender* (or 'structured action') theories, imagine violent acts as 'performances' of hegemonic masculinity by actors who 'multiply (and [are] simultaneously) constrained by the structures of class, race and gender' (Gadd &

Jefferson, 2007, p. 41). Drawing on Giddens (1976), Messerschmidt's work on masculinity (1993, 1994, 1997) observes the way in which 'young men situationally accomplish public forms of masculinity in response to their socially structured circumstances . . . varieties of youth crime serve as a suitable vehicle for doing masculinity when other resources are unavailable' (Messerschmidt, 1994, p. 82). Consider, for example, the enculturation and persistence of 'ghetto specific manhood roles' (Warley, 2011, p. 30) in areas of concentrated poverty, such as public housing developments in the United States (aka 'the projects'). As legitimate avenues for accomplishing masculinity, such as sport and professional employment, remain closed, violence endures as an accessible resource for young men to call upon, 'not only to demonstrate their masculinity but also to restore their masculinity after it has been called into question' (Athens, 2005, p. 643; see also Brezina, Agnew, Cullen, & Wright, 2004; Gadd & Jefferson, 2007, p. 42; Oliver, 2001; Taylor, Esbensen, Brick, & Freng, 2010). As Jerry Heller, manager of rap pioneers Eazy-E and N.W.A., once remarked in relation to this:

> [N]o one survived the streets without a protective mask. No one survived naked. You had to have a role. You had to be "thug," "playa," "athlete," "gangsta," or "dope man". Otherwise, there was only one role left to you. "Victim."'
>
> (Heller, 2007, p. 73)

Measuring prison adjustment

Arguably, to bring about positive changes in serious violent offenders, one needs to move beyond viewing such people through the 'rear-view mirror of their crimes' (Wright, 2004, p. 202) and come to grips with how these people fare across a long sentence. One measure of prison adjustment is the number and type of disciplinary reports filed against a prisoner, or the length of time spent in solitary or punitive detention (McShane & Williams, 1989). Common infractions include disobeying orders, damaging prison property, possessing contraband, returning a positive drug test, and fighting. Other indicators of adjustment include mental health (Toch, Adams, & Greene, 1987), participation in prison activities (MacKenzie, Goodstein, & Blouin, 1987), maintenance of outside relationships (Morris, 1965; Cobean & Power, 1978; Fox, 1981), and work history (Coe, 1961; Wolfgang, 1961). Previous research has drawn a strong link between juveniles sentenced to lengthy terms of imprisonment and increased involvement in (often violent) prison misconduct (Kuanliang, Sorensen, & Cunningham, 2008; Leigey & Hodge, 2013; McReynolds & Wasserman, 2008; McShane & Williams, 1989; Tasca, Griffin, & Rodriguez, 2010). Further, McShane and Williams (1989, p. 266) found that those who were incarcerated for violent offences committed prior to age 17 were almost twice as likely to be problem inmates than their older counterparts aged between 17 and 21, creating 'very specific management problems for prison administrators' and placing 'inordinate demands on expensive segregation facilities'. Such work attests to the largely negative and prolonged effects of sentencing juveniles as adults. In fact, Tasca et al. (2010, p. 246) theorize a difficult adjustment even for those retained by the juvenile justice system until their 18th birthdays, remarking that 'the conditions of confinement in the adult system may actually increase the violent responses of juvenile inmates'. Under these circumstances, concerns have also been raised that teen killers will use their notoriety as currency in adult prisons, attracting bad influences and negating what modest opportunities exist for further treatment and education.

The life sentence as a form of 'social death'

Similarly, commentators speak to the distinct difficulties created by the life sentence, most notably the risk that 'a young person hearing that he may be locked up for 10 or 20 years may have difficulty envisioning an end to that term, easily believing that there is no tomorrow' (Forst, Fagan, & Vivona, 1989, p. 11; see also Flanagan, 1981, 1982). Jewkes (2005) even compares the way in which a life sentence 'seismically disrupts the lifecourse and forcibly suspends future expectations' (p. 366) to the diagnosis of a chronic or terminal illness. Historically, it was feared this would 'result in a new class of "super-inmates" uncontrollable in prison because they have nothing else to lose' (Blair, 1994, p. 213; see also Cheatwood, 1988, p. 53). In line with this, Unkovic and Albini (1969) observed the dramatic reaction of one prisoner who 'could not become accustomed to the idea of losing his freedom and fought to preserve it by rebelling animalistically. He complained of the food, smashed the lights, ripped wooden benches apart, [and] set fire to blankets' (p. 158). Undoubtedly, the ability (and willingness) of correctional staff to respond to such crises in a sensitive and nuanced fashion is constrained when the 'good order' of the prison is under threat (see Halsey & Deegan, 2017). Others take a more optimistic view of the impression lifers cast on the correctional landscape, arguing that these individuals see prison as a home:

> [A]n involuntary one, to be sure – but still a domestic world in which they have an investment . . . [and with] everything to lose since prison is all they have, [they] strive to make the most of the resources available . . . obey the rules and generally stay out of trouble.
>
> (Johnson, 2002, p. 105; see also Wright, 1991)

To this end, Toch (1975, p. 326) describes how 'even environments of stress such as prisons can become settings for survival and milieus for personal growth'. My sense is that the extent to which various custodial climates are fundamentally at odds with the development of effective and prosocial coping strategies in young people remains a critically important question. Certainly, there is good evidence that juveniles enter prison with a limited repertoire of coping skills (Ireland, 2001; Ireland, 2005; Ireland, Boustead, & Ireland, 2005; see also Davis, Bean, Shumacher, & Stringer, 1991) that are readily tested in the presence of older, more experienced prisoners. A wealth of research has focused on the heightened risk of victimization and suicide faced by young people in adult correctional settings (Abramsky, 2001; Beck & Harrison, 2006; Beck, Harrison, & Adams,

2007; Dumond, 1992; Flaherty, 1980; Forst et al., 1989; Memory, 1989; Mumola, 2005). For lifer Paul Crump, in Unkovic and Albini's (1969) study, entering prison was comparable to being transplanted to a jungle: 'If I hadn't been an animal, I wouldn't have survived.' Therefore, displays of toughness and resilience (Nellis & King, 2009), formation of tactical friendships (van der Laan & Eichelsheim, 2013), and other acting-out behaviours can be viewed against attempts to manage the pains of imprisonment (Sykes, 1958) and secure prisoners' safety behind bars.

The problem, of course, is that suitability for housing assignments, work detail, security classification, and, indeed, eventual release on parole is very much dependent on disciplinary history or 'compliance' within the prison. The question of how to predict future dangerousness from a particularly stressful and vulnerable phase in the sentence plan is, accordingly, a difficult one to answer. One way of resolving these issues is to examine whether individuals incarcerated as juveniles remain a persistently antisocial group as they age in prison (Leigey & Hodge, 2013; see also Nellis & King, 2009). Undoubtedly, within my small cohort, there is a mix of views and declarative statements about why the participants were particularly disruptive as juveniles and what motivates them to avoid further serious offending as they enter adulthood and edge closer to making parole. It is fair to say that many feel rehabilitated '*in spite* of prison, not because of it' (Unkovic & Albini, 1969) and that the overwhelming majority conceive of themselves to be fundamentally good people despite varying degrees of public attention and condemnation.

References

Abramsky, S. (2001). Hard-time kids: Handing down adult prison sentences to juvenile criminals isn't solving their problems – Or ours. *The American Prospect*, *12*(15), 16–21. Retrieved from https://prospect.org

Adams, K. A. (1974). The child who murders: A review of theory and research. *Criminal Justice and Behaviour*, *1*(1), 51–61. DOI:10.1177/009385487400100107

American Psychiatric Association. (1994). *Diagnostic and statistical manual of mental disorders (DSM-IV)*. Washington, DC: American Psychiatric Association.

Applegate, B. K., & Davis, R. K. (2006). Public views of sentencing juvenile murderers: The impact of offender, offense, and perceived maturity. *Youth Violence and Juvenile Justice*, *4*(1), 55–74. DOI:10.1177/1541204005282312

Asquith, S. (1996). When children kill children: The search for justice. *Childhood*, *3*(1), 99–116. DOI:10.1177/0907568296003001007

Athens, L. (1985). Character contests and violent criminal conduct: A critique. *The Sociological Quarterly*, *26*(3), 419–431. DOI:10.1111/j.1533-8525.1985.tb00236.x

Athens, L. (1992). *The creation of dangerous violent criminals*. Urbana, IL: University of Illinois Press.

Athens, L. (1997). *Violent criminal acts and actors revisited*. Urbana, IL: University of Illinois Press.

Athens, L. (2005). Violent encounters: Violent engagements, skirmishes, and tiffs. *Journal of Contemporary Ethnography*, *34*(6), 631–678. DOI:10.1177/0891241605280570

Athens, L. (2009). The roots of "radical interactionism". *Journal for the Theory of Social Behaviour*, *39*, 387–414. DOI:10.111/j.1468-5914.2009.00413.x

Australian Bureau of Statistics (ABS). (2015). *4519.0 recorded crime- offenders, 2013–2014*. Retrieved from www.abs.gov.au/ausstats/abs@.nsf/Lookup/by%20Subject/4519.0~2013-14~Main%20Features~Youth%20Offenders~5

Baglivio, M. T., & Wolff, K. T. (2017). Prospective prediction of juvenile homicide/Attempted homicide among early-onset juvenile offenders. *International Journal of Environmental Research and Public Health, 14*(2), 197–210. DOI:10.3390/ijerph14020197

Bailey, S. (1996). Adolescents who murder. *Journal of Adolescence, 19*(1), 19–39. DOI:10.1006/jado.1996.0003

Beck, A. J., & Harrison, P. M. (2006). *Bureau of justice statistics, prison rape elimination act of 2003: Sexual violence reported by correctional authorities, 2005 (NCJ 214646)*. Washington, DC: Government Printing Office. Retrieved from www.researchgate.net/publication/265193552_Sexual_Violence_Reported_by_Correctional_Authorities_2005

Beck, A. J., Harrison, P. M., & Adams, D. B. (2007). *Bureau of justice statistics, prison rape elimination act of 2003: Sexual violence reported by correctional authorities, 2006 (NCJ 218914)*. Washington, DC: Government Printing Office. Retrieved from https://bjs.gov/content/pub/pdf/svrca06.pdf

Bennett, W. J., DiIulio, J. J., & Walters, J. P. (1996). *Body count: Moral poverty- And how to win America's war against crime and drugs*. New York: Simon & Schuster.

Berkowitz, L. (1989). Frustration-aggression hypothesis: Examination and reformulation. *Psychological Bulletin, 106*(1), 59–73. Retrieved from www.apa.org/pubs/journals/bul/

Berkowitz, L. (1993). *Aggression: Its causes, consequences, and control*. Boston, MA: McGraw-Hill Book Company.

Bernstein, J. I. (1979). Premeditated murder by an eight-year-old boy. *International Journal of Offender Therapy and Comparative Criminology, 23*(1), 47–56. DOI:10.1177/0306624X7902300105

Bingenheimer, J., Brennan, R., & Earls, F. (2005). Firearm violence exposure and serious violent behavior. *Science, 308*(5726), 1323–1326. DOI:10.1126/science.1110096

Blair, D. (1994). A matter of life and death: Why life without parole should be a sentencing option in Texas. *American Journal of Criminal Law, 22*(1), 191–214. Retrieved from http://ajclonline.org

Block, C. R., & Block, R. (1993). *U.S. department of justice, national institute of justice: Street gang crime in Chicago (NCJ 144782)*. Retrieved from https://pdfs.semanticscholar.org/17bf/40fc952dc172cf9b0a008675bdf827c3773d.pdf

Block, R. L. (1977). *Violent crime: Environment, interaction, and death*. Lexington, MA: Lexington Books.

Blumer, H. (1962). Society as symbolic interaction. In A. Rose (Ed.), *Human behavior and social processes* (pp. 179–92). Boston, MA: Houghton Mifflin.

Blumstein, A. (1995). Violence by young people: Why the deadly nexus? *National Institute of Justice Journal, 22*, 2–9. Retrieved from www.ncjrs.gov/pdffiles/nijj_229.pdf

Blumstein, A., & Cohen, J. (1987). Characterizing criminal careers (crime-committing patterns as part of longitudinal stochastic process). *Science, 237*, 985–991. DOI:10.1126/science.237.4818.985

Bradford, J. W., Greenberg, D. M., & Motayne, G. G. (1992). Substance abuse and criminal behaviour. *Psychiatric Clinics of North America, 15*(3), 605–623. DOI:10.1016/S0193-953X(18)30227-2

Brezina, T., Agnew, R., Cullen, F. T., & Wright, J. P. (2004). The code of the street: A quantitative assessment of Elijah Anderson's subculture of violence thesis and its contribution to youth violence research. *Youth Violence and Juvenile Justice, 2*(4), 303–328. DOI:10.1177/1541204004267780

Broadhurst, R., Maller, R., Maller, M., & Bouhours, B. (2018). The recidivism of homicide offenders in Western Australia. *Australian and New Zealand Journal of Criminology*, *51*(3), 395–411. DOI:10.1177/0004865817722393

Busch, K. G., Zagar, R., Hughes, J. R., Arbit, J., & Bussell, R. E. (1990). Adolescents who kill. *Journal of Clinical Psychology*, *46*(4), 472–485. DOI:10.1002/1097-4679(199007)46:4<472::AIDJCLP2270460416>3.0.CO;2-F

Bushman, B. J., & Anderson, C. A. (2001). Is it time to pull the plug on hostile versus instrumental aggression dichotomy? *Psychological Review*, *108*(1), 273–279. DOI:10.1037//0033-295X.108.1.273

Carcach, C. (1997). *Youth as victims and offenders of homicide: Trends and issues in crime & criminal justice (No. 73)*. Canberra: Australian Institute of Criminology. Retrieved from https://aic.gov.au/publications/tandi/tandi73

Cheatwood, D. (1988). The life-without-parole sanction: Its current status and a research agenda. *Crime & Delinquency*, *34*(1), 43–59. DOI:10.1177/0011128788034001003

Cobean, S. C., & Power, P. W. (1978). The role of family in the rehabilitation of the offender. *International Journal of Offender Therapy and Comparative Criminology*, *22*(1), 29–38. DOI:10.1177/0306624X7802200103

Codd, H. (2007). Prisoners' families and resettlement: A critical analysis. *The Howard Journal of Criminal Justice*, *46*(3), 255–263. DOI:10.1111/j.1468-2311.2007.00472.x

Coe, R. (1961). Characteristics of well adjusted and poorly adjusted inmates. *Journal of Criminal Law, Criminology and Police Science*, *52*(2), 178–184. DOI:10.2307/1141315

Cohen, L. E., & Felson, M. (1979). Social change and crime rate trends: A routine activities approach. *American Sociological Review*, *44*(4), 588–608. DOI:10.2307/2094589

Cook, P. J., & Moore, M. H. (1999). Guns, gun control, and homicide: A review of research and public policy. In M. D. Smith & M. A. Zahn (Eds.), *Homicide: A sourcebook of social research* (pp. 277–296). London: Sage Ltd.

Corder, B. F., Ball, B. C., Haizlip, T. M., Rollins, R., & Beaumont, R. (1976). Adolescent parricide: A comparison with other adolescent murder. *American Journal of Psychology*, *133*(8), 957–961. DOI:10.1176/ajp.133.8.957

Cornell, D. G. (1990). Prior adjustment of violent juvenile offenders. *Law and Human Behaviour*, *14*(6), 569–577. DOI:10.1007/BF01044882

Cornell, D. G. (1993). Juvenile homicide: A growing national problem. *Behavioural Sciences and the Law*, *11*(4), 389–396. DOI:10.1002/bsl.2370110406

Cornell, D. G., Benedek, E. P., & Benedek, D. M. (1987a). Characteristics of adolescents charged with homicide: Review of 72 cases. *Behavioural Sciences & the Law*, *5*(1), 11–23. DOI:10.1002/bsl.2370050103

Cornell, D. G., Benedek, E. P., & Benedek, D. M. (1987b). Juvenile homicide: Prior adjustment and a proposed typology. *American Journal of Orthopsychiatry*, *57*(3), 383–393. DOI:10.1111/j.1939-0025.1987.tb03547.x

Cornell, D. G., Benedek, E. P., & Benedek, D. M. (1989). A typology of juvenile homicide offenders. In E. P. Benedek & D. G. Cornell (Eds.), *Juvenile homicide* (pp. 59–84). Washington, DC: American Psychiatric Press.

Criminal Law Consolidation Act 1935 (SA). Retrieved from www.legislation.sa.gov.au/LZ/C/A/CRIMINAL%20LAW%CONSOLIDATION%20ACT%201935.aspx

Criminal Law (Sentencing) Act 1988 (SA). Retrieved from www.legislation.sa.gov.au/LZ/C/A/CRIMINAL%20LAW%20(SENTENCING)%20ACT%201988.aspx

Cubbin, C., Pickle, L. W., & Fingerhut, L. (2000). Social context and geographic patterns of homicide among US black and white males. *American Journal of Public Health*, *90*(4), 579–587. DOI:10.2105/AJPH.90.4.579

Cunneen, C., & White, R. (2007). *Juvenile justice: Youth and crime in Australia* (3rd ed.). South Melbourne: Oxford University Press.

Darby, P. J., Allan, W. D., Kashani, J. H., Hartke, K. L., & Reid, J. C. (1998). Analysis of 112 juveniles who committed homicide: Characteristics and a closer look at family abuse. *Journal of Family Violence*, *13*(4), 365–375. DOI:10.1023/A:1022823219276

Davis, D. L., Bean, G. J., Shumacher, J. E., & Stringer, T. L. (1991). Prevalence of emotional disorders in a juvenile justice institutional population. *American Journal of Forensic Psychology*, *9*(1), 5–17.

DeLisi, M., Kosloski, A., Sween, M., Hachmeister, E., Moore, M., and Drury, A. (2010). Murder by numbers: Monetary costs imposed by a sample of homicide offenders. *The Journal of Forensic Psychiatry & Psychology*, *21*(4), 501–513. DOI:10.1080/14789940903564388

DeLisi, M., Piquero, A. R., & Cardwell, S. M. (2016). The unpredictability of murder: Juvenile homicide in the pathways to desistance study. *Youth Violence and Juvenile Justice*, *14*(1), 26–42. DOI:10.1177/1541204014551805

DiCataldo, F., & Everett, M. (2008). Distinguishing juvenile homicide from violent juvenile offending. *International Journal of Offender Therapy and Comparative Criminology*, *52*(2), 158–174. DOI:10.1177/0306624X07303906

Dolan, M., & Smith, C. (2001). Juvenile homicide offenders: 10 years' experience of an adolescent forensic psychiatry service. *The Journal of Forensic Psychiatry*, *12*(2), 313–329. DOI:10.1080/09585180110056858

Donnellan, A. (2015, June 2). *Power to veto parole decisions to be relinquished by South Australian Government.* Retrieved from http://mobile.abc.net.au/news/2015-06-02/power-to-veto-parole-decisions-to-be-relinquished-sa/6515564

Donnerstein, E. (1984). Pornography: Its effect on violence against women. In N. M. Malamuth & E. Donnerstein (Eds.), *Pornography and sexual aggression* (pp. 53–81). Orlando, FL: Academic Press, Inc.

Donnerstein, E., Linz, D., & Penrod, S. (1987). *The question of pornography: Research finding and policy implications*. New York: Free Press.

Dumond, R. W. (1992). The sexual assault of male inmates in incarcerated settings. *International Journal of the Sociology of Law*, *20*(2), 135–157. Retrieved from www.sciencedirect.com/journal/international-journal-of-the-sociology-of-law

Eronen, M., Hakola, P., & Tiihonen, J. (1996). Factors associated with homicide recidivism in a 13-year sample of homicide offenders in Finland. *Psychiatric Services*, *47*(4), 403–406. DOI:10.1176/ps.47.4.403

Ewing, C. P. (1990). *When children kill*. Lexington, MA: Lexington Books.

Fagan, A. A., & Western, J. (2005). Escalation and deceleration of offending behaviours from adolescence to early adulthood. *Australian and New Zealand Journal of Criminology*, *38*(1), 59–76. DOI:10.1375/acri.38.1.59

Fagan, J., & Wilkinson, D. L. (1998). Guns, youth violence, and social identity in inner cities. *Crime and Justice*, *24*, 105–188. DOI:10.1086/449279

Farrington, D. P. (1986). Age and crime. *Crime and Justice: An Annual Review of Research*, *7*, 189–250. DOI:10.1086/449114

Farrington, D. P. (1997). Early prediction of violent and nonviolent youthful offending. *European Journal on Criminal Policy and Research*, *5*(2), 51–66. DOI:10.1007/BF02677607

Farrington, D. P., Loeber, R., & Berg, M. T. (2012). Young men who kill: A prospective longitudinal examination from childhood. *Homicide Studies*, *16*(2), 99–128. DOI:10.1177/1088767912439398

Felson, R. B. (2002). *Violence and gender reexamined.* Washington, DC: American Psychological Association.

Felson, R. B. (2009). Violence, crime and violent crime. *International Journal of Conflict and Violence, 3*(1), 23–39. DOI:10.4119/UNIBI/ijcv.46

Felson, R. B., & Messner, S. F. (1998). Disentangling the effects of gender and intimacy on victim precipitation in homicide. *Criminology, 36*(2), 405–423. DOI:10.111/j.1745-9125.1998.tb01253.x

Felson, R. B., & Steadman, H. J. (1983). Situational factors in disputes leading to criminal violence. *Criminology, 21*(1), 59–74. DOI:10.1111/j.1745-9125.1983.tb00251.x

Felson, R. B., & Tedeschi, J. T. (1993). A social interactionist approach to violence: Cross-cultural applications. *Violence and Victims, 8*(3), 295–310. DOI:10.1891/0886-6708.8.3.295

Fiddes, D. O. (1981). Scotland in the seventies – Adolescents in care and custody: A survey of adolescent murder in Scotland. *Journal of Adolescence, 4*(1), 47–65. DOI:10.1016/S0140-1971(81)80005-X

Flaherty, M. G. (1980). *An assessment of the national incidence of juvenile suicide in adult jails, lockups, and juvenile detention centers.* Champaign, IL: Community Research Forum. Retrieved from https://files.eric.ed.gov/fulltext/ED199625.pdf

Flanagan, T. J. (1981). Dealing with long-term confinement: Adaptive strategies and perspectives among long-term prisoners. *Criminal Justice and Behavior, 8*(2), 201–222. DOI:10.1177/009385488100800206

Flanagan, T. J. (1982). Lifers and long-termers: Doing big time. In R. Johnson & H. Toch (Eds.), *The pains of imprisonment* (pp. 115–128). Beverly Hills, CA: Sage.

Fontaine, R. G. (2007). Disentangling the psychology and law of instrumental and reactive subtypes of aggression. *Psychology, Public Policy, and Law, 13*(2), 143–165. DOI:10.1037/1076-8971.13.2.143

Forst, M., Fagan, J., & Vivona, T. S. (1989). Youths in prisons and training schools: Perceptions and consequences of the treatment-custody dichotomy. *Juvenile and Family Court Journal, 40*(1), 1–15. DOI:10.1111/j.1755-6988.1989.tb00634.x

Fox, G. L. (1981). The family and the ex-offender: Potential for rehabilitation. In S. Martin, L. B. Sechrest, & R. Redner (Eds.), *New directions in the rehabilitation of criminal offenders* (pp. 406–423). Washington, DC: National Academy Press.

Fox, J. A. (1996). *Trends in juvenile violence.* Washington, DC: Bureau of Justice Statistics, U.S. Department of Justice.

Freiberg, A. (2001). Affective versus effective justice: Instrumentalism and emotionalism in criminal justice. *Punishment & Society, 3*(2), 265–78. DOI:10.1177/14624740122228320

Gadd, D., & Jefferson, T. (2007). *Psychosocial criminology: An introduction.* London: Sage.

Garbarino, J. (2000). *Lost boys: Why our sons turn violent and how we can save them.* New York: Anchor Books.

Garbarino, J., & Haslam, R. H. (2005). Lost boys: Why our sons turn violent and how we can save them. *Child Health, 10*(8), 447–450. DOI:10.1080/00377310109517622

Giddens, A. (1976). *New rules of sociological method: A positive critique of interpretive sociologies.* London: Hutchinson.

Glueck, S., & Glueck, E. (1968). *Delinquents and nondelinquents in perspective.* Cambridge, MA: Harvard University Press.

Goffman, E. (1963). *Behaviour in public places: Notes on the social organization of gatherings.* Glencoe: Free Press.

Goffman, E. (1967). *Interaction ritual: Essays in face-to-face behavior.* Chicago, IL: Aldine.

Gottfredson, M. R., & Hirschi, T. (1990). *A general theory of crime*. Stanford, CA: Stanford University Press.

Graham, B. (2018, October 23). *The true cost of keeping killers locked up*. Retrieved from www.qt.com.au/news/taxpayers-1728-million-bill-for-keeping-anita-cobb/3556459/

Green, D. A. (2008). Suitable vehicles: Framing blame and justice when children kill children. *Crime Media Culture: An International Journal*, *4*(2), 197–220. DOI:10.1177/1741659008092328

Griffiths, E., Yule, C., & Gartner, R. (2011). Fighting over trivial things: Explaining the issue of contention in violent altercations. *Criminology*, *49*(1), 61–94. DOI:10.1111/j.1745-9125.2010.00218.x

Guardian for Children and Young People. (2017). *Looking for balance: A response to the Statutes Amendment (Youths Sentenced as Adults) Bill 2017*. Retrieved from www.gcyp.sa.gov.au/wp-content/uploads/2017/08/GCYP-SUBMISSION-Youth-Sentenced-as-Adults-Bill-2017-29-8-17.pdf

Guilliatt, R. (2013, November 22). A spate of random, cruel murders, committed by teens: Coincidence or a sign? *The Australian: Weekend Australian Magazine*. Retrieved from www.theaustralian.com.au/life/weekend-australian-magazine/boys-gone-bad/story-e6frg8h6-1226763676176

Hagan, J., & Foster, H. (2001). Youth violence and the end of adolescence. *American Sociological Review*, *66*(6), 874–899. DOI:10.2307/3088877

Hagan, M. P. (1997). An analysis of adolescent perpetrators of homicide and attempted homicide upon return to the community. *International Journal of Offender Therapy and Comparative Criminology*, *41*(3), 250–259. DOI:10.1177/0306624X97413004

Halsey, M. (2018). Child victims as adult offenders: Foregrounding the criminogenic effects of (unresolved) trauma and loss. *British Journal of Criminology*, *58*(1), 17–36. DOI:10.1093/bjc/azw097

Halsey, M., & Deegan, S. (2015). *Young offenders: Crime, prison and struggles for desistance*. London: Palgrave Macmillan.

Halsey, M., & Deegan, S. (2017). In search of generativity in prison officer work: Balancing care and control in custodial settings. *The Prison Journal*, *97*(1), 52–78. DOI:10.1177/0032885516679380

Hardwick, P. J., & Rowton-Lee, M. A. (1996). Adolescent homicide: Towards assessment of risk. *Journal of Adolescence*, *19*(3), 263–276. DOI:10.1006/jado.1996.0024

Heide, K. M. (1992). *Why kids kill parents: Child abuse and adolescent homicide*. Columbus, OH: Ohio State University Press.

Heide, K. M. (1999). *Young killers*. Thousand Oaks, CA: Sage.

Heide, K. M. (2003). Youth homicide: A review of the literature and a blueprint for action. *International Journal of Offender Therapy and Comparative Criminology*, *47*(1), 6–36. DOI:10.1177/036624X02239272

Heller, J. (2007). *Ruthless: A memoir*. New York: Simon and Schuster.

Hill-Smith, A., Hugo, P., Hughes, P., Fonagy, P., & Hartman, D. (2002). Adolescent murderers: Abuse and adversity in childhood. *Journal of Adolescence*, *25*(2), 221–230. DOI:10.1006/jado.2002.0462

Hirschi, T., & Gottfredson, M. (1983). Age and the explanation of crime. *American Journal of Sociology*, *89*(3), 552–584. DOI:10.1086/227905

Huizinga, D., Loeber, R., Thornberry, T. P., & Cothern, L. (2000). *Co-occurrence of delinquency and other problem behaviors*. Washington, DC: U.S. Department of Justice, Office of Juvenile Justice and Delinquency Prevention. Retrieved from https://pdfs.semanticscholar.org/5622/95f8d85bd7bcbda8d0c8f068d0db10213c0a.pdf

Ireland, C. A. (2001). *Problems in adapting to prison life*. Doctoral thesis, University of Central Lancashire, Preston, United Kingdom. Retrieved from http://clok.uclan.ac.uk

Ireland, J. L. (2005). Psychological health and bullying behaviour among young and juvenile offenders. *Journal of Adolescent Health, 36*(3), 236–243. DOI:10.1016/j.jadohealth.2004.02.026

Ireland, J. L., Boustead, R., & Ireland, C. A. (2005). Coping style and psychological health among adolescent prisoners: A study of young and juvenile offenders. *Journal of Adolescence, 28*(3), 411–423. DOI:10.1016/j.adolescence.2004.11.002

Irwin, J. (2009). *Lifers: Seeking redemption in prison*. New York, NY: Routledge.

Jewkes, Y. (2005). Loss, liminality and the life sentence: Managing identity through a disrupted lifecourse. In A. Liebling & S. Maruna (Eds.), *The effects of imprisonment* (pp. 366–388). Portland, OR: Willan.

Johnson, R. (2002). *Hard time: Understanding and reforming the prison* (3rd ed.). Belmont, CA: Wadsworth/Thomson.

Keller, C. (2014, December 14). State's prisons full, a third on remand. *InDaily: Independent Adelaide News*. Retrieved from http://indaily.com.au/news/2014/12/12/states-prisons-full-third-remand/

Kuanliang, A., Sorensen, J. R., & Cunningham, M. D. (2008). Juvenile inmates in an adult prison system: Rates of disciplinary misconduct and violence. *Criminal Justice and Behavior, 35*(9), 1186–1201. DOI:10.1177/0093854808322744

Labelle, A., Bradford, J. M., Bourget, D., Jones, B., & Carmichael, M. (1991). Adolescent murderers. *Canadian Journal of Psychiatry, 36*(8), 583–587. DOI:10.1177/070674379103600807

Langan, P. A., & Levin, D. J. (2002). Recidivism of prisoners released in 1994. *Federal Sentencing Reporter, 15*(1), 58–65. DOI:10.1525/fsr.2002.15.1.58

Langevin, R., Paitich, D., Orchard, B., Handy, L., & Russon, A. (1983). Childhood and family background of killers seen for psychiatric assessment: A controlled study. *Bulletin of the American Academy of Psychiatry and Law, 11*, 331–341. Retrieved from http://jaapl.org

Leigey, M. E., & Hodge, J. P. (2013). And then they behaved: Examining the institutional misconduct of adult inmates who were incarcerated as juveniles. *The Prison Journal, 93*(3), 272–290. DOI:10.1177/0032885513490270

Lennings, C. J. (2002). Children who kill family members: Three case studies from Australia. *Journal of Threat Assessment, 2*(2), 57–72. DOI:10.1300/J177v02n02_04

Lennings, C. J. (2004). Young offenders who kill: A review of five Australian case studies. *International Journal of Forensic Psychology, 1*(2), 1–13. https://pdfs.semanticscholar.org/a3d6/81bdf7809ccda26544c3c4307d19875cd1bf.pdf?_ga=2.176759971.70681603.1558247839-922822322.1558247839

Lennings, C. J. (unpublished). *Children who kill: A review of seven Australian case studies*. Australian Graduate School of Policing and Law Enforcement, Charles Sturt University.

Lewis, D. O. (1992). From abuse to violence: Psychophysiological consequences of maltreatment. *Journal of the American Academy of Child and Adolescent Psychiatry, 31*(3), 383–391. DOI:10.1097/00004583-199205000-00001

Lewis, D. O., Lovely, R., Yeager, C., Ferguson, G., Friedman, M., & Sloane, G., . . . & Pincusm, J. H. (1988). Intrinsic and environmental characteristics of juvenile murderers. *Journal of the American Academy of Child and Adolescent Psychiatry, 27*(5), 582–587. DOI:10.1097/00004583-198809000-00011

Lewis, D. O., Moy, E., Jackson, L. D., Aaronson, R., Restifo, N., Serra, S., & Simos, A. (1985). Biopsychosocial characteristics of children who later murder: A prospective study. *American Journal of Psychiatry, 142*(10), 1161–1167. DOI:10.1176/ajp.142.10.1161

Liem, M., Zahn, M., & Tichavsky, L. (2014). Criminal recidivism among homicide offenders. *Journal of Interpersonal Violence*, *29*(4), 2630–2651. DOI:10.1177/0886260513517302

Loeber, R., & Farrington, D. (2011). *Young homicide offenders and victims: Risk factors, prediction, and prevention from childhood.* New York: Springer.

Loeber, R., Pardini, D., Homish, D. L., Wei, E. H., Crawford, A. M., Farrington, D. P., . . . & Rosenfield, R. (2005). The prediction of violence and homicide in young men. *Journal of Consulting and Clinical Psychology*, *73*(6), 1074–1088. DOI:10.1037/0022-006X.73.6.1074

Luckenbill, D. F. (1977). Criminal homicide as a situated transaction. *Social Problems*, *25*(2), 176–186. DOI:10.2307/800293

MacKenzie, D. L., Goodstein, L. I., & Blouin, D. C. (1987). Personal control and prison adjustment: An empirical test of a proposed model. *Journal of Research in Crime and Delinquency*, *24*(1), 49–68. DOI:10.1177/0022427887024001004

Malmquist, C. P. (1971). Premonitory signs of homicidal aggression in juveniles. *American Journal of Psychiatry*, *128*(4), 461–465. DOI:10.1176/ajp.128.4.461

Maruna, S. (2001). *Making good: How ex-convicts reform and rebuild their lives*. Washington, DC: American Psychological Association.

May, H. (2000). "Murderers' relatives": Managing stigma, negotiating identity. *Journal for Contemporary Ethnography*, *29*(2), 198–221. DOI:10.1177/089124100129023873

McNeill, F., & Maruna, S. (2008). Giving up and giving back: Desistance, generativity and social work with offenders. In G. McIvor & P. Raynor (Eds.), *Developments in social work with offenders* (pp. 224–339). Series: Research Highlights in Social Work (48). London: Jessica Kingsley Publishers.

McNutt, H. (2010, March 2). Tainted by the James Bulger legacy. *The Guardian*. Retrieved from www.google.com.au/amp/s/amp.theguardian.com/society/2010/mar/03/james-bulger-legacy-disturbed-children

McReynolds, L. S., & Wasserman, G. A. (2008). Risk for disciplinary infractions among incarcerated male youths: Influence of psychiatric disorder. *Criminal Justice and Behaviour*, *35*(9), 1174–1185. DOI:10.1177/0093854808319936

McShane, M., & Williams, F. (1989). The prison adjustment of juvenile offenders. *Crime and Delinquency*, *35*(2), 254–269. DOI:10.1177/0011128789035002005

Memory, J. M. (1989). Juvenile suicides in secure detention facilities: Correction of published rates. *Death Studies*, *13*(5), 455–463. DOI:10.1080/07481188908252324

Merlo, A. V. (2000). Presidential address: Juvenile justice at the crossroads: Presidential address to the academy of criminal justice sciences. *Justice Quarterly*, *17*(4), 639–661. DOI:10.1080/07418820000094701

Messerschmidt, J. W. (1993). *Masculinities and crime*. Lanham, MD: Rowman & Littlefield.

Messerschmidt, J. W. (1994). Schooling, masculine and youth crime by white boys. In T. Newburn & E. A. Stanko (Eds.), *Just boys doing business*? (pp. 81–99). London: Routledge.

Messerschmidt, J. W. (1997). *Crime as structured action*. London: Sage.

Miller v Alabama, 132 S. Ct. (2012). Retrieved from www.courts.ca.gov/documents/BTB_23_THURSDAY_LUNCH_PLENARY_2.pdf

Moffitt, T. (1993). Adolescence-limited and life-course persistent antisocial behaviour: A developmental taxonomy. *Psychological Review*, *100*(4), 674–701. DOI:10.1037/0033-295X.100.4.674

Morris, A. (1965). The comprehensive classification of adult offenders. *Journal of Criminal Law, Criminology, and Police Science*, *56*(2), 197–202. DOI:10.2307/1140506

Muftić, L. R., & Hunt, D. E. (2012). Victim precipitation: Further understanding the linkage between victimization and offending in homicide. *Homicide Studies*, *17*(3), 239–254. DOI:10.1177/1088767912461785

Muftić, L. R., & Moreno, R. D. (2010). Juvenile homicide victimization: Differences and similarities by gender. *Youth Violence and Juvenile Justice*, *8*(4), 386–398. DOI:10.1177/1541204010368235

Mumola, C. J. (2005). *Suicide and homicide in state prisons and local jails (NCJ 210036)*. Washington, DC: Department of Justice, Bureau of Justice Statistics.

Myers, W. C. (1992). What treatments do we have for children and adolescents who have killed? *Bulletin of the American Academy of Psychiatry and the Law*, *20*(1), 47–58. Retrieved from http://jaapl.org/content/jaapl/20/1/47.full.pdf

Myers, W. C., & Kemph, J. P. (1990). DSM-III – R classification of homicidal youth- Help or hindrance. *Journal of Clinical Psychiatry*, *51*(6), 239–242. Retrieved from www.psychiatrist.com/jcp/Pages/home.aspx

Myers, W. C., & Scott, K. (1998). Psychotic and conduct disorder symptoms in juvenile murderers. *Journal of Homicide Studies*, *2*(2), 160–175. DOI:10.1177/1088767998002002004

Myers, W. C., Scott, K., Burgess, A. W., & Burgess, A. G. (1995). Psychopathology, biopsychosocial factors, crime characteristics, and classifications of 25 homicidal youths. *Journal of the American Academy of Child and Adolescent Psychiatry*, *34*(11), 1483–1489. DOI:10.1097/00004583-199511000-00015

National Center for Injury Prevention and Control (Division of Violence Prevention). (2016). *Youth violence: Facts at a glance*. Retrieved from www.cdc.gov/violenceprevention/pdf/yv-datasheet.pdf

Nellis, A., & King, R. (2009). *No exit: The expanding use of life sentences in America*. Washington, DC: Sentencing Project. Retrieved from http://sentencingproject.org/doc/publications/publications/inc_NoExitSept2009.pdf

Newson, E. (1994). Video violence and the protection of children. *Journal of Mental Health*, *3*(2), 221–227. DOI:10.3109/09638239409003802

Oliver, W. (2001). *The violent social world of Black men*. San Francisco, CA: John Wiley and Sons, Inc.

Polk, K. (1994). *When men kill: Scenarios of masculine violence*. New York: Cambridge University Press.

Polk, K. (1999). Males and honor contest violence. *Homicide Studies*, *3*(1), 6–29. DOI:10.1177/1088767999003001002

Posner, M. I., & Rothbart, M. K. (2000). Developing mechanisms of self-regulation. *Development and Psychopathology*, *12*(3), 427–444. DOI:10.1017/S0954579400003096

Post, S. (1982). Adolescent parricide in abusive families. *Child Welfare: Journal of Policy, Practice, and Program*, *61*(7), 455–455. Retrieved from www.cwla.org/child-welfare-journal/

R v Ormonte-Extrada (No. SCCRM-13–263). Retrieved from www.courts.sa.gov.au/sent_remarks/index.html

R v T, J. (No. SCCRM-11–175). Retrieved from www.courts.sa.gov.au/sent_remarks/index.html

Richards, K. (2011). *What makes juvenile offenders different from adult offenders*? Trends and Issues in Crime and Criminal Justice Series No. 409. Australian Institute of Criminology. Retrieved from www.aic.gov.au/publication/current/20series/tandi/401-420/tandi409.html

Rogers, C. (1993). Gang-related homicides in Los Angeles County. *Journal of Forensic Sciences*, *38*(4), 831–834. DOI:10.1520/JFS13479J

Russell, D. H. (1979). Ingredients of juvenile murder. *International Journal of Offender Therapy and Comparative Criminology*, *23*(1), 65–72. DOI:10.1177/0306624X7902300107

Russell, D. H. (1984). A study of juvenile murderers of family members. *International Journal of Offender Therapy and Comparative Criminology*, *28*(3), 177–192. DOI:10.1177/0306624X8402800304

Russell, D. H. (1985). Girls who kill. *International Journal of Offender Therapy and Comparative Criminology, 29*(2), 171–176. DOI:10.1177/0306624X8502900209

Sege, R., & Dietz, W. (1994). Television viewing and violence in children: The pediatrician as the agent for change. *Pediatrics, 94*(4), 600–607. Retrieved from www.researchgate.net/publication/15262122_Television_viewing_and_violence_in_children_The_pediatrcian_as_agent_for_change

Sendi, I. B., & Blomgren, P. G. (1975). A comparative study of predictive criteria in the predisposition of homicidal adolescents. *American Journal of Psychiatry, 132*(4), 423–427. DOI:10.1176/ajp.132.4.423

Sheppard, C. (1971). Towards a better understanding of the violent offender. *Canadian Journal of Criminology and Corrections, 13*(1), 60–67.

Shumaker, D., & McKee, G. (2001). Characteristics of homicidal and violent juveniles. *Violence and Victims, 16*(4), 401–409. DOI:10.1891/0886-6708.16.4.401

Sloan, J. H., Kellerman, A. L., Ready, D. T., Ferris, J. A., Keopsell, T., Rivara, F. P., . . . & LoGerfo, J. (1988). Handgun regulations, crime, assaults, and homicide: A tale of two cities. *New England Journal of Medicine, 319*(19), 1256–1262. DOI:10.1056/NEJM198811103191905

Sorrells, J. M. (1977). Kids who kill. *Crime and Delinquency, 23*(3), 313–320. DOI:10.1177/001112877702300307

South Australia. *Parliamentary debates*, House of Assembly, July 5, 2017, 10434–10435 (John Rau, Attorney-General). Retrieved from http://hansardpublic.parliament.sa.gov.au/Pages/HandsardResult.aspx#/docid/HANSARD-11-27112

Statista: Crime and Law Enforcement. (2016). *Number of murder offenders in the United States in 2016, by age*. Retrieved from http://statista.com/statistics/251884/murder-offenders-in-the-us-by-age/#0

Statutes Amendment (Youths Sentenced as Adults) Act 2017 (SA) (Austl.). Retrieved from www.legislation.sa.gov.au/LZ/V/A/2017/STATUTES%20AMENDMENT%20(YOUTHS)%20SENTENCED%20AS%20ADULTS)%20ACT%202017_67/2017.67.UN.PDF

Statutes Amendment (Youths Sentenced as Adults) Bill 2017 (SA) (Austl.). Retrieved from http://classic.austlii.edu.au/au/legis/sa/bill/sasaab2017499/

Steinberg, L., & Schwartz, R. G. (2000). Developmental psychology goes to court. In T. Grisso & R. G. Schwartz (Eds.), *Youth on trial: A developmental perspective on juvenile justice* (pp. 271–289). Chicago, IL: University of Chicago Press.

Steinberg, L., & Scott, E. S. (2003). Less guilty by reason of adolescence: Developmental immaturity, diminished responsibility and the juvenile death penalty. *American Psychologist, 58*(12), 1009–1018. DOI:10.1037/0003-066X.58.12.1009

Sykes, G. (1999 [1958]). *Society of captives*. Princeton, NJ: Princeton University Press.

Tasca, M., Griffin, M. L., & Rodriguez, N. (2010). The effect of importation and deprivation factors on violent misconduct: An examination of Black and Latino youth in prison. *Youth Violence and Juvenile Justice, 8*(3), 234–249. DOI:10.1177/1541204010366619

Taylor, T. J., Esbensen, F., Brick, B. T., & Freng, A. (2010). Exploring the measurement quality of an attitudinal scale of street code-related violence: Similarities and differences across groups and contexts. *Youth Violence and Juvenile Justice, 8*(3), 187–212. DOI:10.1177/1541204010361297

Tedeschi, J., & Felson, R. B. (1994). *Violence, aggression and coercive actions*. Washington, DC: American Psychological Association.

Toch, H. (1969). *Violent men: An enquiry into the Psychology of Violence*. Chicago, IL: Aldine.

Toch, H. (1975). *Men in crisis: Human breakdowns in prison*. Chicago, IL: Aldine.

Toch, H., Adams, K., & Greene, R. (1987). Ethnicity, disruptiveness, and emotional disorder among prison inmates. *Criminal Justice and Behaviour*, *14*(1), 93–109. DOI:10.1177/0093854887014001008

Toupin, J., & Morissette, L. (1990). Juvenile homicide: A case control study. *Medicine & Law*, *9*(3), 986–994. Retrieved from www.wshein.com

Trulson, C. R., Caudill, J. W., Haerle, D. R., & DeLisi, M. (2012). Cliqued up: The post-incarceration recidivism of young gang-related homicide offenders. *Criminal Justice Review*, *37*(2), 174–190. DOI:10.1177/0734016811434531

Unkovic, C. M., & Albini, J. L. (1969). The lifer speaks for himself: An analysis of the assumed homogeneity of life-termers. *Crime and Delinquency*, *15*(1), 156–161. DOI:10.1177/001112876901500114

van der Laan, A., & Eichelsheim, V. (2013). Juvenile adaptation to imprisonment: Feelings of safety, autonomy and well-being, and behaviour in prison. *European Journal of Criminology*, *10*(4), 424–443. DOI:10.1177/1477370812473530

Vitaro, F., Barker, E. D., Boivin, M., Brendgen, M., & Tremblay, R. E. (2006). Do early difficult temperament and harsh parenting differentially predict reactive and proactive aggression? *Journal of Abnormal Child Psychology*, *34*(5), 685–695. DOI:10.1007/s10802-006-9055-6

Warley, R. M. (2011). *Juvenile homicide: Fatal assault or lethal assault*? El Paso, TX: LFB Scholarly.

Webster, D. W., & Wilson, M. (1994). Gun violence among youth and the pediatrician's role in primary prevention. *Paediatrics*, *94*(4), 617–622. Retrieved from https://pediatrics.aapublications.org/content/94/4/617.long

Weisheit, R. A., & Wells, L. E. (2005). Deadly violence in the heartland: Comparing homicide patterns in nonmetropolitan and metropolitan counties. *Homicide Studies*, *9*(1), 55–80. DOI:10.1177/1088767904271434

Wekinson, M. (1995). Kids who kill: Parricide committed by children. *Australian Social Work*, *48*(2), 3–10. DOI:10.1080/03124079508414070

Wheeler, J. L. (1993). *Remote controlled: How TV affects you and your family*. Hagerstown, MD: Review and Herald Publishing Association.

Widom, C. S. (1989). Does violence beget violence? A critical examination of the literature. *Psychological Bulletin*, *106*(1), 3–28. DOI:10.1037/0033-2909.106.1.3

Wilson, M., & Daly, M. (1985). Competitiveness, risk-taking, and violence: The young male syndrome. *Ethology and Sociobiology*, *6*(1), 59–73. DOI:10.1016/0162-3095(85)90041-X

Wilson, M., & Daly, M. (1993). An evolutionary psychological perspective on male sexual proprietariness and violence against wives. *Violence and Victims*, *8*(3), 271–294. DOI:10.1891/0886-6708.8.3.271

Wolfgang, M. E. (1958). *Patterns in criminal homicide*. New York: John Wiley and Sons Inc.

Wolfgang, M. E. (1961). Quantitative analysis of adjustment to the prison community. *Journal of Criminal Law, Criminology and Police Science*, *51*(6), 608–618. DOI:10.2307/1141648

Woodworth, M., Agar, A. D., & Coupland, R. B. (2013). Characteristics of Canadian youth- perpetrated homicides. *Criminal Justice and Behaviour*, *40*(9), 1009–1026. DOI:10.1177/0093854813482390

Wright, J. H. (1991). Life without Parole: The view from death row. *Criminal Law Bulletin*, *27*, 334–357.

Wright, P. (2017, September 21). Penny Wright: Sentencing repeat juvenile offenders as adults will do little to improve community safety. *The Advertiser*. Retrieved from www.adelaidenow.com.au/news/opinion/penny-wright-sentencing-repeat-juvenile-offenders-as-adults-will-do-little-to-improve-community-safety/news-story/1eebc4b56e3266e908556b08c007d4c

Wright, R. (2004). Care as the "heart" of prison teaching. *Journal of Correctional Education, 55*(3), 191–209. Retrieved from www.jstor.org/stable/23292135

Young, A. (1996). In the frame: Crime and the limits of representation. *Australian and New Zealand Journal of Criminology, 29*(2), 81–101. DOI:10.1177/000486589602900201

Young Offenders Act 1993 (SA) (Austl.). Retrieved from www.legislation.sa.gov.au/LZ/C/A/YOUNG%20OFFENDERS%20ACT%201993/CURRENT/1993.57.AUTH.PDF

Zagar, R. J., Arbit, J., Sylvies, R., Busch, K., & Hughes, J. (1990). Homicidal adolescents: A replication. *Psychological Reports, 67*(3, Pt 2), 1235–1242. DOI:10.2466/PR0.67.8.1235-1242

Zagar, R. J., Grove, W. M., Busch, K. G., Hughes, J. R., & Arbit, J. (2009). Looking forward and backward in records for risks among homicidal youth. *Psychological Reports, 104*(1), 103–127. DOI:10.2466/PR0.104.1.103-127

Zimring, F. E. (1998). *American youth violence*. New York: Oxford University Press.

Zimring, F. E. (2000). Penal proportionality for the young offender: Notes on immaturity, capacity, and diminished responsibility. In T. Grisso & R. G. Schwartz (Eds.), *Youth on trial: A developmental perspective on juvenile justice* (pp. 271–289). Chicago, IL: University of Chicago Press.

Zimring, F. E. (2005). *American juvenile justice*. New York, NY: Oxford University Press.

2 Approach to the field: data

During my employment as a legal aid solicitor, I represented hundreds, possibly even thousands, of individuals arrested overnight on various matters and certified unfit for bail by the local police authority. Lawyers in private practice would also refer anyone in strife direct to me to look after. I was inundated. My days were spent running between police cells and the court house: making bail applications; ordering social background reports; and even entering the occasional guilty plea should stars align on the bench. For example, Mr Churches regularly sat as an auxiliary magistrate, and his was always the best court for someone in trouble in South Australia to appear in, particularly if they were prepared to resolve their matter on the spot. With any luck, defendants went home at the end of the day with their good behaviour bonds and I never saw them again, although the combination of personal and social problems encountered by such people – not to mention their notoriety (and visibility) in the local service area – meant this was sometimes a tall order.

When, in mid-2005, the duty solicitor service was extended to include the prisons, a request for counsel came straight from the deep end of the correctional system: G-Division, Yatala Labour Prison (i.e. maximum-security isolation cells within a maximum-security prison). There I met the young man who would go on to become the inspiration for this study: a 26-year-old lifer who identified strongly with J.M. Barrie's Peter Pan, the free-spirited and mischievous boy spared the degradation of growing old. In this case, however, 'Peter' was only too desperate to outgrow the monotony and inertia of the prison system, replete with its own band of lost boys. In the years that followed, I often gave pause to think about Peter, just two years my senior, and how life might play out for him in the long run, taking into account his incarceration since the age of 15. Given he continues to be incarcerated now into his 40s without any indication of making parole, this remains an open question. Nevertheless, coming to grips with how some teens arrive at and cope with a life sentence at the same time their peers are completing high school or seeking employment *is* a challenge taken up in this book. With this in mind, what follows is a phenomenology of the juvenile lifer. Specifically, I focus on how such individuals view their world with respect to the following:

- Why they are where they are
- How they cope day-to-day
- How they see the future and their place within it

Approval to conduct this research was granted by the Flinders University Social and Behavioural Research Ethics Committee (*Project Number 6876*) and the South Australian Department for Correctional Services (DCS). Various amendments to the ethics applications were sought and approved as the project unfolded.

Research design

From September 2015 to August 2018, in-depth interviews were completed with all individuals who were under sentence or parole supervision in South Australia as a result of having been convicted of murder as youths. Given the State's small population and the low frequency of juvenile homicide offending, this amounted to only 19 persons (18 males, 1 female). However, it goes without saying that murder investigations are complex and do not always result in prosecutions and/or convictions. Therefore, the actual number of young people involved in this type of violent event may be significantly higher.

Each participant was approached via a written letter of introduction and information sheet, and great care was taken to ensure the documents described the study in clear and uncomplicated terms. I introduced myself as a researcher who was interested in the personal backgrounds of juvenile lifers and the latter's perceptions of the events surrounding their crimes and prison sentences. Participation in the research meant committing to three interviews that would be audio-recorded and transcribed verbatim. Assurances were given that the choice about whether or not to do an interview would not influence legal or prison arrangements in any way and that participants' names would not appear in any published material. Included with the letter was a returnable expression of interest document, allowing participants the opportunity to opt in to further involvement. It was made clear that by doing so, individuals gave permission to me to write to them directly and follow up with a face-to-face visit to explain the project in greater detail. There are always concerns about communicating with the incarcerated population. These concerns include how disproportionately low educational attainment, low literacy, and health-related conditions (e.g. traumatic brain injury, substance abuse disorders, and mental illness) influence prisoners' abilities to understand information relevant to their participation. Giving potential research subjects orally presented information about the potential risks and benefits of their involvement prior to recruitment accounted for a range of literacy levels, allowed respondents to ask questions about the project, and ensured each participant had the capacity to give informed consent.

Several months before the mail-out took place, I was asked by the university ethics committee to estimate the number of participants likely to accept my invitation. It was a good question. Would some of the State's most vilified individuals seriously consider exposing themselves to the possibility of further attack? They know – perhaps best of all – just how untenable their world can be. If you make full and frank admissions about the offending, you're a self-confessed killer. If you offer a justification, you're a killer in denial. Neither looks particularly impressive on a parole application. Not to mention that media and political figures have a curious way of inserting themselves into the frame after learning such proceedings are on foot. So why risk it? On the back of these concerns, receiving a positive response rate of 100% was staggering. However, upon reflection, it is completely consistent with the tenor of the vocabularies that followed: these interviews represented, in many cases, the most genuine and sustained interest in their predicaments to date. Some of the respondents had not even participated in their own legal hearings to the same extent. As such, I am fully cognizant that being entrusted with these accounts, particularly in a small city such as Adelaide, is a great responsibility and one I do not take lightly. It is my hope that this work achieves a balanced and nuanced view of the juvenile lifer that is, at the same time, sensitive to the families of their victims.

Of course, the small sample size and description of events around each participant make it impossible to totally eliminate the chance that someone reading this work may recognize certain situations mentioned during interview and be able to identify the people involved. Participants consented to interview on the basis that the risk here is small but real. In the latter stages of the research, one participant asked if I would put my perspective on record in a documentary that sought to put a human face on youth homicide offending. In this instance, the young man signed a separate consent form, acknowledging that this would very likely mean his involvement in the research would become public knowledge and that I could no longer reasonably be expected to protect his identity.

In all, 63 interviews (lasting between 45 minutes and 2 hours) were completed with the juvenile lifers over the period September 2015 to August 2018. The majority ($n = 15$) were interviewed three times during that period. Four individuals were interviewed on further occasions (three on four occasions; and one on six occasions), taking into account these individuals' particularly detailed responses and institutional timetables. Five additional community-based interviews were conducted in mid-2018, after Stefan, Eddie, James, and Toby were granted parole. All other interviews were conducted in prison and, to a much lesser extent, pre-release settings ($n = 8$ interviews). The cultural backgrounds of the participants were diverse (Indigenous, Caucasian, African, Asian, Middle Eastern, and Spanish), with all but four born in Australia. The youngest participants ($n = 2$) were 14 years old at the time of the murder, while the average age at the time of the offence was 16 years 9 months. Consequently, all participants had served time in both juvenile facilities and prison. As at their first interview, participants were aged 18–64 years (18–24 = 10; 25–34 = 3; 35–44 = 3; 45–54 = 2; 55–64 = 1) and were serving minimum prison terms ranging from 5 to 20 years, with an average non-parole period of 12 years and 6 months. It is important to note, however, that over half of the cohort ($n = 10$) had already served between two and seven years *in excess of* their non-parole period despite continued recommendations from the Parole Board in favour of release. This means that for many juvenile lifers, the duration of their prison 'bid' (slang for a prison sentence) will outstrip their time spent in the community prior to arrest. In the words of one juvenile lifer (Ben), they are the State's 'career prisoners' (as distinct from 'career criminals'). Three participants (James, Cody, and Derek) were noticeably older than the rest of the sample. Both Cody and Derek had been returned to prison following the cancellation of their parole several years earlier (one for breaching parole conditions, the other for further serious offending), whereas James's offending did not come to light until he was in his mid-30s.

Most people appreciate that family members, particularly mothers and fathers, might continue to support their children in the face of horrendous offending. However, underlying these dutiful but often fraught commitments are substantive issues for the family members – issues that can result in significant loss of income, valued personal relationships (Griffiths, Yule, & Gartner, 2011), and standing within the community (see, e.g., Halsey & Deegan, 2014). Arguably, the emotional and financial resources required to support those prisoners serving life sentences remain unparalleled. As part of this study, I have also interviewed various persons nominated by the juvenile lifers as playing significant and ongoing roles in their lives. These one-off interviews were designed to elicit data on the nominated significant others' (NSOs') experience of events that transpired before and after their young person's involvement in a murder. Such conceptions, as I will show, heavily influence the level of commitment NSOs have towards supporting the prisoner in his quest to build a positive future. Not surprisingly, all but one nomination involved persons drawn from the lifer's immediate family (including grandparents). In one instance, an older brother was interviewed in prison, as he was completing a minimum of 20 years in relation to his own murder conviction arising from the same incident. Ten males and 11 females were nominated, resulting in 16 interviews (4 of which were conducted jointly with, for example, the mother and father of the juvenile lifer participant). Four lifers were estranged from all avenues of potential support on the outside and were unable to nominate someone for interview.

Given the nature and impacts of a murder conviction, select representatives of the DCS were also interviewed about opportunities for juvenile lifers to engage in meaningful educational, vocational, counselling, and leisure activities whilst incarcerated. Specifically, one-off interviews with Offender Development Managers (n = 6) and members of the Serious Offenders Committee (n = 4) were completed to ascertain how they engender a sense of hope or achieve rehabilitative goals against wider pressure to punish or write off serious violent offenders. These DCS staff were also asked to identify factors that motivated long-term prisoners to either avoid or engage in 'trouble' within the prison setting and the ramifications of such behaviour (i.e. receiving disciplinary action for disobeying orders, possessing contraband, failing drug tests, and fighting and/or assaulting other prisoners).

In total, 96 interviews were conducted for the *Lives and Adjustment Patterns of Juvenile Lifers* project. Consistent with previous findings on the Australian Research Council project *Generativity in Young Male Offenders: Caring for Self, Other and Future within Prison and Beyond* (2009–2013), 'delving into the struggles – the lived experience of the pain, hopes, and fears – of highly marginalized people' (Halsey & Deegan, 2015, p. 32) can be quite confronting, both for the person telling the story and for the listener. During interviews, fathers openly wept for the lives (and crimes) of their sons. Some mothers spoke to their time in psychiatric care, as the gravity of their children's circumstances was finally sheeted home to them. And no family member was immune from the campaigns of ostracism and harassment that arose from a variety of intra- and extra-familial sources: the return to work of one long-serving police officer was marked by a roll of crime scene tape and a pair of crime scene gloves placed conspicuously on his keyboard (see Chapter 5). Time as a healer of all wounds was anathema to the men and women forced to grieve their own social deaths alongside those of their children. In these moments, it was hard to avoid the conclusion that interviews for this project were one giant catalogue of trauma. Nevertheless, for participants to talk to someone who was outside the situation appeared to drain some of their despair and pain.

The question of *who* in the encounter performed the lion's share of emotional labour might be moot when the emotional toll is related to the 'strain of witnessing and sharing the anguish of the informant, and the strain of coping with the feelings they release in oneself' (Booth & Booth, 1994, p. 422). Kelly and Totten (2002, p. xii) make the valid point that researching violent and often cruel murders can lead to symptoms of vicarious (or secondary) trauma, including 'nightmares and anxiety; obsessive thoughts about the offenders, their horrifying actions, and the brutal deaths of the victims; and feelings of hopelessness, sorrow, and anger'. I found having and maintaining separate recreational interests – generally physical activities – to be particularly helpful outlets during this time.

In any case, the ethical issues faced by sensitive researchers, it is true to say, go deeper than the manner and preparation involved with conducting interviews (Melville & Hincks, 2016, p. 11). Accepting rapport as a form of moral currency, it made intuitive sense to want to 'give back' or show a tangible degree of care towards participants, even after the project was completed (Melville & Hincks, 2016; see also Bahn & Weatherill, 2013, p. 33; Halsey & Deegan, 2015, p. 32). Taylor's (2002, p. 156) work similarly calls for a sustained and ongoing commitment to participants as a means to reduce suspicion and restore trust in the researcher and scientific process. One way I did this was to follow up with handwritten letters after each interview and to provide participants with periodic updates on the progress of the study. Christmas cards and the occasional birthday card were also sent. One prisoner commented that it was the first one he had ever received. He was in his 50s. As I quickly learnt, prisoners (and their family members) would not hesitate to ring and tell me about their successes (and failures) within the prison system and beyond. Others wrote letters to express their fears of institutionalization and to ask me to second-guess their prospects of receiving and/or surviving on parole. As described in a previous study, these responses were taken as a tangible measure of the trust established over the course of the project (see Halsey & Deegan, 2015, p. 32). My responses, in turn, were aimed at encouraging prisoner participants to maintain a sense of composure and to do 'good time' in hopes of a positive outcome.

Perhaps more significantly, approval from the Flinders University Social and Behavioural Research Ethics Committee was given to me to write letters of support concerning lifers' applications for parole. These letters provided the Parole

Board with some background relating to participation in the study and were used to convey – using predominantly the applicant's own words – what parole would mean to him/her and how each had worked hard to reflect on the factors that led to their situation. Letters did not attempt to put a gloss on participants' offending or the occasions where they made their sentences more difficult for themselves. At the same time, most prisoners were also at a stage in their lives (and sentences) where they too were very well aware of not wanting to make excuses for their behaviour.

Interview data informing this book was supplemented by relevant material located on the court file of each participant (e.g. sentencing remarks, pre-sentence reports). These items were used as a means to gauge the objective seriousness of the offending and provided the factual basis on which matters were ultimately settled. As might be expected, aspects of the prosecution case were sometimes disputed. Bear in mind that many prisoners convicted under the doctrine of joint enterprise maintain their innocence and refuse to show remorse for a crime they feel they did not commit. Whether the evidential bar remains too low in these cases is presented in some depth in Chapter 3. However, at no time did a respondent present an account of events that was at odds with conviction in the legal sense.

The chapters that follow, which synthesize several dozen vignettes with detailed case studies of life-sentenced juveniles, emerge from a grounded analysis of interview transcripts (see Dey, 2007). As D'Andrade (1991, as cited in Ryan & Bernard, 2003, p. 9) has remarked, 'anyone who has listened to long stretches of talk knows how frequently people circle through the same network of ideas'. In the first instance, topics, or potential themes, that occurred and reoccurred (Bogdan & Taylor, 1975, p. 83) were earmarked across all transcripts. Next, through my continual comparisons of the transcripts, themes were refined until a saturation of key issues was determined (Carson, Gilmore, Perry, & Gronhaug, 2001; Glaser & Strauss, 1967; Strauss & Corbin, 1998). The process of manually cutting and sorting quotes 'into piles at different levels of abstraction' (Ryan & Bernard, 2003, p. 103) continued until issues arising from interviews could be assumed under central or sub-themes as appropriate (Barkin, Ryan, & Gelberg, 1999). I do not, however, make the claim that each and every subject broached by the participants is tested here. As Athens (2005, p. 651) reminds us, 'during a single study, researchers can seldom fully digest every slice of their data, especially if it is replete with "thick descriptions"'.

Research limitations

Several limitations to this research must be acknowledged. First, given that juvenile homicide is such a rare phenomenon, the validity of research in this field is almost always restricted by small sample sizes and individual case studies without comparisons or control groups (Cornell, Benedek, & Benedek, 1987; Darby, Allan, Kashani, Hartke, & Reid, 1998; Ewing, 1990; Hardwick & Rowton-Lee, 1996; Hill-Smith, Hugo, Hughes, Fonagy, & Hartman, 2002; Shumaker & McKee,

2001; Vries & Liem, 2011). Nevertheless, certain themes, issues, and ideas *can* be extracted from 'detailed, *descriptive* accounts ('thick descriptions') of particular events' (Gadd & Jefferson, 2007, p. 8; see also Mitchell, 2000, p. 170; Stake, 2000 at 22; Gluckman, 1964) that allow 'the "how?" and "why?" questions to be adequately broached' (Gadd & Jefferson, 2007, p. 6). In fact, a distinct advantage of this methodology is that unique or distinct features of cases can inform theory to a similar extent as details shared with other cases. In other words, 'each case tells us something new, and new observations are always valuable, whether they confirm previous theory or add something unexpected' (Stiles, 2007, p. 123).

A second limitation is that this research focuses almost exclusively on the lives and adjustment patterns of a cohort of male (ex-)prisoners. As authors correctly identify, there is very little information available about the experiences of female adolescents who commit murder (Sellers & Heide, 2012) or enter adult prisons generally (Pomeroy, Green, & Kiam, 2001). In particular, questions have been posed regarding whether 'paths to aggression, violence, criminality, and murder' vary markedly between boys and girls (Hill-Smith et al., 2002). As previously noted (see Halsey & Deegan, 2014), despite pioneering work by Carlen (1988), Smart (1976, 1989), and Edwards (1981, 1984), the visibility of females in the context of research on offending, victimization, and post-release support remains relatively low. Regrettably, this study is unable to contribute significantly to the dearth of material regarding this population, as only one life-sentenced juvenile in the South Australian context, during the research period, was female. Nevertheless, her story is significant and is included here.

Finally, the research relies, to a great extent, on self-report data. While I have no reason to regard (ex-)prisoner respondents as inaccurate historians, there remains the possibility that recall of (distant and/or traumatic) events will be imprecise. It also makes sense that prisoners will be disinclined to talk behind bars about negative experiences, where any indication of vulnerability could be problematic (Leigey, 2010, p. 263). Certainly, exaggerated levels of 'toxic masculinity', as a barrier to mental health treatment in male prisons, are well documented by Kupers (2005). Strict assurances were given to participants in the current study regarding the participants' confidentiality, along with anonymity in published works. The depth and breadth of the disclosures that followed, including instances of physical and sexual assault, inspire confidence that participants provided honest and upfront accounts of their experiences as life-sentenced juveniles.

References

Athens, L. (2005). Violent encounters: Violent engagements, skirmishes, and tiffs. *Journal of Contemporary Ethnography*, *34*(6), 631–678. DOI:10.1177/0891241605280570

Bahn, S., & Weatherill, P. (2013). Qualitative social research: A risky business when it comes to collecting "sensitive data". *Qualitative Research*, *13*(1), 19–35.

Barkin, S., Ryan, G., & Gelberg, L. (1999). What paediatricians can do to further youth violence primary prevention: A qualitative study. *Injury Prevention*, *5*(1), 53–58. DOI:10.1136/ip.5.1.53

Bogdan, R., & Taylor, S. J. (1975). *Introduction to qualitative research methods*. New York: John Wiley.

Booth, T., & Booth, W. (1994). The use of depth Interviewing with vulnerable subjects: Lessons from a research study of parents with learning difficulties. *Social Science and Medicine*, *39*(3), 415–424. DOI:10.1016/0277-9536(94)90139-2

Carlen, P. (1988). *Women, crime and poverty*. Milton Keynes: Open University Press.

Carson, D., Gilmore, A., Perry, C., & Gronhaug, K. (2001). *Qualitative marketing research*. London: Sage.

Cornell, D. G., Benedek, E. P., & Benedek, D. M. (1987). Juvenile homicide: Prior adjustment and a proposed typology. *American Journal of Orthopsychiatry*, *57*(3), 383–393. DOI:10.1111/j.1939-0025.1987.tb03547.x

Darby, P. J., Allan, W. D., Kashani, J. H., Hartke, K. L., & Reid, J. C. (1998). Analysis of 112 juveniles who committed homicide: Characteristics and a closer look at family abuse. *Journal of Family Violence*, *13*(4), 365–375. DOI:10.1023/A:1022823219276

Dey, I. (2007). Ground theory. In C. Searle, G. Gobo, J. Gubrium, & D. Silverman (Eds.), *Qualitative research practice* (pp. 80–94). London: Sage.

Edwards, S. (1981). *Female sexuality and the law*. Oxford: Martin Robertson.

Edwards, S. (1984). *Women on trial*. Manchester: Manchester University Press.

Ewing, C. P. (1990). *When children kill*. Lexington, MA: Lexington Books.

Gadd, D., & Jefferson, T. (2007). *Psychosocial criminology: An introduction*. London: Sage.

Glaser, B. G., & Strauss, A. L. (1967). *The discovery of grounded theory: Strategies for qualitative research*. Chicago, IL: Aldine.

Gluckman, M. (Ed.). (1964). *Closed systems and open minds*. London: Oliver & Boyd.

Halsey, M., & Deegan, S. (2014). "Picking up the pieces": Female significant others in the lives of young (ex) incarcerated males. *Criminology and Criminal Justice*. Retrieved from http://crj.sagepub.com/content/early/2014/03/12/1748895814526725.ref.html. DOI:10.1177/1748895814526725

Halsey, M., & Deegan, S. (2015). *Young offenders: Crime, prison and struggles for desistance*. London: Palgrave Macmillan.

Hardwick, P. J., & Rowton-Lee, M. A. (1996). Adolescent homicide: Towards assessment of risk. *Journal of Adolescence*, *19*(3), 263–276. DOI:10.1006/jado.1996.0024

Hill-Smith, A., Hugo, P., Hughes, P., Fonagy, P., & Hartman, D. (2002). Adolescent murderers: Abuse and adversity in childhood. *Journal of Adolescence*, *25*(2), 221–230. DOI:10.1006/jado.2002.0462

Kelly, K., & Totten, M. (2002). *When children kill: A social-psychological study of youth homicide*. Ontario: University of Toronto Press.

Kupers, T. (2005). Toxic masculinity as a barrier to mental health treatment in prison. *Journal of Clinical Psychology*, *61*(6), 713–724. DOI:10.1002/jclp.20105

Leigey, M. (2010). For the longest time: The adjustment of inmates to a sentence of life without parole. *The Prison Journal*, *90*(3), 247–268. DOI:10.1177/0032885510373490

Melville, A., & Hincks, D. (2016). Conducting sensitive interviews: A review of reflections. *Law and Method*, 1–25. DOI:10.5553/REM/.000015

Mitchell, J. C. (2000). Case and situation analysis. In R. Gomm, P. Hammersley, & P. Foster (Eds.), *Case study method* (pp. 165–168). London: Sage.

Pomeroy, E. C., Green, D. L., & Kiam, R. (2001). Female juvenile offenders incarcerated as adults: A psychoeducational group intervention. *Journal of Social Work*, *1*(1), 101–115. DOI:10.1177/146801730100100107

Ryan, G. W., & Bernard, H. R. (2003). Techniques to identify themes. *Field Methods*, *15*(1), 85–109. DOI:10.1177/1525822X02239569

Sellers, B. G., & Heide, K. M. (2012). Male and female child murderers: An empirical analysis of U.S. arrest data. *International Journal of Offender Therapy and Comparative Criminology*, *56*(5), 691–714. DOI:10.1177/0306624X11411152

Shumaker, D., & McKee, G. (2001). Characteristics of homicidal and violent juveniles. *Violence and Victims*, *16*(4), 401–409. DOI:10.1891/0886-6708.16.4.401

Smart, C. (1976). *Women, crime and criminology: A feminist critique*. London: Routledge & Kegan Paul.

Smart, C. (1989). *Feminism and the power of law*. London: Routledge.

Stake, R. (2000). The case study method in social inquiry. In R. Gomm, P. Hammersley, & P. Foster (Eds.), *Case study method* (pp. 19–26). London: Sage.

Stiles, W. B. (2007). Theory-building case studies of counselling and psychotherapy. *Counselling and Psychotherapy Research*, *7*(2), 122–127. DOI:10.1080/14733140701356742

Strauss, A., & Corbin, J. (1998). *Basics of qualitative research: Techniques and procedures for developing grounded theory*. Thousand Oaks, CA: Sage.

Taylor, J. Y. (2002). Talking Back: Research as an act of resistance and healing for African American women survivors of intimate male partner violence. *Women & Therapy*, *25*(3–4), 145–160. DOI:10.1300/J015v25m03_11

Vries, A. M., & Liem, M. (2011). Recidivism of juvenile homicide offenders. *Behavioral Sciences & the Law*, *29*(4), 483–498. DOI:10.1002/bsl.984

3 Accepting the challenge

Male-on-male confrontational violence

> We were all kind of the 'bad kids' of the neighbourhood . . . and [there were] other groups [as well]. . . . [S]o [we'd] have the clash, you know. *[We'd]* want to be the best and *they'd* want to be the best, and that's how it all started, like, 'All right. Meet us here'.
>
> (Mike)

> With guys that age it's like you're just hungry for it. . . . [S]o drama and just like blues would just be over the smallest little things: look at somebody the wrong way or something and yeah, it would pop off.
>
> (Sonny)

This chapter deals with scenarios of confrontational violence as a well-travelled, but no less problematic, route to a murder conviction. These cases, by their nature, typically involve young men, the demographic most likely to get themselves into these sorts of situations. Indeed, Australian researchers Tomsen and Crofts (2012, p. 424) observe that 'male on male attacks are so frequent as to form the bulk of all homicide cases'. A recent analysis by the Australian Institute of Criminology used 25 years of data from the National Homicide Monitoring Program to describe the characteristics of homicide incidents perpetrated by offenders aged 10–17 years. Bricknell and Bryant (2018, p. 3) demonstrated that the majority of young homicide offenders in Australia were male (88%) and cite evidence that 42% of all juvenile homicide incidents were acquaintance homicides, with a third of all incidents (33%) classified as stranger homicides and a fifth as domestic homicides (21%). By contrast, only 11% of all homicide incidents perpetrated by adults over the same period involved the death of a stranger (p. 6). In the following, I suggest that what often sets (juvenile) stranger incidents apart from other homicides is the absence of a long-term plan to inflict harm on anybody. Rather, things spiralled out of control very quickly once my participants confronted – or were confronted by – the victim. The association between cause of death and whether the youth was acting alone or in company was also substantial. Stabbings (38%) and beatings (35%) were the most frequent cause of the victim's death in all homicides perpetrated by juvenile offenders. However, beating deaths became even more common (54%) when the homicide incident involved a group of young offenders, as opposed to a young person acting alone. The fact that group-perpetrated homicides primarily occurred in a public location – usually a street or other open area (43%) – is testimony enough that young people 'are attracted to public spaces with different physical and spatial qualities. They like to be where there are other people and where special things happen' (Lieberg, 1995, p. 723). Unknown people and situations open up new horizons and prosocial networks but can also bring teenagers into conflict with adults, other youth, and youth groups. As Lieberg (1995, p. 722) observes in relation to youth:

> They also take over a public space by marking it in some way (such as graffiti) or by their own way of using the objects and furnishings of the place. Just by appearing in public spaces or through their dress, ways of moving, and ways of expressing things, teenagers attract attention and cause irritation.

With two notable exceptions, the nine individuals whose voices feature in this chapter had no formal antecedent history prior to their involvement in the death of the victim. However, by their own admission, each interviewee was in a state where their criminal conflict was escalating and violent conflict was always a possibility – if not a probability. The motivation to engage in violent incidents ranged from retaliation against perceived transgressions or affronts to their person, to involvement in groups or 'crews' that clashed over bragging rights in the local area, to petty street crime that exploded as their victims – also young males – refused to acquiesce and unexpectedly fought back. Some cases involved a measure of all three. To a much lesser extent, certain of the young men had possessed handguns to intimidate and threaten in the course of more organized criminal activities. Interestingly, none of the shootings in this book was rooted in the context of such dealings, as opposed to interpersonal tensions that were taken to fatal and tragic conclusions by the perpetrators' untimely access to firearms. In any event, it is obvious that all of the juveniles in this chapter had seen a lot of fighting and been involved in a lot of fights, which had decreased their fear of these events over time.

Different factors, at different times, caused the confrontations in this chapter to take sudden and catastrophic turns. What is clear right now is that the impact of unresolved trauma and loss at individual-neighbourhood levels left these young men with virtually no shot of developing as conventional, responsible, and mature young adults. This was underlined by a long-time pervasive pattern of reckless, dangerous, and impulsive acts resulting in multiple suspensions and sanctions. One variable that seems firmly in the mix here is a regression to the basic need for survival at any cost during critical moments surrounding the crimes – even though none of the young men intended or wanted for death to occur. This circumstance brings sharply into focus many of the key problems facing a much larger group of teenagers who fail to appreciate what might result from their ill-conceived, aggressive actions. This includes, first and foremost, how a youth who is not pursuing a murderous plan can get himself into a nasty predicament in which a life is lost and the lives of many others (including his own) are instantly and irrevocably transformed. I join a small but critically informed literature that foregrounds the psychodynamics of youth offending and the highly effective way the common law doctrine of common purpose (like felony murder and extended joint enterprise) is used to convict secondary parties to a homicide. Such work links the frailties (increased attraction to novel and exciting experiences, impulsivity, recklessness, and so on) of the adolescent brain to, among other aspects, a burden of proof low enough to allow those 'who are simply too morally remote from the crime, bit-part players or not even players at all, to be swept up in a prosecution and convicted on the basis that they were all "in it together"' (Coleman, 2016, p. 2). Together they function to structure discussion of how the mandatory life sentence will impact the various trajectories of those young people who don't fit neatly into the murderer category.

Growing up 'gangsta': upbringings in situations of violence, including the use of weapons

What is immediately striking from the accounts of juveniles involved in male-on-male confrontational violence is such males' early exposure to, or experience of, significant violence in the home, neighbourhood, or wider community. Without doubt, the most extreme examples were gleaned from those born in developing countries. For instance, Will came from Northeast Africa and was subject to many atrocities there while a civil war raged. During this time, police, army, and government officials would enter Will's house at night, unannounced, leaving his family terrified. His mother, a single parent, described the raids as life and death situations in which Will and his seven siblings were routinely hit on the head, back, and arms with rods or canes when they cried, leading to nightmares and intrusive thoughts about those visits. As Will reflects in the following, travelling to Egypt at the age of 7 proved far from the reprieve that his family had hoped for:

> [I saw] stabbings, fucking people getting run over . . . all kinds of shit, people getting kidnapped. . . . Rich people, like, wealthy people [would] steal them for their organs, stuff like that. . . . I almost had that happen to me actually.
>
> There was no cops, none of this, you know, police, no. Zero. Coming to your house to write a report? There's none of that shit. The police only come to someone's house if somebody gets killed or raped – barely even then. So you deal with your own shit, you know what I mean?

Similarly, Nick was born in a small township historically synonymous with police oppression in South Africa under apartheid. According to official crime statistics, his region has long been regarded as the murder capital of the country, a fact not lost on his older brother Marcus (also convicted of murder arising from the same incident), 'You see people getting killed from a young age. Things like that are happening all the time.' Coming from a comparatively wealthy family in the Eastern Cape – their father had a good job, they owned their own home, and even employed the services of a housekeeper – only reinforced a sense of being suitable targets for crimes of opportunity. As he told me, 'People are poor there. So if you, [or] if your family, do all right and do okay for yourself there's always someone hungrier than you that wants to come and take what you've got.' To Marcus's mind, far from being a rejection of mainstream cultural values, this social reality, in fact, left no choice *but* to anticipate and outmanoeuvre potential threats from early childhood, endorsing attack as the best form of defence.

At interview (part-way through his life sentence), now a 28-year-old man, he regularly made reference to the 'code of the street' – a code where you just don't back down from fights, you go headlong back into them to show your mettle.

> Even in primary school you had people carrying knives and things like that – *in primary school!* And if you couldn't fight you [would] always be the victim no matter what . . . and that would just open the door for everyone to [exploit you]. So you would always have to be confident and be able to take things head on . . . otherwise, you wouldn't survive.

A world away, in some of the most deprived communities within Adelaide's northern and western suburbs, the net effect was not altogether dissimilar, as all of the young men remembered seeing people on the streets being knocked out or unconscious and bleeding on numerous occasions. At some point, all had experienced being outnumbered and set upon in the public spaces around their homes, such as ovals, sporting, and community centres, often requiring them to seek out hospital treatment:

> I used to live at Pennington and that was all right; that was pretty safe. But then when I went down to Taperoo, I got bashed by eight people when I spent a day there and woke up in hospital. . . . I had a broken nose and a fractured jaw.
>
> (Leo)

While hardly an 'inner city warzone' in the sense contemplated by studies of densely populated urban centres like Chicago, Baltimore, or Detroit, Mike's projections of his area as akin to 'the Bronx' often played out in some very violent ways. In one such scenario, he reported experiencing the Western suburbs 'weapon of choice' – the 'trolley-pole' – an improvised baton made from the dislodged steel handle of a supermarket trolley/cart.

> I've seen, you know, stabbings, bashings. A lot of weapons, you know, poles, knuckle-dusters . . . eight balls in a sock, that sort of stuff. I got hit with a trolley-pole once in the back of the head, but it didn't really – it cut me open – but it didn't really do any serious damage or anything. . . . They'd seen me on my own in Mansfield Park . . . [and] that's the prime opportunity. . . . They didn't take anything from me; they just bashed me.
>
> (Mike)

Further complicating this picture, several of the young men had also been subject to displays of their fathers' violent and unpredictable moods, heightened by the use of amphetamines and other criminal activity around the home. One of the most vivid examples was provided by Leo, who recalled accompanying his father, from around the age of 7 or 8, to the homes of various 'debtors':

> I was pretty young and I can just remember someone lying on the front of their fucking doorstep, on the ground, and Dad's just smashing them with a hammer. . . . I was just screaming, crying, yeah.

In each juvenile's narrative, victimization – or the threat thereof – preceded the decision to possess, collect, and/or carry items that were capable of being used as weapons, such as poles, decorative knives/swords, throwing stars, and so on. As described by Tyson, who had acquired a small armoury of weapons, these items were common currency amongst young people and could be bought just about anywhere:

> Every day [my friends would] bring some sort of weapon down [to the community centre] and this person wants to show that he's got a more deadly weapon than the others and then . . . they started bringing like machetes and knives and ninja swords. . . . It was [easy] for me to get these items . . . because my uncle used to own a deli and . . . *The Picture* magazine used to have this page where you could buy BB guns and throwing knives . . . and I used to get my uncle's [credit] card down and I'd put it on there and . . . they would just send the item to my shop.

On the nights the victims were killed, the motivation to go equipped with such articles ranged from incidental or 'just in case' reasons to the more deliberate scenarios where earlier events or discussions foreshadowed that a confrontation was about to take place. In the latter cases, forewarned was most certainly forearmed. As Sonny's and Mike's accounts so deftly illustrate, the very reason parliament has legislated offenses such as 'carrying an offensive weapon' (see s21C(1)(a) *Summary Offences Act*, 1953 [SA]) – even if people do not use the weapons – is the very real risk that they *will* be used, regardless of an individual's intentions when setting out with such items.

> I used to mostly get around unarmed but towards the end, because of dramas [with other groups] and all that, I'd get around with a pool ball wrapped up in a couple of stockings. I used to make like a nice little cosh out of it with a handle and that. But my mates all had knives.
>
> (Sonny)

> We went there for a fight, you know, like as usual, as we normally do. We'd always take poles – never knives – we've never really stabbed, any of us. . . . It was always poles or bats and stuff like that but never knives. And I thought the knives [on this occasion] were just to scare them, you know, until I saw him get stabbed and then I knew it was serious. That's why we took off straight away.
>
> (Mike)

Related to this, several of the males described themselves as being sensitive to their ethnic origins and influenced by American music and film, in which minorities are featured and involved in street fighting and/or criminal activity, including the films *Scarface* and *Boyz n the Hood* and entertainers N.W.A, Tupac Shakur, Bruce Lee and the like. These observations pull together two aspects I see as being important in relation to those young men disposed to carry weapons capable of inflicting serious injury or killing a person. The first is identification with the hero; in violent entertainment, the hero is often portrayed as someone who has a just cause and is allowed to use whatever is necessary to follow through with his/her goals and aims. Indeed, Kopak and Sefiha (2014) remind us of an entertainment reality:

> [S]ome of the most memorable lead characters from crime-related television series (e.g. Vic Mackey (Michael Chiklis) in *The Shield*, Emily Thorn (Emily VanCamp) in *Revenge*, and Dexter Morgan (Michael C. Hall) in *Dexter*) and film (e.g. Frank Castle (Thomas Jane) in *The Punisher*, Nick Hume (Kevin Bacon) in *Death Sentence*) include those who consistently challenge moral and legal norms.
>
> (p. 95)

Obviously, it is far too broad to state that anybody who views or listens to this kind of material will then go and perpetrate violence. The key is that it is in vulnerable people, such as those who feature in this book, that violent games, movies, and/or blood sports can have a significant impact. As Kathleen Heide (1999) observes, this material portrays robbing, killing, and raping as 'part of everyday life in "the hood" for low-income members of society, particularly African Americans' (p. 43). Without any current stake in conformity and conventional activities (school, sport, work, etc.), many of the young people she evaluated 'fashioned themselves as "players" in the game of life . . . [who] were out to have "a good time"' (p. 48). In this regard, Sonny, of Tanzanian extraction, remarked that 'from a very young age, I did want to be a gangster'. On the night the victim (a Caucasian male) was killed, Sonny recalled how he (aged 15) and his friends had been influenced after watching films in which African American protagonists were involved in street crime. He recalled that his group big-noted themselves and assumed the role of gangsters for the night. Here, he reflects on the curious way the issue of race emerged during his sentencing hearing:

> Even the victim's mother in the victim impact statement brought up that [she] thought [the crime] was like, racially motivated. And there was an element of racism, right. Because at some point in our lives we had all copped racial abuse . . . to the point I used to wish I was born white . . . with straight hair and all of that.

I elaborate on the issue of racist attitudes and bullying in detail later in Section 'Kicking against the pricks: seeking justice through violence'.

The second factor I see as important here is that the movies that so often appeal to adolescent males, such as the *Die Hard*, *Fast and Furious* or *Rambo* franchises, present an account of violence with an unrealistic optimism about the level of insult a human body can withstand. Put simply, the boys in this chapter were totally ignorant as to just how *easy* it can be to kill a person, even with weapons involved. At times, this naivety was substantiated by medical evidence to the effect that very little force was required to inflict the fatal injury, which was certainly not inflicted with the maximum force available to the young offender. These one-strike injuries were often consistent with an act of bravado, an intention to cause serious – but not lethal – harm (i.e. 'Here's something to go home with: Don't tangle with X, Y, Z again'). Something of this reality seems to have resonated with Tyson, Sonny, and Mike in the following excerpts:

> I pointed the knife . . . and it hit him in the back of the shoulder blade and . . . it killed him instantly. . . . I just panicked and in that one motion I jabbed it towards whatever I saw in front of me. . . . I didn't know that a puncture wound to the shoulder blade would kill a person.
>
> (Tyson)

> At that age you don't understand the consequences. . . . If you're carrying a knife and you stab somebody, it's very easy to kill that person, you know what I mean? So, yeah, what has dawned on me is how naive I was. . . . It's like I was playing a grown-up's game but with the mind of a child.
>
> (Sonny)

> I never used to think about [the outcome]. It was like, 'Who cares?', you know, 'He's not going to die.' You never think about that until you go [through] something like [this].
>
> (Mike)

Not surprisingly, previous involvement in violent encounters that ended 'well' did little to deter the young males from entering all-in brawls on the days or nights the victims died. One of the young men told me,

> I got attacked at the Salisbury skate park. . . . It wasn't really bad; I got a broken arm and a broken leg. . . . [I was conscious] until right at the end when I got hit in the head and knocked out.
>
> (Luke)

His indifference to an assault causing harm with intent points to the destructive effects of childhood trauma, and, specifically, to the likelihood of criminality for those who carry the weight of current and historic as well as personal disadvantage.

Relevant here is previous work by Kelly and Totten (2002), who report the way in which 'many youth homicide offenders espoused a "violence-as-normal" attitude and indicated that their victims died from a level of violence that they felt was "normal"' (as cited in Woodworth, Agar, & Coupland, 2013, p. 1019). Eddie, for example, had this to say about the matter: '[I'd been in] a couple of fights that were *worse* but didn't really [have any consequences] . . . yeah, some of them got really out of hand. *Really bad.*' The fact that victims were still standing and/or conscious and talking as the juveniles decamped the scenes gave way to the perpetrators' confusion, panic, and regret upon learning, days or hours later, that the victims had, in fact, died in hospital:

> The last time that I saw this guy, he was on his feet. He was alive. He went onto the road 'cause there was a taxi coming. . . . Him and his mate jumped in the taxi and I've jumped in [our] car. . . . I never thought that this guy was going to die; that's not what I wanted at all. I understand that he died as a result of my actions but I never meant for that to happen.
>
> (Stefan)

> [The police] turned the camera on, said the bloody date, asked me my name and he was like, 'William De Villiers, we're charging you with murder: first-degree murder.' And I was like, 'What? You're joking me,' and he's like, 'No. So what have you got to say?' . . . I still couldn't believe it. My body just fucking went numb and I was like, 'Who fucking died?'
>
> (Will)

Organized for disorganization: families who are economically, geographically, linguistically, and/or culturally isolated with few, if any (prosocial), friends or support

It is obvious that for the vast majority of young men who find themselves before the courts, after responding quickly and violently to relatively trivial altercations, life was a struggle from a very early age. These young men's formative years were generally characterized by chaotic, highly unstable, and transient lifestyles, resulting in multiple placements and an ongoing lack of supervision and boundaries. In fact, even for the young men who cited membership of a close-knit, 'functional' family, there was little evidence of support during the course of their trials or subsequent imprisonment, endorsing the opinion that these men have often had to survive life under their own steam. Despite the (reported) efforts of some parents, it is clear that their sons were able to keep them ignorant about the trouble they had been in from time to time. In any case, the common thread binding these males is varying degrees of economic, geographic, linguistic, and cultural isolation, with few, if any, positive role models or support. It is hardly surprising, then, that none of the individuals in this chapter was regularly attending school at the time of the offence, and this detail forms an all too familiar backdrop to crimes of violence on the street and in public places. As shall become evident, with little to no assistance from a father figure or a wider network of teachers, employers, and the like, the gravitational pull towards the group or gang was undeniable. As Mike explains, leading an aimless existence and having a poor self-concept and time on his hands was symptomatic of the situation he was in, along with many of his friends at the time of the offence:

> It was bound to happen, not so much to murder somebody, but seriously hurt someone, you know, stab somebody, something like that. It was getting to that point. The only way I could have stopped it was to just branch off from [my friends] . . . but the lifestyle I was in, it was so good, it was so appealing to me that it was just too hard to do that. . . . [We were] sort of like a little family, you know, because I didn't have my mum or my dad or anything like that – they weren't really interested – so they kind of made up for that. It was like a brotherhood sort of. It was like having all these older brothers which I never had and if anyone disrespected me . . . they'd be the first ones into it, so I kind of felt like I was someone, which I didn't have before.

Typical of this cohort, Mike had a historically difficult relationship with his parents, who had separated before his first birthday. The subject of several child protection notifications in relation to his mother's excessive use of intravenous drugs, Mike would frequently leave the house without knowing if his mother would be alive or dead upon his return. Mike recalled her admission to a closed psychiatric ward when he was around 6:

> She had her own priorities. She didn't really worry about [her] kids; she kind of done her own thing . . . methamphetamines a lot. Smoked marijuana. But it was the meth that really damaged her.

Over the next few years, Mike cycled between the homes of his maternal aunt, his maternal grandmother, his father, and his paternal grandparents. Pre-sentence reports indicate he was homeless in the sense that he had no particular place to call home, with placements in each location quickly breaking down for a variety of reasons. This was not an uncommon scenario, with several of the young men relinquished or removed to their grandparents' homes due to parental issues with alcohol and illicit substances. Eddie told of his unfortunate start in the following terms:

> I was only with my parents for maybe two, three weeks due to substance abuse, like alcohol, and then neglect. . . . I remember my grandparents telling me that when they [found me,] it was a real hot day and I was in a cot, just left by myself . . . breathing heavily and I had sores all over my body. So back then, I was in hospital a lot.

Grandparents interviewed for this study confirmed their grandchild's very unsettled and unhappy family backgrounds, marked by their own child's regular abuse of alcohol and other drugs and subsequent indifferent approach to parenting. Under these circumstances, Dorothy reported that it was not uncommon for her grandson to be 'dropped off' for months on end with no contact from either parent to enquire as to his whereabouts, activities, or welfare:

> His parents both had issues with drugs. And his mother couldn't look after him. She turned around and told us she has no maternal instincts: couldn't

> cope. His father was just always around drugs. He tried to be a good father but it just didn't work and they couldn't cope looking after children. So the boys were always dropped off, like Leo and his brothers were usually dropped off to us to look after, could be a couple of hours or, as previously stated, I had Leo for 14 months [on one occasion] before I seen his mother again.

Another grandfather went further to add that, at one point in time, he was raising 17 of his grandchildren under the same roof to spare them from being declared wards of the state. While the young men spoke with fondness for their grandparents, many found it difficult to adjust to household rules and expectations in their teenage years, as such practices were foreign to them. In short, most had never heard the word 'no' until they commenced living in their grandparents' care. Consequently, attempts to rein them in generally came up short, as the adolescents would find their way to their friends' couches or back to their parents, where their behaviour could remain unchecked. One of the fathers himself had this to say in relation to his son:

> I was hooked on cocaine and fucking taking acid like you wouldn't believe [so] I didn't really pay much attention . . . like I didn't sit back and look, 'Oh, okay, have they got any problems?' or anything like that. All I knew was that when Dad was around, they were happy and that's all I seen. So, to me, they were happy.
>
> (Dean)

Instead of being an alternative site for happiness, school turned out to be a series of dismal failures for all the young men. Attending a total of nine primary schools, Mike advised that he initially loved going to school to meet with friends and escape from his home life. By high school, however, already experimenting with alcohol and poly-drug use, Mike found that his enthusiasm and attendance waned as he grappled with feelings of being abandoned and disenfranchised from his family. Despite testing at above average intelligence, he was suspended on several occasions for swearing and excluded for a period of ten weeks in Year Nine after becoming involved in a physical altercation. The final straw was an ill-fated decision to enrol him in a very large, predominantly middle-class school, despite Mike's protestations that he would not fit in with the general student demographic. Instead, Mike felt that this decision was motivated by his stepmother for reasons of convenience, given she already had a child attending the school. As Mike recalls, he was soon singled out by other students due to his different behaviours and physical presentation, which included tattoos and an electronic monitoring anklet:

> When I got there . . . everyone was like 'Whoa! *What* is this bloke here? He's got tattoos in high school. He's got a Home D bracelet on.' That sort of stuff. . . . The boys there didn't like it 'cause it took the attention off them but a lot of the girls gave me a lot of attention 'cause they wanted to know; they

> were *very* interested . . . and I had a bit of drama here and there, you know, but I was only there for about three weeks and I got kicked out. It just wasn't the right school.

Even for males who indicated consistent (prosocial) parental care, it is apparent that their early years were marked by dislocation, instability, and poverty, factors that were often compounded by racial attitudes. The most common disruptions included moving house and school on numerous occasions, which left a trail of broken educational and behavioural milestones.

Floyd considers his relationship with his family, who had migrated together as political refugees, to be of a different quality from that of many of his peers in the juvenile and adult prison environments. He was first subjected to racial comments at school. He told me, 'Reception was the first time I experienced bullying. . . . They would [say] . . . "Go back to where you come from," or "Why is *he* playing here? He's black" . . . or "He's a wog".' His strategy was instinctive and unambiguous:

> [I]t would upset me and it would hurt my feelings but . . . you can't lose face. That's the mentality I had back then. . . . I had to defend myself, my people, my honour. . . . I would stand my ground. I didn't like being walked over.

Tyson, of Vietnamese heritage, adopted a similar tack: 'I've always managed to get my face [i.e. honour] back. Even if I had to lose a fight . . . I've never let anyone hit me and get away with it. Ever.' Not surprisingly, these young men's face-saving behaviour led to occasions where the conflict escalated into physical fights that sometimes involved suspensions and expulsions in their teenage years. Floyd estimates he was suspended from school on no fewer than six occasions due to fighting. But, as a talented sportsman, he was subsequently accepted and formed bonds of friendship with his schoolmates. However, this process had to be repeated each time he moved to a new school – something Floyd accepted but completely detested:

> We were always renting houses and . . . sometimes the landlord would decide that 'Oh, I'm selling the house' and . . . we'd have to move wherever my dad could find accommodations . . . so I had to change schools pretty regularly. . . . When you're settled, you know, you've established friendships with people at school, on your soccer team and then I've got to move again and yeah, that was that.

As Floyd explained, adopting a stance that indicated to others he would not be oppressed by them became particularly useful in his current incarceration in an adult prison, as he knew how to stand up for himself without fear:

> When you get to the new school or the new gaol you can identify . . . where the food chain [is] if . . . you want to word it like that. And you would either

> get into a fight with that guy or you become friends with that guy . . . [so] you . . . can elevate straight [in with] . . . the popular kids sort of thing. . . . If you win a fight with that guy then *you* become the alpha. . . . I wasn't planning on that but I think that's how it sort of eventuated.

Will's and Sonny's families, each headed by a single mother, also lived in high-density, low-income housing in several of Adelaide's more crime-ridden areas. Will's father, who remains in Sudan, never made much effort to meet him and – despite Will's claims to the contrary – I suspect anger over being abandoned continues to weigh heavily on him: 'It doesn't make any difference to me if he is here or he's not. I haven't had him [then] so it wouldn't make any difference to me [now].' Of course, as Psychologist James Garbarino points out in his book *Lost Boys: Why Our Sons Turn Violent and How We Can Save Them* (2000), when boys grow up without fathers, there is always a possibility that the boys will be drawn into the role of the man of the house. Garbarino observes (pp. 55–56) in relation to this:

> Without stable partners in their lives, some mothers turn to their sons for intimacy or protection. This is not necessarily a problem in and of itself. But premature responsibility and responsibility that is too big for a child to shoulder gracefully can cause big problems in the long run. . . . This kind of role reversal – where the child is the protector and the parent is needy – is common in the lives of violent boys.

As with several of the young men described in Garbarino's book, it was not uncommon for males in the current study to sell their limited possessions or use the proceeds of low-level criminality to provide household items for their mothers. In any event, for Will, the irony was stark; he had survived several of the world's deadliest provinces and yet there he was, out of control in Adelaide's inner-north.

> That's where the shit hit the fan, you know, Kilburn's a shit area . . . fucking, it's a ghetto. I don't know if you've heard about it but Kilburn's fucking where trouble starts. If you're born there, you're born into a life of crime.

Instead of playing sport or engaging in academic pursuits, Sonny described hanging out on the block as a way to have fun and reduce boredom: 'We moved to a unit in a big block of units . . . [with] a tiny little back yard and it meant I was sort of like out on the streets . . . from quite a young age.' At interview, his mother Lorraine agreed that, despite her best efforts, Sonny had no real childhood to speak of: no positive male role model; no good routine; a miserable experience of school; few (if any) conventional friends; and few opportunities to do what other families do (go on holidays, watch Dad go to and return from work, and so on).

> Even from primary school, he was targeted with racial vilification . . . and he didn't tell me until the end of the year, after he'd copped 12 months of it. . . .

> The things [they] used to say to him every day . . . [like], 'Your [skin] colour is the colour of shit,' [and] 'You have no father.' . . . He was crying and not wanting to go to school and I didn't understand *why*.

Instead, Sonny had to improvise. And by this, Lorraine meant that Sonny taught himself to get what he needed to survive, physically and emotionally:

> He wanted to have fun and socialise with his friends. He didn't have a father . . . and we were really poor. We were very, *very* poor. We couldn't afford holidays and I couldn't afford to take time off work. So what joy or happiness did he have in his life? He didn't have the family holiday to look forward to.

Over time, distress and anger at his father's rejection gave way to Sonny's growing sense of despondency over his lack of disposable income: 'I've always been poor. I never had a dollar to my name. The only way I did was if I stole it.' The subject of racial taunts at school and resentful about having less money than his friends, he gravitated towards a group of individuals who were given to rebellious behaviour and petty street crime. After stealing a motorcar during the holidays and driving about the city somewhat aimlessly, talk amongst the group turned to "rolling" someone to get their hands on a mobile telephone. Sonny had absorbed the widespread message of the American (or Australian) 'Dream'. By his own reckoning, everything was about the money.

> I came from a broken home. My parents divorced when I was like two years old. I was raised by my mother and she was out of work until I was like 11 so I was raised on social security. And this was the main reason I found myself dabbling in crime. It was just [that] I was unable to find a job, no matter how many times I applied. Until by the end of it I was like 'I'm going to have to go rob somebody, aren't I?'

Not unlike several of the parents at the centre of this book, Sonny's mother, Lorraine, consistently lamented the lack of an effective means for turning an impending and readily identifiable disaster into a personally and socially safe scenario:

> I would say to Sonny, 'I don't give you permission to go out. I don't want you going out tonight.' But teenage boys they just say, 'Yeah whatever' and they waltz out the door. What can you do to keep your child from leaving the premises? What legal rights does a mother have to keep a teenage child on the premises at night-time? What can we do and what supports can we get to keep them here? If I would have deadbolted – like locked ourselves down – he would have broken glass to get out.

With all avenues for assistance exhausted (help lines, family members, fellow church parishioners, government and non-government organizations), this mother was left to wrestle with the following conclusion: 'He's economically disadvantaged, he's a racial minority, and he doesn't have a father. Was he ever going to make it? I don't think he was ever going to make it' (Lorraine).

Kicking against the pricks: seeking justice through violence

The third relevant dimension of confrontationally violent juveniles is their sense of personal power and supreme confidence to take excessive responsibility for matters affecting them or their significant others. When wronged, as Heide (1999, p. 47) argues, 'they become consumed with rage and feel compelled to strike back'. Persecution arose from a variety of sources and served largely to entrench the outsider status experienced by the young men, who became inclined to act impulsively even *before* being subjected to any taunting or humiliating abuse. Frequently, questions of justice (and a particular kind of masculine script) completely obscured any alternative strategies aimed at de-escalating conflict, such as walking away or calling police/a responsible adult. In essence, these young people had become distrustful, developed some elements of grandiosity, felt betrayed, and were angry. Indeed, Athens' (1992, p. 27) account of the creation of violent offenders recognizes the way in which 'coarse and cruel treatment at the hands of others' produces 'a lasting and dramatic impact upon the subsequent course of their lives', a four-stage process Athens terms *brutalization.* Again, it is difficult to conceive of a more extreme chain of events than those narrated by Will, who had escaped war and abject poverty in Sudan and Egypt as a refugee. Arriving in Australia, he was bullied, firstly because of his colour and secondly because he was so far behind in his academic studies. His first teacher and mentor, Pamela, noted the South Australian school system as unable, or unwilling, to deal with the specific problems suffered by children such as Will, viewing him as just another problem student:

> I remember a lot of them [i.e., African kids] saying, 'I don't care if I get punished.' . . . It wasn't that; that wasn't the problem. The problem was if they received a [time] out and the other [i.e., white] child didn't. So they wanted to be treated equally and . . . and that's why they used to get more upset and angry and therefore think, 'No-one's supporting me, so I'm going to . . .' Because don't forget, they were fresh in the country. You're not going to switch that off; that was a survival mode . . . that's what they were used to doing. Like, 'If someone's going to hurt me, I'm going to hurt back or even if *I think* they're going to hurt me, I have to protect myself.'

At interview, Will was pragmatic: 'A lot of people prefer white people over black people.' At the same time, he conceded that as he grew older, he became more frustrated and less able to cope. Will was typical of the young men in this chapter: his initial quest for justice ultimately became an attempt to forge a hostile identity that could stand up to those who sought to marginalize and dismiss him. Katz (1988) notes the seductive and empowering lure of crime, with 'the ways of the badass' announcing, in effect, the following:

> Not only do you not know where I'm at or where I'm coming from, but, at any moment, I may transcend the distance between us and destroy you. I'll jump you on the street, I'll 'come up side' your head, I'll 'fuck you up good'. (p. 81)

As the following conversation with Will underscores, becoming badass required 'an overarching focus on gaining and maintaining respect . . . [as] a form of social capital that provides both status and protection earned by exuding dominance through one's physical presence, volatile actions, and in some special cases, violence' (Kopak & Sefiha, 2014, p. 98).

WILL: I don't just turn around and chuck shit at people. No, no . . . I was getting into fights with boys at school and then they were getting away with certain things and . . . I was angry. It was just a vibe, you know.

SIMONE: Did you ever feel like, 'This isn't really right: [the fact] that I'm *so, so* angry?'

WILL: No, I liked it actually, to be honest with you . . . when I'd get into a fight [and] sort of lose the plot, black out . . . [and] go into a rage mode. . . . [Having that] reputation, yeah, that was part of it as well. . . . [When] people know [you're] a nutcase: 'Don't fuck with him or he'll lose the plot'; this and that. I had that [reputation] since I was in Egypt as well. . . . [It] sort of developed who you [were] as a person around your peers. Where you fit in in the group was, you know, 'How well can you fight?', 'How well can you defend yourself?', 'How smart are you in the street?', 'How much money can you make?' All this bullshit, like that was literally imprinted into me since I was in Egypt. That's how I knew how to do certain things. It's how I knew how to get respect in a way.

SIMONE: So where did you fit in that pecking order?

WILL: Usually it's either at the top or just below the top. That's where I tend to aim at; it's either not to be fucked with or to be cautious with, you know? If I can't beat you, I have to stab you, you know: I have to hurt you some way.

SIMONE: So did you get some respect here in Australia for being that way?

WILL: I got respect or fear so either way I got something. It didn't faze me. The point is I don't want people fucking with me. That was pretty much the aim, plus whatever comes with it.

From interviews, it appears that confrontation and intimidation were devices that the young men could rely on to have their needs met when all others had failed. Almost 20 years since his arrest, Tyson recalled the exact moment he resolved that he was, as Athens put it, 'ready and willing to injure badly or even kill someone, should the proper circumstances arise' (1992, p. 60):

> I said to myself that I would never let any of these guys pick on me ever again, at all costs. I don't care if they have to beat me to death – *they will have to beat me to death* – because no-one is ever going to hit me again. . . . I didn't want to become a victim. I would rather become the offender instead.

Consistent with Polk's (1994) account of violent male-on-male encounters, these initial provocations often (but not exclusively) centred around the racism of so-called old Australians aimed at recently arrived Africans, Afghans, and Vietnamese. Floyd told of this reality in the following terms:

> [There was a group called] 'No Fucking Asians, Arabs, or Africans' [or] 'N.F.A.' That's what they used to graffiti up in the area . . . but then when you would approach them they would say, 'Oh nah nah nah: it stands for "No Fucking Around".' . . . But that was how the vibe was. Even in Rundle Mall, there was a group called 'National Action' and they were these skinheads and they sort of followed [the politician] Pauline Hanson and they hated Asians and wogs. And so, for us growing up, if we went to Rundle Mall, we had to fight with these people and in the end, when they stopped hanging around, it was like: we won.

On occasion, a racial presence was felt in the courtroom itself. Tyson recalled that the opening of his trial was attended by a neo-Nazi mob:

> Pauline Hanson [the politician] had come out with all her racism comments about getting swamped by all these Asians. And then you had all these people watching Romper Stomper with Russell Crowe and everything just all went into one. They decided to have a little protest.

That was, until, in Tyson's words, 'They realised that the person charged is an Asian boy and he killed another Asian boy so, "Oh, let it go." '(Tyson).

Angry, powerless boys turn to violence when they feel there is no legitimate recourse available to them. Or they turn to those who can be counted on to provide equally bad advice. From the perspective of Athens' (1992, p. 46) violentization theory, completing the brutalization process requires that subjects undergo violent instruction, 'usually by an older person who puts himself into the role of coach'. Far from acting as censuring agents, some parents were the prime movers in their sons' subsequent resort to violence.

> Sonny was being teased, being threatened by . . . a gang, a racist gang . . . and I told him, 'You should go to the police. You need to tell somebody about what's happening.' But Owen, [my partner] whom I was with at the time, said, 'Oh, the police won't do anything. That's a waste of time,' and kind of laughed and smirked at that and said that when he was bullied as a kid, the way that he earned respect was to be able to defend himself very effectively, you know, to be able to fight to defend himself. And that was the worst possible advice that he could have given him.
>
> (Lorraine, mother)

That's also how the wheels really started to fall off for Leo. He was battling anxiety, being harassed by other students due to his obesity issues, and he was living with his grandparents because his parents were unable to consistently care for him on a full-time basis primarily due to their issues with drugs and alcohol. The pressure was getting to him, but on the other hand he found acceptance with a negative peer group and, soon enough, his father was back on the scene.

Later, when I asked Dean about Leo's difficulties in the classroom, a telling observation was made about the so-called bullying crisis occurring at local high schools:

> In the schoolyard there's a lot of bullying. Whether you're big, small, or whatever, you get a group of kids; they'll bully ya. Well teachers don't do shit. So the next best thing is you make out you're scared, you lure the kid to where there's no witnesses and you kick the shit out of them and then deny, deny, deny. And that's how [my kids] went along. That's how they got through school. . . . Leo copped it 'cause he was just so big, so big and clumsy. And when I started teaching him Brazilian Ninjutsu and all that, he learnt he could break people. And he was knocking out adults at 13.
>
> (Dean, father)

Naturally enough, Dean sensed the romance of a 'crazy', 'wild', or 'killer' social identity (Fagan & Wilkinson, 1998, p. 151). It resurfaced in successive tales of how he had managed to turn the tables on many a flat-track bully. 'I was at school one day and I got punched in the arm and I was that skinny that it fractured my arm bone', Dean said.

> So I hammered the weights and I got on to this HGH – Human Growth Hormone – and it just sent me bonkers. And, yeah, I was just itching to fight all the time, yeah, like my old man wouldn't even go anywhere with me, yeah.

For Athens (1992, p. 64), 'as important as the circumstances surrounding the subject's violent performance is the immediate outcome of his performance'. And, as Athens continues, 'if the subject scores a major victory, there is always the possibility of his moving on to the next higher stage of violence development' (1992, p. 64). Nowhere is the relationship between a 'clear-cut win' and the penchant for further violence more evident than in Leo's construction of an impermeable, volatile identity. As apparent from his following remarks, 'adoption of a badass presentation becomes one of the few ways for youth to demonstrate critical cultural values such as manliness, adulthood, power, intelligence, and safety' (Kopak & Sefiha, 2015, p. 97).

> You have a few [fights] and you feel like you're on top of the world. You feel unstoppable. And you see someone just get knocked out, like, before they hit the ground . . . so then you want to, you know, look for the next one. . . . You feel like you're on top of the world. You feel unstoppable and I guess it just gets to your head and you think you can keep going, bigger and badder.

When asked whether *he* was ever bashed or further victimized in the course of these more proactive endeavours, another young lifer, Sonny responded, 'Nah, nah. That's the whole thing; that's the whole thing, right. That's like why you do it: so that it *doesn't* happen to you.'

Upping the ante: victim precipitation and forward panics

An equally prominent theme to emerge from interviews and qualitative analysis of homicide more generally is the concept of 'victim precipitation' (see Polk, 1994, 1997; Wolfgang, 1958) or those 'incidents in which a physical attack by the victim provokes the offender's lethal attack' (Felson & Messner, 1998, p. 406). Obviously, the displacement of blame onto victims has a long, contentious history, and it is a truism that the question of 'Who started it?' becomes an issue of immense significance wherever juveniles are concerned. Nevertheless, support for this position comes from several studies that show victims and offenders as drawn from the same population, with similar behaviours and life experiences (Broidy, Daday, Crandall, Sklar, & Jost, 2006; Mustaine & Tewksbury, 2000; Sampson & Lauritsen, 1990, p. 110; Singer, 1981; Wolfgang, 1958), including the proclivity to commit violent offences (Jennings, Piquero, & Reingle, 2012; Rivara, Shepherd, Farrington, Richmond, & Cannon, 1995). Authors also note the reluctance of 'offender-victims' (as distinct from 'nonoffender-victims') to engage police assistance, suggesting the former group can be victimized with relative impunity (Sparks, 1982). Something of this mentality is conveyed by Marcus, who became involved in an incident in the mistaken belief that one of the victim's group (a man well known for violence in the area) was responsible for injuries to his younger brother and one of his brother's friends several hours earlier. As Marcus described, the story had spread to the point where the five who stood trial, along with three others, had assembled to seek retribution for what some of them thought had been done to one of their numbers earlier that day. Receiving a panicked call for help, Marcus arrived on the scene (equipped with a baseball bat) just as the confrontation exploded into chaos. To try and diffuse the situation, as he explained, would have been futile.

> [It's] very easy for someone on the outside to say [we had other options] but while you're in that mindset of, this bloke just stabbed your mate [and] you need to go and fucking . . . get some sort of revenge . . . police is the last thing on your mind. . . . It doesn't register on my radar at all. . . . That's [not] how I work.
>
> I don't think it's about the fight as . . . [much as] . . . well, now they feel vulnerable; one of theirs got attacked . . . so, it's like, 'We have to do something . . . he's our mate.' But, yet again, they're kids: . . . when they're like that, hyped up and things like that, good luck to you to get any sense out of anything that's going on with them.

Even the authority and formality of the Supreme Court failed to interrupt displays of pure aggression and hostility directed between the opposing groups, with several mistrials caused by the types of behaviour illustrated in the following:

> The [victim's friend] stood up in court and pointed at us and . . . threatened to kill us. He said, 'This man here, he stabbed my friend and I'm going to kill him. 'Cause in my country, I'd kill all of you.' And he [made] out a [machine] gun [with his arms] and started shooting like this, like 'brrrrrrr brrrrrrr', making the noises. . . . And I was the closest to him; I was [sitting] in the glass. I just kind of, I thought he was going to come over [the dock]. He came right up to the glass and I just kind of sat back and grabbed a pen in case he came over.
>
> (Mike)

Of particular significance to my analysis, Rivara et al. (1995) found that the involvement of assault victims in criminal activity was especially striking for persons younger than 17 years of age. Such work attests to the higher risk of victimization faced by juveniles who engage in delinquent behaviour 'as a direct result of both their own offending and their association with other offenders' (Lauritsen, Sampson, & Laub, 1991, p. 268). In the current study, it was obvious to the young men that they were about to engage in a volatile situation, where they were confronted by a larger, often older group of men whom they believed were armed with knives, machetes, and other weapons. In all but one instance, the teenagers, having experienced conflict with these individuals in the days or hours before the crime, expected reprisals from the other group's members but naturally did not know the timing or the circumstances of such. Yet, in account after account, it was the teenagers who ended up with the murder weapon(s) and who were the ones to up the ante and take events to such fatal and tragic conclusions. As a prime example of 'homicide as a form of conflict resolution' (Polk, 1994, p. 113), Floyd approached the occupants of a vehicle who were acting suspiciously on his street two days before the fatal shooting occurred. Antagonized by the volley of racial epithets that greeted him, he produced and discharged a firearm into the ground, telling the victim's group 'to leave my street and do their crime somewhere else'. Unaware that one of the groups had received an injury when the bullet Floyd had fired had ricocheted into the stranger's leg, Floyd told me, 'They left and I thought I had resolved the situation.' On the night of the murder, Floyd arrived home to notice the same group of males with poles and bottles, sitting down and standing on the footpath outside his home. Immediately, his thoughts turned to the well-being of his family members, asleep only a stone's throw away:

> This particular incident was like a spur of the moment thing. I wouldn't say wrong place, wrong time, because it happened at my house, like on my street. I think that sort of made me a bit more, I wouldn't say *territorial*, but sort of more defensive in regards to [the fact] my family was inside sleeping at the time and there had been a previous altercation where I'd spoken to these people before and so [now] they had came back a second time . . . for retribution. . . . And I didn't know if they had already been inside my house with my family sleeping and so that's probably what made me go a bit overboard.

Exiting his vehicle, Floyd was immediately struck to the side of the head, causing him to fall to the ground. He heard one person say, 'I'm going to kill this cunt. He shot me.' It was at this point he learnt that the round he had previously discharged had grazed the leg of one of the men. A scuffle ensued, until which time a machete was swung – only narrowly missing its mark. Outnumbered and unarmed, Floyd ran home, located his firearm, and returned to the scene. Viewed forensically, he fully acknowledges that the execution-style killing of one and wounding of another was completely out of proportion to the men's conduct. Furthermore, it would appear that Floyd had opportunities to reflect on the circumstances before obtaining and discharging the firearm. The first arose when he reached his own home, as the obvious course of action would have been to simply remain there where he had the protection of being in secure premises and, if necessary, call the police. The second opportunity occurred as Floyd fired shots at the victim who was running away from him, constituting no threat to him at that time. Indeed, it was on the latter basis that any potential claim of self-defence was doomed to failure. Again, there is much here that fits Polk's (1994) pattern of masculine confrontational homicide, in which one or another of the parties breaks off the immediate conflict to bring a weapon into the scene. Deeply ashamed and remorseful of his actions, Floyd offered the following explanation for his hot-headed and impulsive response:

> Even though they wanted retribution on me, I feared it would escalate to them hurting my family. I presumed they might have a firearm too because they had been shot [previously]. All sorts of thoughts were going through my head. The victim was 23 years old and the others were like 25, 24, and I was 17. . . . They already had weapons in their hands and I'm fighting with [bare fists] . . . ducking and dodging this way, that way and that way. So I sort of tried to even out the numbers a bit by introducing [a firearm] into the scene. . . . It felt like a lifetime at the time, but [it was] probably under a minute, 30 seconds, yeah, no more than a minute or two, like for the whole thing [to be over].

Immediately following the event, Floyd perceived that everyone had run away and that the immediate danger was gone. He stated, 'I saw one person lying on the floor and my automatic reaction was to help him. I called the police and ambulance and handed myself in.'

As an exploratory variable, the concept of a 'forward panic' offers one plausible explanation for how tables can turn so excessively, quickly, and gratuitously on would-be offenders. Developed by Randall Collins (2008), the term is adopted from French military researcher Ardant du Picq, who called it a '"flight toward the front" – a pattern of emotional release like a panic retreat but in this case rushing towards a fallen enemy no longer able to resist' (Collins, 2009, p. 572). As Collins (2009, p. 572) observes, these situations are marked by protracted tension 'during which both sides [do] little damage . . . followed by an event which [makes] one side weak and unable to defend itself'. In practical terms, this emotional surge often occurs 'when one side runs away, has been caught, handcuffed, fallen down, or been isolated from support, etc.' (Gross, 2016, p. 245). Noting that 'the tension is prolonged and built up . . . [and is] striving toward a climax' (2008, p. 85), Collins observes the way actors enter an 'emotional tunnel of violent attack' and a 'moral holiday' (2008, p. 87), which supports behaviour that is otherwise socially (and personally) unacceptable. Under these conditions, 'unstoppable frenzies centered on rage, in which incredibly violent acts and "overkill" – the carryover of violent acts well past the point of victory – occur frequently' (Gross, 2016, p. 243). The entire four-stage sequence that typifies the forward panic scenario (including 'Build up of Tension/Fear', 'Sudden Resolution in favor of one side', 'Piling on' and 'Overkill' [Gross, 2016, p. 243]) can be seen in Mike's depiction of collective violence that culminated in murder:

> We kind of just grabbed weapons [and] walked around the corner. And as soon as we walked around the corner it was almost instantaneous. They knew what was happening as well. They just jumped up. They started running at us. One of them got hit in the face with a pool cue, he dropped and then it was just warfare after that. . . . It was just scatter, everywhere over the whole oval, you know. People over here being stabbed, people over there being bashed. It was pretty full on. And then Eddie – he didn't have any weapons, he just had his fist – [was] fighting one and another one come up and bit him. So I hit him in the back of the head with a pool cue and he ran. I chased him down and I hit him in the leg and he fell over and we started beating him up and then someone come over the fence and stabbed him, four times in the kidney. . . . He got stabbed four times in the kidney, then four times in the heart, and then one in the neck . . . and the one in the neck, that's what killed him: it hit his jugular and just blood came out everywhere, like you see in the movies, you know. You picture it as fake but it actually happens.

Brothers in arms: extended joint enterprise

Broadly speaking, the stories in this chapter revolve around groups of young men who were minded to enter an affray with another group of males and to assault the members of that group. They are the cases where mutual aggression between two opposing groups results in a situation 'where what is going on is a fight in which the fighters have willingly joined in, whether to carry out or settle a quarrel, or for some other reason' (*R v Nguyen* (1995) 36 NSWLR 397 at 407). In these moments, as Nick articulated, 'You had to pick somebody or that guy was picking you.' Authors such as Polk (1994) appropriately postulate such a scenario as a type of battle. However, as the accounts of the young men indicate, there are different types of battle you can enter. You can enter a fistfight. You can confront some people without knowing what will occur. You can enter a fight with sticks or you can enter a knife fight. Or you can enter what you think is going to be a fistfight, perhaps with some weapons, but it turns out to be far more serious than that because someone, unbeknownst to you, goes further and does something you did not anticipate. People in a group can, and often do, have very different expectations. What you expect depends very much on what you know. This becomes of critical importance in cases involving juveniles and the law of joint enterprise to which I now turn:

> I didn't understand the law of joint enterprise. Nobody explained that to me. I was approached with a deal: guilty plea to manslaughter prior to the trial . . . [and] 'If you're lucky, you might do 10 years.' I'm 16 when [my lawyer's] telling me this, right: 10 years might as well have been forever. . . . Back [then] I was only looking forward to my 17 birthday. And I was like, 'How can I plead guilty to killing somebody when I didn't kill them?' You know what I mean? I just didn't understand the law. So if I want [people] to know anything [about me], it would be the fact *that I did not kill the person. I never intended to kill anybody and I didn't even see the possibility that anybody could be killed* when I was setting out to do this.
>
> (Sonny)

As Sonny highlighted here, murder can take a number of forms. In its most basic form, it is the deliberate and unlawful killing of a person with an intention either to kill the deceased or to cause the deceased grievous bodily harm. Grievous bodily harm means highly serious bodily harm. However, the common law doctrine of joint enterprise was developed to allow more than one person to be charged with and convicted of the same crime, regardless of the role they played in its commission. This allows the prosecution to build a case when it is unknown which of the injuries (or offenders) had caused the victim's death. It is about working together as a team, with a shared or common intention, a shared or common plan. Once a joint criminal enterprise has been found to exist, every act done to implement the agreement or understanding is at law done by all of the group. That is the general principle (see *Gillard v The Queen* (2003) 219 CLR 1; *Markby v The Queen* (1978) 140 CLR 108; *McAuliffe v The Queen* (1995) 183 CLR 108). Further, it is not necessary to prove anything in the nature of a formal or express agreement between the defendants, as an agreement for this purpose may be the result of a carefully worked out plan or it might be made on the spur of the moment. It may be reached only just before the commission of the act that constitutes the crime, with merely a nod, a wink, or a quick word (see *R v Bosworth & Ors* (2007) 97 SASR 502).

To this effect, Leo reflected on the evidence presented at his trial: 'The prosecutor said that we all knew what was going to happen; that without even saying a word, we knew what was going to happen. And I don't . . . I don't believe that.' As he implies, the difficulty in these cases arises where a person reaches an agreement or understanding with another or others to simply assault a person but in the course of that assault, one of the parties goes beyond the scope of the agreement or understanding and commits the crime of murder. In that situation, a person can still be found guilty of murder if, when he commits the crime of assault, he foresaw the possibility in the course of that assault that the other party might unlawfully kill the deceased with murderous intent (i.e. intending to kill or do grievous bodily harm) and the person continued to participate in the joint venture with that degree of foresight (*McAuliffe v The Queen* [1995] 183 CLR 108). This means that, unlike any other sort of case in the entire criminal calendar, extended joint enterprise refers to and requires foresight rather than intention. It requires only foresight of a *possibility* that something might happen (see *Clayton and Ors v. The Queen* [2005] 159 A Crim R 1). Practically speaking, this requires only that Person A thinks that Person B *might do something*. It does not matter if Person A does not want that outcome or thinks that there is little chance of it happening: 'as long as it is possible, they are liable' (Hayes & Feld, 2009, p. 29).

Eddie gave a detailed account of the events on the day the victim was killed. He neither exaggerated nor appeared to minimize his own conduct or that of others who were part of his group. At trial, it was accepted that he was unarmed and that the extent of his actions comprised some punches exchanged with one of the victim's groups. As Eddie explained, 'I was involved in a fight but I didn't, you know, stab or hurt anyone. I was just trying to get away and save my own life.' However, the prosecution submitted that Eddie's group was party to a common purpose to engage in a fight with the victim's group, knowing that members of each group were armed and contemplating that serious injury could result. Undoubtedly the least culpable of the group, Eddie was convicted of murder and sentenced to life imprisonment. As a matter of logic, a fistfight would seem a remarkable and counterintuitive basis on which to find a 16-year-old child guilty of the most serious offence under criminal law.

Of course, by virtue of their age and immaturity, as well as their unfortunate backgrounds, many youths simply have poor judgement. As Heide (1999, p. 48) points out, 'when invited to accompany a group "out for a night of fun," [juveniles] are sent cues that something bad might happen, but these indications go undetected'. Nick was also 16 at the time of the offending and was not privy to any previous incidents with the victim's group. He added that he did not know the group members. During interview, he described being collected by his friends en route to the nearest hospital to get treatment for one of the boys in the vehicle. Somewhere along the journey, his plans were dramatically changed. Here, Nick speaks to the state of helplessness and confusion that preceded his decision to follow a domineering person on a mission he did not properly understand:

> The only reason that I left in the car that day was to take my friend to the hospital. . . . Nothing was ever said about going to get the guys that [had just] stabbed [him]. And then the driver of the car ended up making a decision; he's said, 'Nah, fuck it. Let's go to the oval now and we'll get these cunts,' basically. And so me sitting in the car just went with it . . . because I've always been let down all my life and I felt like I didn't want to let anybody down on this day.

Accordingly, there can be no dispute that this group of teenagers embarked on a mission to administer a beating to members of the victim's group. Such ill-will, as it turned out, was keenly reciprocated:

> When we got there, one male, he was like the eldest one out of all of them, just jumped up and said, 'What, you want a fucking war?' And that was it; the rest of his mates jumped up and [ran at us].
>
> (Nick)

However, while Nick expected that a variety of weapons, capable of causing various types of harm to others would be used, he described the use of a knife as a complete departure from the common purpose in circumstances where he contemplated a fight in which the weapons used were limited to poles, sticks, and other implements only capable of causing injury by a blunt force.

> I had no knowledge that one of the guys I was with had a knife. I had no knowledge. . . . If I knew that . . . I could have made a decision *then*. . . . I might have been a young kid but I'm not dumb. You know what I mean? I would have made [that] decision for myself. . . . Like I said, I thought it was just a fight we were going to. . . . When I first saw the knife, I knew that it had been used . . . [and] that's when I really started thinking, 'Fuck!'

Reflecting from prison, Nick was clearly struggling to accept his conviction and subsequent imprisonment for murder. His frustration and resentment towards the principal offender was ubiquitous:

> It's been six years, going on to seven years now. . . . No justice. Nothing. . . . And that's what stumbles me every day when I think about it . . . and it crushes me, it hurts me . . . to think I'm doing fucking time for *him*.

Ten years earlier, Sonny, aged 15, was also convicted for murder under accessorial liability. In his case, a foolhardy and relatively impetuous decision to acquire a mobile phone took an appalling and tragic turn when his co-offender stabbed the victim without warning as they fought on the side of the road. While making no attempt to avoid responsibility for his part in the death of the victim, Sonny consistently expressed a view that his conviction and sentence for murder were in some way illegitimate.

SIMONE: [Do] you maintain a sense that despite . . . [being involved in a murder] you were fundamentally . . . a good person?

SONNY: Well whether I was or not I don't know but I've certainly paid my debts. . . . I didn't actually commit the murder. I didn't stab the bloke. . . . I was just out to rob somebody. The first cell I moved into at [Magill Training Centre] I've looked at the pin board, and the last guy living in the cell has [his sentence] written on there: 'Robbery with violence: six months [imprisonment]' right? Which, had the things gone to plan, that's what it would have been; it would have been robbery with violence. Had I have been busted, I would have got six months.

These findings align with research by Crewe, Liebling, Padfield, and Virgo (2015) suggesting that prisoners convicted under joint enterprise 'acknowledged that they were guilty of *an* offence, but did not consider themselves guilty of murder' (p. 266). For secondary offenders in my study, the thought of any calculated, predatory, and/or deranged killing was repugnant. As Moore, Tangney, and Stuewig (2016, p. 208) observe, 'perceived stigma may not always lead to agreement with stereotypes, and therefore may not threaten the self and cause internalized stigma (i.e., "People think criminals are dangerous, but I don't think that about criminals or myself")'. Mike and Eddie reflected this type of scenario:

> [Do I see myself as a murderer?] Definitely not. I just see myself as being young and dumb, you know. And that's what I tell people here when they say, 'Oh, Mike,' – they'll introduce me to people and say, 'Oh he's a murderer,' you know. And I tell them that 'No. I'm *not* a murderer. I'm here for murder, you know, but *I* didn't do it; I didn't kill somebody. I was just involved, you know.' Yeah, I think it will have a big effect on the outside, you know: it's how people look at you, you know. As soon as they hear the word 'murder' – he's in gaol for murder – automatically they give you a label: you know, 'He's violent,' you know, 'He'll kill you', 'He'll do this, he'll do that', you know. And I don't think that's fair.
>
> (Mike)

> I don't think I'm a dangerous person. . . . When I was younger, I think [like] all young men . . . you're trying to stamp like your place [in the world] . . . trying to be masculine and . . . you sort of think, 'Oh, that's just what young men do.' . . . But I never thought that [I was dangerous]. I thought that I was more of a – I still do – I think I'm a supporting, loyal friend . . . rather than, 'Oh, he's, you know, violent, dangerous,' 'cause yeah, to be honest, that's the last shit I think of.
>
> (Eddie)

In such circumstances, prisoners believed their life-sentences to be fundamentally unjust.

> I refused to go to sentencing. I just couldn't sit there and hear that, you know. I knew I was getting a life sentence . . . but it was just that I couldn't sit there in the court with my family in there and have to look at them and [have] them listening to that. . . . That would have sent me mental.
>
> (Mike)

These perspectives stood in stark contrast to the views of those who admitted being the people who actually stabbed and killed their victims: 'I totally deserved what I got and . . . I've never really complained about it. . . . I still have my life and he lost his life [so] I've got no right to complain' (Stefan). Related to this, there is the further consideration that individuals on the periphery will be subject to a host of plainly irrelevant and inappropriate treatment and sanctioning whilst in prison (and on parole). As a matter of nomenclature, those found 'guilty by association' reported receiving little by way of dispensation or understanding beyond that afforded to autonomous, premeditated killers. As Sonny commented, 'In here, everybody is a convicted criminal and not many of the staff have such a background to be able to understand that not everybody in here is a low-life scumbag. But that's how you get treated.' Such conceptions, as described by both Marcus and Sonny subsequently, actively worked against wider aims to promote rehabilitation and give some hope and encouragement that these men would become productive members of society. Of course, as the excerpt from Sonny articulately reminds us, one year to a teenager equates to a greater period of time compared to adults in terms of attitudinal shifts that may occur:

> Murder is a scary thing . . . but not a lot of people are interested in the *details* of it . . . what your part [in it was] or what [actually happened]. . . . Like, 'Oh yeah, I'm doing life for murder,' [but] no-one's interested in me doing life for being joint enterprise, *just for being there*, no-one's interested in that. But you say murder: 'Wow!' . . . That's something I can't deal with.
>
> (Marcus)

> In reality I should not have been given this long. . . . If you want a juvenile to get out rehabilitated, you don't give them that long. You don't have to. After my three-year stint in juvenile [detention] I *was* rehabilitated. . . . Had I got out after that, I would have completed my studies. . . . I would be legit today and I would be happy. And I've always done my best to be the best person I can be. I've certainly improved and all that. But after all that good work, they threw me in gaol for another 12½ years and I'm getting treated like any other scumbag, right. When you do that to somebody who is trying to do their best to be a good person – the outcome – you're not going to get a good person at the end of that. That *was* a good person. But you just go and treat them like shit for like [a decade] you know what I mean?
>
> (Sonny)

In sum

The experiences of Leo, Sonny, Mike, Eddie, Floyd, Tyson, Stefan, Will, and Nick resonate through the entire juvenile and criminal justice system. Although their cases operate at the extremes, unwillingness to back down from conflict followed by unwillingness to cease aggressive behavior (most likely transference from past situations during early childhood) are typical of thousands of immature young men who see violence as an acceptable expression of their masculinity. Many will be encouraged by a parental figure to take a stand in circumstances where the young men are feeling bullied and compromised. The extent to which these responses may be compounded by the men's current incarceration remains to be seen when they are eventually released on parole. Clearly possessed of normal intelligence, these young men also shared a number of protective factors prior to their involvement in lethal violence: namely, they were not entrenched in an offending lifestyle; they generally did not use drugs; and they had no identified mental health issues. Had the victim survived, it is impossible to predict with any certainty where the offenders' criminal trajectories would have taken them.

I agree that the decisions of some participants in this chapter to arm themselves with weapons such as trolley poles and pool sticks was foolish in the extreme. Still, to be fair, not everyone equipped themselves in this way when they joined in the assault. Where it was entirely reasonable that a particular young person had no knowledge that some members of the group were armed, the matter took on an entirely different character. However, the law of joint enterprise entails that those who are minded to participate in such group violence will inevitably be obliged to accept responsibility, not only for their own actions, but also for the actions of other group members when crimes such as these are committed. The present research adds to a growing body of literature that calls into question such a low threshold for culpability in light of the mandatory life sentence a conviction for murder automatically attracts. Significantly, a tough stance on crime and punishment ensures that 'the life sentence is exactly that – even if they are eventually released, lifers remain under license until they die, liable to recall to prison if they breach the demanding terms of their license' (Crewe et al., 2015, p. 255). Such a scenario graphically illustrates the need to assign criminal liability by reference to proven moral culpability rather than cases where immaturity and impulsiveness have led young people into error. Instead, as critics rightly point out, joint enterprise 'casts the net of liability for murder too widely . . . [catching] potentially weak and vulnerable secondary offenders' and fixing them 'with very serious criminal liability because they were in the wrong place at the wrong time in the wrong company' (*Clayton v The Queen* [2006] HCA 58 per Kirby J at 119; see also Crewe et al., 2015; Hayes & Feld, 2009; Krebs, 2017).

As the experiences of the young men in this chapter demonstrate, 15-, 16-, and 17-year-old boys frequently act, and indeed live their lives, with little thought for the ramifications of their actions and with little foresight about what another person might do. Such boys often cannot foresee what they themselves are going to do, particularly under conditions of immense stress. Against this backdrop, establishing the state of mind of another (or others) takes on an entirely different complexion when members of 'the group' are themselves virtual strangers, having met only minutes before the violence erupted: 'The first few times I went to court for this, I'm thinking, "Who the hell am I standing next to in the dock? I don't even recognise these people"' (Marcus).

Recent work on child development continues to demonstrate that 'explosive outbursts – like other maladaptive behaviour – occur when the cognitive demands being placed upon the child (or person) outstrip that person's capacity to respond adaptively' (Greene, 2010, p. 17). To this extent, 'when there is a poor fit between the task/environment and the child, the child will try to take control either by avoiding the task, escaping the task, or railing against it' (Gruener, 2014, para. 4). Certainly, as Tyson remarked, 'If I was in a confrontation . . . out of fear, I would explode and give it everything I had to get away unharmed.'

References

Athens, L. H. (1992). *The creation of dangerous violent criminals*. Champaign, IL: University of Illinois Press.

Bricknell, S., & Bryant, W. (2018). *Co-offending among young homicide offenders in Australia*. Australian Institute of Criminology: Statistical Bulletin 12. Retrieved from https://aic.gov.au/publications/sb/sb12

Broidy, L. M., Daday, J. K., Crandall, C. S., Sklar, D. P., & Jost, P. F. (2006). Exploring demographic, structural, and behavioral overlap among homicide offenders and victims. *Homicide Studies, 10*(3), 155–180. DOI:10.1177/1088767906288577

Clayton v The Queen [2006] HCA 58. Retrieved from http://eresources.hcourt.gov.au/downloadPdf/2006/HCA/58

Coleman, C. (2016, February 18). *The complex case of Joint Enterprise*. Retrieved from www.bbc.com/news/uk-30817269

Collins, R. (2008). *Violence: A micro-sociological theory*. Princeton, NJ: Princeton University Press.

Collins, R. (2009). The micro-sociology of violence. *British Journal of Sociology, 60*(3), 566–576. DOI:10.1111/j.1468-4446.2009.01256.x

Crewe, B., Liebling, A., Padfield, N., & Virgo, G. J. (2015). Joint enterprise: The implications of an unfair and unclear law. *Criminal Law Review, 4*, 252–269. Retrieved from www.sweetandmaxwell.co.uk

Fagan, J., & Wilkinson, D. L. (1998). Guns, youth violence, and social identity in inner cities. *Crime and Justice, 24*, 105–188. DOI:10.1086/449279

Felson, R. B., & Messner, S. F. (1998). Disentangling the effects of gender and intimacy on victim precipitation in homicide. *Criminology, 36*(2), 405–423. DOI:10.111/j.1745-9125.1998.tb01253.x

Garbarino, J. (2000). *Lost boys: Why our sons turn violent and how we can save them*. New York: Anchor Books.

Gillard v The Queen (2003). 219 CLR 1. Retrieved from http://eresources.hcourt.gov.au/showCase/2003/HCA/64

Greene, R. (2010). *The explosive child: A new approach for understanding and parenting easily frustrated, "chronically inflexible" children*. New York: HarperCollins Publishers.

Gross, M. (2016). Vigilante violence and "forward panic" in Johannesburg's townships. *Theory and Society, 45*(3), 239–263. DOI:10.1007/s11186-016-9271-1.

Gruener, C. (2014). *Tips for parents: Executive functioning- what is it, why we need it, and how we as parents can support our children's development*. Retrieved from www.davidsongifted.org/Search-Database/entry/A10822

Hayes, R., & Feld, F L. (2009). Is the test for extended common purpose over-extended? *University of New England Law Journal, 4*(2), 17–32. Retrieved from www.austlii.edu.au/au/journals/UNELawJl/2009/2.pdf

Heide, K. M. (1999). *Young killers*. Thousand Oaks, CA: Sage.

Jennings, W. G., Piquero, A. R., & Reingle, J. M. (2012). On the overlap between victimization and offending: A review of literature. *Aggression and Violent Behavior, 17*(1), 16–26. DOI:10.1016/j.avb.2011.09.003

Katz, J. (1988). *Seductions of crime: Moral and sensual attractions of doing evil*. New York: Basic Books.

Kelly, K., & Totten, M. (2002). *When children kill: A social-psychological study of youth homicide*. Ontario: University of Toronto Press.

Kopak, A. M., & Sefiha, O. (2015). Becoming badass: Teaching Katz's "ways of the badass" using the *Breaking Bad* Television Series. *Journal of Criminal Justice Education, 26*(1), 94–111. DOI:10.1080/10511253.2014.928337

Krebs, B. (2017). Accessory liability: Persisting in error. *The Cambridge Law Journal, 76*(1), 7–11. DOI:10.1017/S00081973000150

Lauritsen, J. L., Sampson, R. J., & Laub, J. H. (1991). Link between offending and victimization among adolescents. *Criminology, 29*(2), 265–291. DOI:10.1111/j.1745-9125.1991.tb01067.x

Lieberg, M. (1995). Teenagers and public space. *Communication Research, 22*(6), 720–744. DOI:10.1177/009365095022006008

Markby v The Queen (1978) CLR 108. Retrieved from www.austlii.edu.au

McAuliffe v The Queen (1995) 183 CLR 108. Retrieved from www.austlii.edu.au

Moore, K. E., Tangney, J. P., & Stuewig, J. B. (2016). The self-stigma process in criminal offenders. *Stigma and Health, 1*(3), 206–224. DOI:10.1037/sah0000024

Mustaine, E. E., & Tewksbury, R. (2000). Comparing the lifestyles of victims, offenders, and victim-offenders: A routine activity theory assessment of similarities and differences for criminal incident participation. *Sociological Focus, 33*(3), 339–362. DOI:10.1080/00380237.2000.10571174

Polk, K. (1994). *When men kill: Scenarios of masculine violence*. New York: Cambridge University Press.

Polk, K. (1997). A reexamination of the concept of victim-precipitated homicide. *Homicide Studies, 1*(2), 141–168. DOI:10.1177/1088767997001002004

R v Bosworth, Gibbins, Nance & Richards (2007) 97 SASR 502. Retrieved from www.austlii.edu.au

R v Nguyen (1995) 36 NSWLR 397. Retrieved from www.austlii.edu.au

Rivara, F. P., Shepherd, J. P., Farrington, D. P., Richmond, P. W., & Cannon, P. (1995). Victim as offender in youth violence. *Annals of Emergency Medicine, 26*(5), 609–614. DOI:10.1016/SO196-0644(95)70013-7

Sampson, R. J., & Lauritsen, J. L. (1990). Deviant lifestyles, proximity to crime, and the offender-victim link in personal violence. *Journal of Research in Crime and Delinquency, 27*(2), 110–139. DOI:10.1177/0022427890027002002

Singer, S. I. (1981). Homogeneous victim-offender populations: A review and some research implications. *The Journal of Criminal law and Criminology, 72*(2), 779–788. Retrieved from https://scholarlycommons.law.northwestern.edu/cgi/viewcontent.cgi?article=6240&context=jclc

Sparks, R. F. (1982). *Research on victims of crime*. Washington, DC: Government Printing Office.

Summary Offences Act 1953 (SA) (Austl.). Retrieved from www.legislation.sa.gov.au/LZ/C/A/SUMMARY%20OFFENCES%20ACT%201953.aspx

Tomsen, S., & Crofts, T. (2012). Social and cultural meanings of legal responses to homicide among men: Masculine honour, sexual advances and accidents. *Australian and New Zealand Journal of Criminology, 45*(3), 423–437. DOI:10.1177/0004865812456854

Wolfgang, M. E. (1958). *Patterns in criminal homicide*. New York: John Wiley and Sons Inc.

Woodworth, M., Agar, A. D., & Coupland, R. B. (2013). Characteristics of Canadian youth- perpetrated homicides. *Criminal Justice and Behaviour, 40*(9), 1009–1026. DOI:10.1177/0093854813482390

4 Misfits, murder, and the 'monster child'

> [We] were going out . . . [and] breaking into houses. But every time we went to a house, no-one was ever home. There was nothing ever there. But [then] we broke into *that* house . . . [and] someone was home. It wasn't meant to happen.
>
> (Ben)

> Gears of War, Call of Duty, Modern Warfare, Unchartered, Oblivion . . . they're the games I mainly played. In Gears of War you can do some pretty nasty take-downs . . . cut someone in half with a chainsaw gun. Yeah, you shoot bullets at them and then if you get really close, you can cut them right in half. Organs and fucking guts and ribs come out. Shotguns and rifles can blow arms and legs off. It's fucking hectic. . . . You could fucking mince everyone in that. Yeah, I did some horrible things to people in that game . . . [turned] people into pink mist.
>
> (Aaron)

The discussion thus far has focused on violent activity explicable only in terms of juvenile bravado: instantly regrettable and foolish demonstrations of hegemonic masculinity by young men preoccupied with not appearing weak. In these cases, a confrontation presented itself and the decision was made to engage in a fight that ultimately proved fatal. As such, the death of the victim was neither an explicit nor an implied goal of the venture. In a sense, as previously described by Fiddes (1981, p. 51), these hooliganesque events are 'the "normal" murders against which the more problematic cases stand out'. By contrast, the killings in this chapter exhibit many of the factors that are commonly used to justify the most severe condemnation. They are unique in their history and also unique in their seriousness. The seven young males and one female acknowledge that they knowingly and willingly participated in what can only be characterized as a horrific sequence of events, with a plan to commit a crime (e.g. robbery, trespass, theft, rape or, in one case, murder itself), progressing through a period of de facto imprisonment of the victim, to physical assault and culminating effectively in an execution to ensure silence. The victims' last moments must have been a time of abject terror, as they would have known they were about to die. All of their injuries indicated savage and prolonged attacks. Though neither the initial crimes nor, indeed, the killings were premeditated for very long, both were plainly calculated rather than purely spontaneous and, in regard to both the initial offences and the murders, the juveniles clearly knew what was going to happen and why. With only one exception, all of the teenagers were acting along with co-accused – some with older men who were dealt with in the adult system, some with other youths who were charged with similar or lesser offences. Under these circumstances, it was accepted that certain of the juveniles were neither the initiators nor the main offenders in the crime of murder. However, whichever way one looks at it, no-one amongst these young people tried to stop what was occurring or even report to the authorities (anonymously, if need be) what was happening.

In what follows, I focus on four key themes to describe how and under what conditions young people could get involved in these matters and how such an empathy deficit towards others could arise. Although these people's stories are complex and not totally consistent, a general pattern appears to emerge. Again, only three of the young people in this chapter had a formal offender history prior to the murders they were involved in, in spite of the overwhelming majority having a long history of behavioural problems and leading deeply unsettled lives. As shall become clear, these young people's antisocial attitudes were often justifications for survival and escalated over time, exacerbated by ready recourse to alcohol and drug abuse and identification with delinquent peers.

'Family ties and other crimes': upbringings in appalling family circumstances, including difficulties maintaining parent–child bonds

The existent literature on child development addresses a 'myriad of developmental, physical, and psychological difficulties' (Sprinkle, 2007, p. 134) associated with violence in the home. Several of the children in this chapter had appalling family circumstances, marked by physical abuse and the deprivation of normal love and affection. The respective families of James, Luke, Cody, and Derek stand out among the most unhappy and disturbed. Consistent with this view, none of these men was willing or able to nominate a significant other for interview. Cody described his father's incarceration as the highlight of an otherwise harrowing childhood:

> Everything was going really great and then my father got released from gaol. . . . It was for something kind of bad but I can't recall what it was. . . . [He] was [gone] for about seven years . . . [and] I can honestly say that our life was actually A-OK during that time.
>
> (Cody)

While Cody was quite unprepared to talk in candid terms about his father's offending, court reports revealed that his father was convicted and served a sentence of imprisonment on charges of rape/incest relating to his two daughters. Regrettably, there are other links in the chain of events that led to Cody's offending that probably would have been broken had there been appropriate intervention to protect him from the serious harm occurring within the home. It is pertinent to mention here that when Cody was nine, his elder brother Martin (aged 11) bludgeoned another child to death with a rock in the course of an argument. Martin was convicted of murder and imprisoned until his early 20s. Given the following, it is perhaps not surprising that both boys learned from a tender age that adults coped with life by using violence:

> I can't remember once having a good time whatsoever. I don't remember having a birthday, a Christmas or anything at all like that. . . . I never really heard of anyone else having a childhood like mine: it was pretty violent. I can't remember ever having a day where either I wasn't hurt or my mum wasn't hurt or something like that. . . . No-one [stepped in] whatsoever; no-one at all. And I can remember going to primary school and high school with like black eyes, cracked lips, bruising all over me, and I can't remember anything ever happening [about it].
>
> (Cody)

James's biological father committed suicide when James was aged 3. James was raised by his mother in a sole parenting role until the age of 5. He depicted his stepfather as an alcoholic and described a considerable amount of domestic violence within the home. On one occasion, James, his mother, and the other children left and were accommodated in a women's shelter, returning to find the family home wrecked as a result of a violent outburst from his stepfather:

> My stepfather was an alcoholic and he used to beat up Mum practically every week sort of thing [and] . . . sometimes he beat us as well. . . . They split up at one stage for a while and he got drunk and we were all at a women's shelter and he trashed the place. He went through everything, he smashed everything so, yeah. Then he took off to Mount Gambier where we had relations and then a couple of months later he come back and she took him back in and went on as if nothing happened.

Against this backdrop, James developed an anxiety disorder that manifested in enuresis (bedwetting) until a relatively late age. Severely lacking in confidence, he regarded himself as being 'a bit of a loner' and was socially isolated from his peers at school, leaving as soon as he could at the age of 15:

> I didn't like school . . . I don't know why: I [just] didn't like it. I didn't seem to fit in with the other kids and stuff like that, so yeah . . . it was more to do with the kids and not the work.

At the same time, he perceived his mother to be emotionally abusive, often telling him that he reminded her of his natural father. This sorry state of affairs was all but confirmed by his mother during an interview with police shortly after James's arrest for murder.

> James was the black sheep of the family. I guess I conveyed that to him virtually all his life because he was the only one who was the image of his father and I suppose I never forgave my husband for doing what he did and leaving me with five children, and I was only 25 years old when he died. I remember James used to sulk just like his father did and when he did, I used to say things like, 'Just like your father.'
>
> (Christine, mother)

In fact, when James turned himself in, 16 years after the murder, his mother rejected him altogether and blamed him for the killing, refusing to accept that her eldest son, Robert (by that time deceased), could have had anything to do with it:

> [My brother had] committed suicide not long after [the crime] happened and he had an insurance policy and it bought them a house and a car and everything else, so from then on, he was a saint. . . . When I told them [what we'd done,] they said, 'Well, we don't believe that Robert would have anything to do with this: we think it was all you.' It was *his* car, *his* rifle, *his* shovel, everything, but it was all *my* fault. So I haven't talked to them since. . . . When they first heard it they [actually] said that I'd get into trouble for wasting police time and making a false claim or whatever. But it's not something you'd make up.
>
> (James)

Derek's memories of his early childhood were similarly filled with bitterness:

> When I was a kid, all I remember is that I just wanted to be loved. . . . [But instead] I was raped for the first time at the age of five because I used to walk the streets a lot, you know, just to get away from the house.

Court-ordered reports confirm that Derek absconded from home, first at the age of 4 and then again at 9, only to be returned by the police on each occasion. More distressingly, in light of the physical, sexual, and emotional abuse that he described as occurring at his house, it simply cannot be said that the street was, in fact, a particularly unsafe option:

> All kids get a slap on the arse. All kids get yelled at by their parents and all that. But not all kids get thrown through glass doors. Not all kids have knives put at their throats. Not all kids get raped. Not all kids get, you know, belted with a closed fist. Not all kids get their boots slipped into their guts . . . [so my] life's been pretty fucking different.
>
> (Derek)

Until Derek was 10, his father lived at the house (between prison stints), where he abused alcohol and marijuana and subjected Derek and his mother to emotional and physical abuse on a recurring basis. Derek's well-being was further set back by a congenital deformity that was corrected by leg irons and braces over the first four years of his life. At the age of 8, he developed another serious illness that led to his hospitalization for a nine-month period, followed by an extended stay in a convalescent home for disabled children. At no point during admission did Derek's father either visit or maintain any form of contact. Essentially, as Derek explained, his father was unable to accept his son's difficulties and rejected him, violently, from an early age:

> For the first five years of my life . . . I had to have plaster on both legs up to my waist because I was born with hip dysplasia [and] clubfoot. And when the plaster came off, I then had to wear calipers. . . . The assaults started on me at the age of two when I was thrown through a glass door by my father . . . [who] was a very, very hard man . . . [and] I was so absolutely shit-scared of copping floggings from my father [that] I had this bedwetting problem that lasted until about the age of 12.

By contrast, Derek's relationship with his mother was less strained but also problematic. Struggling to make sense of a sexual assault that occurred at her hands, he recalled lying in wait to assault (and possibly kill) her, a causal factor in his subsequent placement under the Guardianship of the Minister:

> I loved my mother. I respected my mother and for that to happen to me . . . I remember my thought pattern changing that night and I'd fucking had enough. And two nights later I waited for my mother. . . . I waited for Mum in the back seat of a car and I was going to fucking throttle her, you know, for what she'd done to me. . . . I don't know [exactly] what I was going to do but I certainly wanted to hurt her like she hurt me.

I do not dwell on it here but make the observation that Derek's victim, a mature-aged female unknown to him, was strangled from the back seat of her vehicle during a botched robbery when Derek was 17. Earlier on, when Derek was 10, his parents had separated in circumstances involving a great deal of domestic tension that had continued for many years. With two notable exceptions (see Section '"Out of the blue": when "good" kids do (really) bad things'), this was a background feature common to all of the young people in this chapter. Ironically, establishing whose 'inadequate, defective or bad [parenting] was the key correlate to the anti-social and offending behavior of their offspring' (Halsey & Deegan, 2014, p. 4) would provide the ultimate fodder for the rehashing of familiar plots, as Aaron's father demonstrates: 'She [the mother] squarely put the blame on me. Until I turned around and said, "Well, it's funny that. He's lived with you all but six months of his life and you're fucking blaming me?" That shut her up' (Vincent, Aaron's father). Additionally, in Derek's case, his father adopted a bizarre approach to his son's upbringing by regularly taking the boy out bush and forcing him to work on cattle stations and factories in an attempt to 'make him a man'. Apparently, this formed part of a wider campaign of strict discipline, although, paradoxically, he paid his son with cannabis rather than cash for his efforts. Making his first appearance in the juvenile court around this time (aged 10), Derek was already experimenting with intravenous drug use and exhibiting very aggressive and antisocial behaviour. It was evident that parental care remained in seriously short supply:

> I was at the Port Adelaide Courts and I got Mum down there and I said, 'Please get me out of here.' You know, 'Bail me out.' She said, 'Nope. You're staying in there. You're going back into the Boys' Home and that's it.' And the judge turned around to Mum and . . . he said to her, 'What? Can't you look after your own kids?' And she just got her back up and bailed me out.

Luke also described the parental modelling he received from a violent father and an ambivalent mother. He noted his father was a very big, intimidating, and heavily tattooed man who worked as an interstate truck driver. Luke's mother often accompanied him on the road and, as such, Luke was left to look after himself on weekends and quite often during the week as well. A heavy amphetamine user, Luke's father's physical punishments were generally brought on by his ever-increasing use of speed. It bothered Luke immensely that his mother was loyal to her husband and never sought to intervene when Luke had 'the crap belted out of [him]' once or twice a month:

> My dad was pretty violent a lot of the time . . . towards me mostly. . . . If I did the wrong thing, obviously I would cop a few smacks around the head and that . . . I used to just run away, get into trouble and get locked up and it would be all right when I came back eventually. My mum and my sister wouldn't do anything because it was my dad . . . [and] it made me angry.

Diagnosed at a young age with ADHD, Luke also came to realize that his scripts for Ritalin were being filled, yet he never received the medication, observing that his parents were 'doing something with it'. The upshot was that Luke struggled to contain his boundless energy and had a history of impulsive behaviour, commenting that he 'would always need to be moving; otherwise, I'd get restless and bored'. In common with the cohort generally, Luke's educational attainment was further undermined by his attending numerous primary and high schools due to his parents' frequent relocations and, in later years, his own aggressive and unacceptable behaviour:

> I was expelled from like five different schools . . . for fighting and stuff like that. . . . When I was young I had a really short fuse and a bad temper. People would say something and I'd take it the wrong way. . . . [So] I went to schools for people that got kicked out of other schools.

As is true for other cases within this pattern, at the age of 14, Luke left school and commenced 'couch-surfing' with various friends and associates in order to escape his father's violence. Unable to access welfare payments, Luke would support himself by breaking into cars and occasionally buildings to steal cash, along with anything easily saleable that he could offer people in lieu of rent. To this end, his antecedent report records convictions for serious criminal trespass, aggravated assault, illegal use of a motor vehicle, larceny, and some minor drug and traffic offences. Tenuous at best, these living arrangements were generally short-lived, with Luke conceding that '[I] wore out my welcome at a few places'. Unemployed and of no fixed abode, he was also heavily addicted to cannabis: 'I just smoked pot; that's it. . . . I smoked a fair bit, like about half an ounce . . . [which costs] about 120 bucks a day.' Although Luke escalated his offending very quickly on the night of the murder in a way that moved from affecting people's property in the main to actually ending someone's life, it is clear that his lifestyle was one of day-to-day survival. For young men such as Luke, who essentially would be regarded as a thief, crime was seen as an entirely 'logical response to life's challenges' (Halsey, 2008, p. 107) and as a means to ingratiate themselves with an antisocial peer group: '[I admired] a couple of my friends [but] not for the right reasons. . . . They were just always getting in trouble and that, always getting in fights, and when I was younger, I thought that was cool.' He spoke, as homicide offenders often do, of how 'a deviant lifestyle, and the participation in a cluster of criminal offences . . . [ultimately] became part of the lethal violence' (Polk, 1994, p. 98). Against this backdrop, Luke became involved with the other offenders on this particular evening. As his comments illustrate, knowledge of the victim and the presence of money was a central feature of their project:

> My friend came and picked me up and said that he owed money; he owed about 20 grand to someone and they were going to get him if he didn't pay the money . . . and [the victim] was supposed to have money in his house.
>
> (Luke)

Numerous homicide studies confirm the tendency for youths to be involved in concurrent crime that leads to their behaviour as charged. In the US context, this relationship is thought to occur in approximately half (Cornell, 1993) to two-thirds (Roe-Sepowitz, 2009) of all killings committed by juveniles. More recent work by Woodworth, Agar, and Coupland (2013) reports that homicide committed by Canadian youth involved concurrent crimes almost half (46%) of the time.

With his ascending states of criminality and propensity for violence, Luke was enlisted to accompany two adult friends to a farm where lots of migrant workers were, in the expectation that there would be cash there, perhaps hidden in different places. He had been to the property previously, and '[he] knew where there were things to be found'. Exactly what happened when they got there and exactly who did what cannot be articulated precisely, given Luke's reluctance to discuss the behaviour of the other men involved. He prefers, it would seem, to protect his co-defendants out of his keen attentiveness to *prison law*, a system that

> occupies the day-to-day consciousness of prisoners and governs such decisions as who it is safe to speak to and be seen with, who can deal particular types of drugs and so forth . . . [and] has as its main objective the physical survival of each prisoner.
>
> (Halsey & Deegan, 2012, p. 348)

> I wasn't the ringleader. I was the youngest of them there . . . [but if you talk], you get labelled a 'dog' and if you still try and hang around with the same people, you just get attacked. . . . And if I did dog, then the people that I was hanging around with, they'd be able to find me no matter where I was.

What *is* clear is that things spiralled out of control very quickly once the victim, understandably agitated and having armed himself, confronted the trio, resulting in a frenetic attack that left him incapacitated and/or unconscious. Regrettably, as soon as the group left, the decision was made to return to the property, as part of a replica firearm had been left behind. There was then a second assault on the victim who, in total, sustained in excess of 70 injuries. While there is no suggestion that Luke went there that night looking to kill or cause grievous bodily harm, a confrontation arose and he admits to using a spade and a piece of wood to hit the victim. He also accepts responsibility for stomping on the man's chest while the man was on the ground. From Luke's perspective, such an aggressive response was motivated by elements of panic, self-preservation, and negative peer pressure: 'I went there to try and help someone but it didn't play out right. . . . [T]he guy's come out with a knife . . . tried to stab my friend, tried to stab me and we ended up attacking him.'

As glib and unsatisfying as this explanation may be, particularly in terms of the second attack, the role of *people* rather than the 'things' they want is paramount in the context of thinking about murder that occurs in the course of other crime. In the tradition of symbolic interactionalists such as Blumer (1962) and Athens (1997, 2005), the experiences of the young people in my research demonstrate that explanations of violent crime are not solely reducible to the makeup of the offender or the community in which the violence occurs. In line with these researchers, I contend that violent criminal acts, as with all human action, are *situated* and linked to would-be perpetrators' definitions and interpretations of scenarios as they unfold. It is on the basis of those interpretations, informed in no small part by antecedent factors, such as an abnormal personality, violent/dysfunctional upbringing, drug/alcohol intoxication, and so on, that different courses of action can arise. In circumstances where (multiple) offenders encounter a victim inclined to resist the 'specific course of action that the perpetrator[s] [sought] to carry out' (Athens, 1997, p. 36), participants repeatedly told of an explosive atmosphere with few, if any, circuit breakers: 'It was heaps quick. . . . They had camera footage of [our] car rocking up and we were there for like two and a half minutes' (Luke).

For those juveniles in the company of older, more established and much more motivated offenders, the position was particularly unenviable. In recognition of these circumstances (despite wide variation among interviewees), Athens (1997, pp. 32–40) determined that the interpretations of situations in which violent criminal acts are committed fall into four distinct types: (1) 'Physically Defensive' interpretations, which assume, from the demeanour of the victim, that a retaliatory, physical attack is imminent or already underway; (2) 'Frustrative' interpretations, formed when the victim's gestures indicate resistance to the *specific* course of action the perpetrator seeks to carry out; (3) 'Malefic' interpretations, which indicate to the perpetrator that the victim is deriding or badly belittling them, supporting a conclusion that the victim is an extremely evil or malicious person; and (4) 'Frustrative-malefic' interpretations, which combine features of the previous two types.

The following three passages are extracted from interviews I conducted with Luke and James in their respective prison settings. The first speaks to a 'physically defensive interpretation', where the perpetrator, in grave fear of serious harm, 'sees violence as the only means of preventing another person from inflicting physical injury on him or an intimate' (Athens, 1997, p. 34). To this formulation, I would add the elements of anxiety, desperation, face-saving, single-mindedness, and a determination to follow through with an act that the perpetrator had previously discussed and started to enact. The second and third passages refer to the 'frustrative interpretation' formed when violence is seen 'as the most appropriate way to . . . block the larger act that the [victim] wants to carry out – for example, calling the police or arresting the perpetrator' (Athens, 1997, p. 36). James's account also touches on the potential for socially and/or psychologically damaged youth to be overborne and submissive to the demands of more robust, violent, and antisocial personalities. This notion is in accord with previous work highlighting the propensity for ostracized or marginalized individuals 'to conform with a norm, comply with a request, and obey an order from an authority figure' (Ren, Wesselmann, & Williams, 2018, p. 35).

> There wasn't anyone supposed to be there. We were supposed to just go there and get the money. This bloke's come out with a knife and we were cornered and the only place we could go was straight through him. He wasn't supposed to be there.
>
> (Luke)

> I asked him what he was doing. He said that she had seen us and that he couldn't let her go. He told me to get his rifle out of the boot. I got the rifle out of the boot.
>
> (James)

> I was in a state of complete shock. I was crying; I kept asking him why he was doing it. When I went and got the rifle out and gave it to him, I was doing what he told me to do. I always did what he told me to do. He was my brother. He was my hero.
>
> (James)

What is also striking here is the interplay between an ill-considered criminal enterprise ('I'd never robbed a person in my life and I didn't know what I was going to do or how I was going to do it' [Derek]) and the resort to fight, as opposed to *flight*, when things went awry: 'I just lunged at her and grabbed her' (Derek). Criminal incompetence is something I return to later in this chapter (see Section '"Out of the blue": when "good" kids do (really) bad things'). But on that count, it comes as little surprise that the offending described in this chapter generally travelled in tandem with significant alcohol, cannabis, and/or amphetamine consumption:

> I was using cocaine, speed, LSD. . . . [That night] I had probably about half a bottle of Scotch and a few pills.
>
> (Derek)

> He was buying alcohol and kept forcing it onto me, so I was pretty drunk when he came up with the idea of abducting a girl and raping her.
>
> (James)

> I was already smoking pot and taking acid, smoked ecstasy on a couple occasions, pills occasionally, like pharmaceutical pills. And I also dabbled in heroin and mainly meth and just drinking myself into oblivion – if I could take pills with it, all the more better. . . . I was a regular taker of drugs [and] I had started using needles and such before I came to gaol.
>
> (Lucy)

Loeber and Farrington (2011, p. 120) echo similar sentiments, with approximately 68% of their juvenile offenders reporting drug use prior to the homicide and 45% disclosing the consumption of alcohol. Alcohol and cannabis are both depressants of the nervous system (i.e. 'downers') but also serve to produce a degree of disinhibition, or the removal of normal impulse control. Ecstasy (MDMA) is a stimulant and, as with amphetamines, can increase impulsivity and alertness (Australian Government Department of Health, 2017). When drugs are combined, a typical behavioural profile of the drug-taker is of someone who is easily angered, impulsive, and disinhibited in their behaviour. Paranoia often accompanies stimulant use, with distortion in perceptions and paranoid interpretation (Drinkaware, 2016).

Of course, not all potentially violent situations will end in violence. Sometimes, an individual is able to *redefine* the situation and, on the basis of their new definition, abandon their will towards violence; this is recognized as a 'restraining judgment' (Athens, 1997, p. 45). For example, this might occur where a victim is physically superior and a successful 'take down' is by no means guaranteed. It could also happen where there is an understanding of an act combined with an ability to view and appreciate other factors: 'If I do this, how's it going to impact on the victim, his/her family, my family?' Other individuals such as Aaron, to whom I now turn (see Section "Childhood, Interrupted': histories of psychological/psychiatric presentation from early years), will suffer a kind of 'intellectual tunnel vision' and find it hard, once they have something in their mind, to divert themselves onto another course.

'Childhood, interrupted': histories of psychological/psychiatric presentation from early years

Historically, it has been assumed that children who kill derive from psychiatric populations; however, very few studies actually confirm their adolescent homicide perpetrators as psychotic (Cornell, Benedek, & Benedek, 1987; Hardwick & Rowton-Lee, 1996; Myers & Kemph, 1990). This viewpoint, based more on popular discourse than empirical investigation, tends to surround the most horrendous crimes that attract a great deal of publicity and is often used to justify a knee-jerk punitive response. While the participants in this study go some ways to dispel some of these stereotypes around youthful homicide offending, a high proportion of those in this chapter first came to psychiatric/psychological attention in early childhood at the instigation of parents who thought their children had behavioural disorders. There is a constant theme in these participants' development where suicidal ideation, suicide attempts, and self-harming behaviour took over when initial displays of hyperactivity, poor concentration, and inappropriate attitudinal presentation left off:

> How am I going to kill myself? That was all that was going through my mind the whole time.
>
> (Toby)

> She's done some self-harm [over] the years. . . . She's had stuff on her arms. She's got scars . . . they're really quite [obvious] now because as your skin fades they get quite prominent. . . . She's pushed her hand through the wall and cut her hands and gone to hospital, you know, so she's done some stupid things.
>
> (Vanessa, mother)

> I'd just had enough. I just grabbed a knife and put it to my wrist and I was going to cut it but some other kid walked past and looked at me . . . [so] I stuck the knife back in the bag and went out and played. And then at 14 . . . [life] was starting to mess with me and people weren't getting along with me and I was just like, 'Fuck this,' so I tried to cut my throat but it was a plastic knife so it didn't do shit . . . [but] the intent was there.
>
> (Aaron)

Indeed, there were several situations where the young people found themselves admitted to or detained in psychiatric wards on account of the types of self-destructive behaviour described in the preceding passages. These ideas are taken up strongly by Darby, Allan, Kashani, Hartke, and Reid (1998), who found that juvenile homicide offenders are more likely to have prior suicidal ideations and/or attempts, with 30% of their sample evaluated by a mental health professional prior to the crime. However, as is readily apparent, decoupling participants' problematic behaviour from their disadvantaged or unorthodox living situations often proves a complex, if not impossible, task. By all accounts, Lucy had a particularly difficult upbringing, characterized by a long history of conduct issues, including ADHD and violent mood swings: 'I never knew why but I always felt like I was different. . . . I was always doing weird and obscure things.' But even this assessment fails to capture the true extent of the ordeal that played out at home, with Lucy's parents employing restraints and Phenergan, an anti-allergy medication with strong sedative properties, to get the preschooler to sleep at night. In fact, as time wore on, both her mother and father exhibited authoritarian violence to their daughter in trying to come to grips with how to manage her, and excessive discipline appears to be an undercurrent in Lucy's childhood:

> When the family punishment came down, I copped the brunt of it. . . . I [always] knew what was going to be in store for me and I hated my dad. Hated him. He just had this very regimented [ideal] of being a certain way and I couldn't match up to it.
>
> There was one incident where my dad inflicted enough force on me that it actually required . . . medical intervention and he's never forgot about it. I've haven't forgotten about it. We have sat down and spoken about it since I've been in [prison] but for me . . . there's still scars. I can still feel it.

From the age of 2–15, Lucy was subject to a battery of medical and psychiatric evaluations in an attempt to curb her restless, impulsive, and boundary-pushing behaviour – but to no avail. Already strained by her challenging behaviours, Lucy remarked how these processes only served to further exceptionalize and alienate her from the family unit:

> I felt like I was just dragging them down: that I had consumed too much of their time as a kid growing up. I kind of felt like a lot of their energy was focused on me because I was this broken, fractured child, you know, that there was always something wrong. Carting me off to doctors and all sorts of shit and it's just it was one thing after the other since the age of about eight. This team of psychiatrists, psychoanalysts . . . psychologists, pediatricians: it just went on and on . . . [and] it was unwanted attention that I felt was being taken away from my brother and my sister. . . . I thought they'd be better off without me in their lives.

Similarly, Aaron grew up with the impression he was different: 'People didn't like me, the way I was.' Classmates thought of him as strange and morbid. Others described him as psychotic or schizoid and as someone who enjoyed listening to the violent and sexually explicit lyrics of Eminem and D12. As he continued, 'I obsessed about killing people. From Year One to Year Eight I've just had thoughts about killing people and when I get angry today, when I get *really* angry, I still think about it.' Understandably, sentiments like these brought him under the supervision of some fairly significant professional services from around the time he started school. As is well documented, Aaron suffered substantial cognitive difficulties that impaired his ability to perform at a satisfactory level academically: 'I refused to read for like four-and a-half years. I couldn't handle it. I didn't like it. I always felt stupid when people were trying to teach me it.' In fact, the general conclusion at sentence was that Aaron's cognitive impairment placed him in the bottom 1% of children in his age group, or, as Aaron bluntly surmised, 'They had the audacity to say that I was mildly retarded.' Unfortunately for Aaron, a number of implications flowed from his (diagnosed) intellectual disability. As mentioned, he performed very poorly at school and, in turn, consistently displayed the behavioural issues that one might expect to see in relation to his level of intellectual functioning:

> I wasn't conforming to the way *they* did school. They all did their little fucking quizzes and all their little bullshit. I'd walk outside, plug in my iPod and sit there and watch the clouds go by for days at a time. I couldn't read, I couldn't write. I used to get severe headaches in class and it did my head in. I couldn't handle the pressure of it . . . trying to keep up with everyone.
>
> (Aaron)

But, more importantly, Aaron's cognitive difficulties also diminished his social competence and ability to integrate with his peers. The desire to connect socially with others is a well-researched dimension of psychology, and there is good evidence to suggest that ostracism and other forms of social exclusion are associated with a range of negative physical and psychological outcomes (Ren et al., 2018; Wesselmann, Butler, Williams, & Pickett, 2010; Wesselmann et al., 2016a; Wesselmann, Ren, & Williams, 2016b). More specifically, individuals are recognized to experience pain on account of their ostracism (Eisenberger, Lieberman, & Williams, 2003), with increased negative affect (i.e. anger, jealousy, sadness, and shame) (Chow, Tiedens, & Govan, 2008; Peterson, Gravens, & Harmon-Jones, 2011; Westermann, Rief, Euteneuer, & Kohlmann, 2015); heightened cortisol (i.e. stress hormone) levels (Dickerson & Kemeny, 2004; Gunnar, Sebanc, Tout, Donzella, & van Dulmen, 2003); feelings of dehumanization (Bastian & Haslam, 2010); and a tendency towards physical and social aggression (Buckley, Winkel, & Leary, 2004; Warburton, Williams, & Cairns, 2006). While it was standard fare for school to be a source of isolation and unhappiness within the cohort, the level of bullying Aaron received on a daily basis cannot be underestimated. He was repeatedly teased, abused, and sometimes beaten. As his father Vincent described, the treatment meted out to Aaron began virtually the day he commenced school and continued to when he was suspended on the day of the victim's death.

> School was shit to him; school wasn't very nice. In fact, kids are fucking royal arseholes. . . . I don't like the little fuckers. I fucking don't. They're cruel, self-centred little shits and their parents let them get away with murder. . . .

> [They were always] teasing him for whatever it was; yeah, he hated school. It was never going to be a happy ending at school.
>
> (Vincent, father)

Arguably, few children possess the emotional reserves sufficient to cope with rejection and ostracism of this magnitude, let alone when a significant disability enters the mix. In Aaron's case, developing in school as a social outcast appears to have shaped his attitudes towards all people, save for a smattering of individuals – largely comprised of his immediate family – he viewed as on his side. Everybody else, by stark contrast, was seen as a potential enemy, with themes of hatred, violence, retribution, and aggression marking his interactions with people from the outset of his formal education. In these circumstances, he found it very difficult to empathize with others:

> I was clouded by anger and hatred of people . . . 'cause I was treated badly for no reason for a long time and, yeah, there were some things that I couldn't help when I was younger and I got targeted for it.

While Aaron humoured his father's early attempts to engage him in more traditional pursuits, he did so without enthusiasm:

> It was always hard for him to . . . let go of whatever he was transfixed on at the time, whether it be one particular game or one particular movie. . . . He'd start talking of violence and I'd cut it off: 'I'm not interested, mate.'
>
> 'Imagine this Dad – '
>
> 'I don't want to know, Aaron,' you know? 'Let's talk about something else. . . . Let's watch a good comedy or something like that.'
>
> (Vincent, father)

> I was forced to [play sport] actually. . . . My dad said you've got a choice of either football or cricket . . . [but] I didn't enjoy sport at all. I was antisocial. I had no reason to really communicate with people outside my house. . . . They all fucking thought I was [no good]. A lot of people in my neighbourhood . . . didn't really want to hang out with me, so I didn't really care. It didn't really affect me.
>
> (Aaron)

Aaron's issues around social dysfunction developed steadily to the extent that he reported being suspended from school over 50 times. But more to the point, he soon became disenchanted with whatever embryonic attempts he had made to go along to get along. Consequently, he vowed to set the standard instead of lowering the tone:

> If people are going to accuse me of stuff, I'm going to act like it. Yeah, I grew up with that mentality. Fucking people [were] accusing me of being a

> monster, so I showed them a monster. . . . When I was younger, I'd show them that: 'If you want to see me be nasty, I *will* be nasty . . . [and], well, you're going to have fun trying to deal with me then.'

At that moment, Aaron was referring to the origin of his mistrustful and aggressive attitudes, but in hindsight, it was a prescient observation about the days ahead: when people would cease to see the 14-year-old amid the headlines and outrage that soon surrounded him. But to focus on Aaron's claims that such intense rejection and torment had no major impact on him is to ignore so much else of what is known about him. It ignores the fact that Aaron retreated deeper into a solitary world of violent movies, pornography, and video games such as Grand Theft Auto and Saints Row, in which people were killed in explicit and overtly brutal ways. It ignores the fact that his exposure to and interest in this kind of material was such that a notice of concern was registered with family services: 'I talked to other people about killing people. . . . I used to make a lot of jokes, a lot of references towards killing people and that' (Aaron). And it ignores the fact that his father, having sought the school's intervention in relation to his son's bullying and on not being satisfied with that intervention – and clearly at wit's end – encouraged Aaron to express his anger and frustration in a violent manner:

> I've gone down [to] the school and said, 'How dare you suspend my child when he's been antagonised? This is crap. You're pushing *my* buttons now.' And [the response was], 'Oh, we've done it for Aaron's safety as well because there's other boys involved.' And I said, 'Well, why weren't they all suspended? Not just Aaron? . . . My kids deserve the same protection at school. And if you can't protect them because there's bullies in the school, the bullies need to be got rid of, not the other way around.' But it wasn't very much longer that all this shit went down.
>
> (Vincent, father)

> He got rejected a lot by other kids and I felt sorry for him and there's not a lot that a parent can do about that; you can't make kids play together. . . . But he was [also] picked on and that wasn't addressed as far as I was concerned; stuff that he done in primary school was still being picked on two years down the track [in High School] . . . kids wouldn't let it go. And then it got a little bit physical. And that's when I said he has the inherent right, if a kid comes and pushes him, to plant one straight on his chin. He'll stop. Pick the biggest one and *hit*.
>
> (Vincent, father)

Here, it is difficult to argue that inability to get Aaron the right help in a timely fashion played no part in the tragedy that eventually occurred. Whilst writers acknowledge that angry, frustrated individuals are 'less likely to consider the long-term consequences of their behavior' (Agnew, 2006, p. 33), the school system – no doubt trying to deal with its own strains – appears to have let a disturbed young man fall straight through some very wide cracks:

AARON: What did I used to talk about more than anything, fucking, in the world? Oh, yeah, 'I'm going to kill this fucking person, I'm going to kill that person, I'm going to become a mass murderer, fucking, I want to be a hit man.' They thought it was just me being angry. But it's 'cause I wanted to do all of it.

SIMONE: You did? You were serious: you wanted to?

AARON: I wasn't fucking around. . . . I was in the principal's office, looking at the assistant and I was like, 'You haven't got a .45 by any chance?' She's like 'Why?' And I said, 'So I could knock everyone in my class. Go shoot them out.'

SIMONE: Were you serious [about doing that]?

AARON: Back then I was. If she'd said yes, I would have gone for it.

While Aaron did not go on to commit a high school shooting, two risk factors are consistently identified in those who do: 'The first, perpetrators often have a fascination with weapons and they have all had access to guns. The second is disclosure of assault plans, referred to as *leakage*. The perpetrators of many shootings have provided clues about their plans' (Wike & Fraser, 2009, p. 164). Aaron was an avid player of 'first-person shooter' games, so called because players take on the killer's point of view with a projectile weapon (Hollingdale & Greitemeyer, 2014); these games tend to feature prominently in the course of such investigations. While the literature is somewhat equivocal in relation to the effect of first-person shooter games on the arousal of violent and aggressive behaviours (but see APA Task Force on Violent Media, 2015), it seems fair to say that given Aaron's particular vulnerabilities, this kind of material, combined with the violent coaching he received, promoted aggressive strategies as a means for re-empowerment in situations where he felt disempowered:

> I didn't talk about my problems. They [all] knew about the problems I was going through but they didn't know what to do. . . . [I was] unfairly treated in life. . . . I didn't get any respect . . . everyday shit was really fucking with me and I was angry.
>
> It was an escape of reality and I'd get invested in it and fucking start – I'd fucking start taking on the characters, start acting like them. Yeah, and it fucked with me. . . . I played all the time. Fucking as soon as I got back from school, before I went to school, fucking, all the time. If I wasn't playing videogames or watching movies I was watching porn. So I didn't have a very healthy lifestyle. I shut everyone out from what I was doing or what I was thinking or feeling 'cause, fucking, people didn't want to hear it. Fucking, everyone thought it was a phase and, fucking, they were wrong in the end.

Problems continued at school and, on the day of the murder, a confluence of immediate triggers appear to have set the forces in motion. Particularly angry and distressed about the circumstances in which he was suspended ('Well, he belted one of the kids or something like that' [Vincent, father]), Aaron spent the afternoon with another youth who, coincidentally, was also suspended that day following displays of aggressive behaviour. Into the night, there was heavy involvement with violent videogames in tandem with significant alcohol consumption, which was accessed after Aaron's father retired for the evening. For the most part, the boys were content to play games and fantasize about life as the 'street thug' they personified in Grand Theft Auto: 'Jacking people for cars; running people over; killing people; bashing people; banging ho's; slinging drugs. The usual' (Aaron). But, at some point, things took a more disturbing turn, according to Aaron's father:

> Another kid and they might have talked about stealing a car and egged each other on to [do that]. Stealing Dad's car, stealing Mum's car, taking it for a joyride. I don't know. But they egged each other on and it was particularly about murdering somebody.
>
> (Vincent, father)

During the sentencing process, forensic psychologist Luke Broomhall testified that Aaron, having become 'fixated' with the idea of taking the victim's life, found it 'almost impossible' to renege on the situation given his cognitive deficits. Wesselmann et al. (2016b, p. 157), drawing on the work of Twenge, Baumeister, Tice, and Stucke (2001) and DeWall, Twenge, Gitter, and Baumeister (2009), observe in relation to paradoxical behavioral responses to ostracism:

> Aggression is not simply retaliatory. Indeed, ostracism elicits a retaliatory response toward the *source* of ostracism . . . as well as *bystanders* . . . and *innocent targets*. . . . Even simply recalling a time when one had been ostracised is enough to evoke an aggressive response.

This goes some way to explaining how an elderly woman (who was, by any view of it, completely defenceless) came to be murdered in her own home. Ironically, for Aaron, there was a feeling that demonstrating this kind of commitment to an extreme and shared goal would bring about the acceptance and friendship that had previously eluded him (see Goldman & Hogg, 2016). This was not to be:

> My co-accused that got away with it, he was involved. . . . He got found not guilty' by the good people of South Australia and I haven't heard anything of him [since]. . . . I hate him with a passion and I hope he dies in a car crash.

Reflecting from custody, Aaron spoke of his inability to deal with anger and despair in a socialized or an acceptable way and the role of screen violence in providing a desensitizing precursor to a real-life event:

> I don't know where the fuck it come from but my first response [to bullying] was like, 'I'll fucking kill you,' and that: 'Test me. I'll kill you.' And then

> watching all these violent movies and videogames and with all my anger and that, I just started thinking about doing it and I just brooded on it, thought about ways I could do it and how to get away with it. And then, yeah, just one day I did it. And it was the most stupidest decision of my life. . . . I [still] don't know why [I did it]. The way I was thinking wasn't controlled. The way I was thinking wasn't right: wanting to do that for seven years, or even longer, it's just not right. . . . And then someone that didn't deserve any harm, [that] did nothing wrong by me, ended up copping all the anger I had.

'Dying to fit in': finding refuge in all the wrong places

Very closely related to their extremely unsettled, disrupted, and miserable experiences at home and at school – in fact, flowing from it – was the overarching desire of these juveniles to be accepted by their peers, most of whom had in common some negative traits. The overwhelming majority of participants knew of and spoke to the fact that their low self-esteem, passivity, and a willingness to comply contributed to their involvement in the unfortunate series of events: 'Ultimately . . . [I needed to] extricate myself from the situation but I didn't feel like I had the courage, the power – the will power – and the determination to think for myself and just [leave]' (Lucy). A strongly recurrent theme here was the perception of parents that their child was, in essence, a follower who went along with others in an attempt to cement an identity within the group, obviously in a manner that was reprehensible:

> [Ben's] not a leader; he's a follower. He always has been. You do something, he's going to follow you into it. So whatever Henry did, *he* did. . . . Henry wanted to be a chef; *he* wanted to be a chef. . . . [It's] just [that] Ben was more [driven]; when he gets his mind set on something, he'll want to do it.
>
> (Bianca, mother)

> Easily led, you know, he's not the . . . he might tell you he's the pack animal or like the Alpha male, but he very rarely is.
>
> (Colin, father)

> Other kids, you know, they [load] the gun up; Lucy's always the one that fires it and gets caught. . . . [She's] always been a bit of a follower. Not an independent person, you know: she'd follow where other people led and she just [walked] right into all of this.
>
> (Vanessa, mother)

Throughout their children's upbringing, parents observed their children thriving on the attention of others and needing intense one-on-one contact with people. When attempts to be part of the group failed – as they often did – young people were thrust into a state of despondency and despair, feelings that they carried into the secure care setting: 'When she puts herself out there, she gets quite crushed when it goes [bad]' (Vanessa, mother). In Lucy's case, getting 'crushed' was synonymous with rampant alcohol, cannabis and amphetamine consumption, and the requisite degree of self-loathing. When newly incarcerated, she wrote herself the following note:

> Why do I have to be born? . . . [I'm] fucked in the head, a reject, I am so dumb. I don't know what I am doing, I fucked up myself. I should have murdered myself instead. I am a freak. I am so different, ugly, unpopular.

Such comments go to the obvious but critically important point that happy, well-adjusted teenagers rarely find themselves in the midst of a murder enquiry. And the participants' romantic relationships, where they occurred, afforded a particularly significant opportunity for participants' families, already deep in crisis, to edge closer to the brink:

> As soon as he met her, he didn't care about anything, anybody, other than what Claire wanted. And he even left home because of her. . . . Everything revolved around her. He wouldn't listen to anything I said: 'I'll do what I like.' He'd just take off whenever he wanted to. His whole attitude changed. Every single detail of his life was, 'Claire this, Claire that', 'I'm going to do this with Claire, I'm going to do that', and it's like, 'Oh my god. How can someone have such a strong hold on someone?' That was my thought. But then again, obviously he was looking for a different sort of love than what a mother gives, so I don't know. . . . And they got a flat together at Para Hills. And that was just disastrous, totally disastrous. That's when he started getting into trouble, like stealing a car and just doing really silly things.
>
> (Karen, mother)

> [When they broke up] I know that affected him quite badly. He was very withdrawn and I think he just grasped at anyone and, unfortunately, it was a girl named Sarah who then introduced him to all the others: the others who were at *that* house. So he moved in there against my [wishes] . . . and then it just went *kapoof!*
>
> (Karen, mother)

One of the most common grievances, as identified in the preceding extracts, was the perceived ease with which juveniles left home and bounced from different social welfare drop-in places and assisted housing schemes, ultimately ending up at the murder locations a short time before the murders happened. Sometimes, establishing the true reasons for juveniles initially leaving home was difficult due to different perceptions held by the various parties. Putting this issue aside, it is clear that these lodgings functioned for young people as places to test their fledgling adult capabilities and often, unfortunately, as some kind of sanctuary for getting high:

> In the last couple of months I had changed various addresses from couch-surfing to a bed at halfway houses and stuff like that. . . . It was perceived to

> be a bit more freedom for me. I didn't have adults watching over my every move and if I came back stoned or off my face on something or other, I wasn't questioned to within an inch of my life. . . . I thought it was so much more liberating than where I was living because you had to be back by a certain hour and all this kind of shit and it was just draining my life away so to speak. . . . So that attracted me and then naturally other people started gravitating there . . . suppliers, dealers and the like and . . . I was looking to get on basically.
>
> (Lucy)

Mothers, while relaying frustrated attempts to locate their children or to be heard as to their growing concerns, clearly blamed government agencies (whose specific remit was to offer support) for events that ensued:

> [They] had put her into this unit at Queenstown . . . and I'd been over there every day and I'd hammer on their door and I said, 'Look, I'm trying to find my daughter.'
>
> 'Nope, she's [considered] an adult. We can't give you any information rah, rah, rah.'
>
> I said, 'Look, put it [on the record]: if anything happens to her, I hold you accountable.'
>
> (Vanessa, mother)

> He eventually ended up having to go to a halfway house at Tapleys Road in Alberton and from there he met this crew that he got into trouble with. . . . [And] I have no idea what was going on in that house: none at all. All I know is that I never went there and whatever those four were doing has led to calling the [victim] and doing all of *that*.
>
> (Karen, mother)

A major problem with emergency accommodation, as noted by Halsey (2008, p. 1225) is the tendency for these 'to be occupied by the "kinds" of people who would be more, not less, [willing] to engage in crime or to respond to minor forms of conflict with disproportionate amounts of violence'. Apparent in this study are the similar lifestyles being led by all those who were present where each of the killings occurred. To a great extent, police were led to a group of basically young homeless people, mostly unemployed, with a long history of bespoke trauma, behavioural problems, and spiralling drug use.

Lucy had known her co-offenders (a drug dealer and four drug users) for about two weeks before a series of sustained assaults on the victim at a local 'doss house' shifted into the crime of murder, precipitated by some argument over money. In no meaningful way, however, did the initial motive bear any relevance to the horrendous ordeal that developed over a period of hours and hours, during which time the whole object of the exercise became to do away with the poor girl in question. Lucy, not a central figure in anyone's account, recounts how concern for her own position ultimately overrode whatever duty she thought she might have to seek help for the victim or disabuse the others from proceeding with their plan:

> It was just a very eclectic group of people which I think wouldn't have met under any circumstances other than a desire for drugs, [social] connection and the need to prove oneself. Unfortunately in my case, these people I didn't particularly know and I thought, 'Fuck. If this is the way it's going to go, it might well be me [that dies] if I decide to walk out now.'

Here, one begins to see the writing on the wall in terms of the volatility of such living arrangements and the complexity of the experiences (insecure attachment and bonding, domestic violence, excessive discipline, psychological disturbances and abnormalities, miserable experience of school, etc.) of those forced to confront them. Given the kinds of stories participants related during interviews, the situations were not easy to prevent, and it is realistic to assume that highly troubled youth will, from time to time, get caught up in situations not of their making. The reality, of course, is that all of these young people actively participated – albeit to varying degrees – in crimes that plainly fall into the worst category, and failure to report them to police, from a safe distance, must tell against them in some regard. There is no easy response to this kind of scenario, but it is probably necessary to deal with the question of remorse because its absence is a major plank of the argument that children who kill are exotic, cold-blooded, and irredeemable individuals without a future as eventual members of our community. Somewhat counter-intuitively, nearly all participants pleaded guilty at an early stage and 'accepted "their lot" in terms of the requirement that they be punished [severely] for what they had done' (Halsey, 2007, p. 349). The following quotes from participants support this:

> Mine was a fucked-up crime and I'm happy to have a life sentence.
>
> (Aaron)

> Everything I did back then was my choice. Whether or not there was that goal at the end [i.e., to cause the death of the victim] . . . it doesn't matter. There was still a choice all the way and I chose wrong . . . [and] they can put [me] behind as many fences as they like; the hardest thing every single day when [I] wake up is knowing that [I've] killed someone. That's the hardest. It makes no difference what DCS [does] to [me] or what anybody else does to [me] and not a lot of people realise that.
>
> (Toby)

Some even offered to give evidence against the other defendants, many of whom were less than sympathetic to colleagues who cooperated with police: 'When I arrived [in prison] . . . there was [a] list of people waiting to beat the crap out of me all because Zoe had set it up that way' (Lucy). In a bold and significant move on his part, James took the unusual step of voluntarily coming forward to confess many years after the murder, knowing he was thereby committing himself to a long period of imprisonment. He went to a priest first and then to the police: without his confession, he would never have been discovered. As distinct from the feelings of remorse that might, in part, be induced by a fear of the consequences shortly after an offender is arrested, for James, the prospect of a life sentence had both an atoning and redemptive dimension:

> I wish we had of been caught [at that time] because I spent a lot of time, as I say, in a bottle. . . . I was having blackouts all the time through the alcohol [and making] heaps of wrong decisions. I tried a few times to take me own life so, yeah, I decided that I'd go forward and tell the police what had happened. So I went to see a priest and then . . . a lawyer [and] then I went to the police. . . . I was feeling pretty calm because it was finally coming to an end. . . . When I talked to the lawyer he sent me off to another lawyer to talk about what was going on and his secretary made a mistake and sent the paperwork to the police before the whole meeting had finished. So he said, 'We can stop it and deny everything and there's nothing they can do about it,' and I said, 'No. We'll keep going forward.' . . . I was very sorry for what I'd done. That's the only thing I wanted [to demonstrate] and maybe get some closure for her family sort of thing: to see someone punished for what had happened. . . . In a way it was a relief, now that it's all done and dusted, because it needed being paid for.
>
> (James)

Comments like these hint at the untold potential for this group of young people, with the right kinds of therapeutic intervention, to rejoin the community at some point as empathetic, socially responsible adults. Having said as much, the vast majority of participants, 'whilst understanding the *right* to punish – could not grasp how the conditions to which they were sentenced could in any way assist them to become a "better person"' (Halsey, 2007, p. 349), which is something I elaborate on in Chapter 6. It is also not to suggest that recognizing the enormity and gravity of their actions and the devastating impact they had on so many people was necessarily axiomatic. Reaching this point, as participants themselves observed, was a process that could take years, even decades, to fully accept:

> Every person has that ingrained sense of what's right and what's wrong, and [this] was wrong immediately afterwards. But the gravity of it didn't sink in for years and years and years and years and years. It gave me nightmares, it gave me flashbacks. It had me spiralling into a deep depression. . . . It took a while [to sink in] and it comes in dribs and drabs. Sometimes it's periodical, like at certain times of the year, a certain smell, or a certain something will trigger something in my head. . . . But, yeah, it does resonate with me that it's my cross to bear. It's my burden. It's my fault. At the same time I don't take all of that guilt myself because I was involved with other people. But the defining point is that it shouldn't have happened. No-one deserves that.
>
> (Lucy)

> I've come to terms with it, you know, getting [sentenced to] life and being locked up but how do you come to terms with killing someone? . . . I still have my ups and downs and I still have nights where, you know, it'll just pop into my head when I'm trying to sleep . . . yeah, there was a lot of blood.
>
> (Henry)

> People keep telling me that I should feel more. Like I feel bad, I feel sorry but I've never ever been good at putting emotions into words and saying sorry. I can say sorry as much as I want or as someone wants me to but after the first one, I can't do anything [more]. . . . You want me to be more apologetic but I physically can't without, you know, looking like a mockery. . . . I can't change it. I can't fix it. I literally can't do anything. . . . And I know some people think that's not remorseful enough and a million other things, but I can't fix it [so] I'm going to move on.
>
> (Ben)

'Out of the blue': when 'good' kids do (really) bad things

There are a handful of special cases, as Polk (1994, p. 157) deftly points out, 'where what happens between key actors is so odd, bizarre, or unusual' as to frustrate efforts to understand exactly *why* the interaction resulted in murder. In what follows, I draw on the case of Henry and Ben, who had generally unremarkable childhoods *with* the benefit of stable family upbringings devoid of abuse or trauma. It is perplexing because there seems to be no explanation we can relate to in terms of how two average suburban teenagers came to shock the public conscience of South Australia so completely as to warrant record sentences for youthful murder in this State. Henry himself noted in relation to his normalness:

> I was just a typical teenager until I did it and for the rest of my life now, I'll be labelled as a murderer. . . . I won't step out of gaol or do anything significant with my life for at least the next [20] years.

While their case has some common features with earlier accounts involving simultaneous other offending, it differs in several critical respects, relating to both the transaction that occurred between the victim and offenders and the personal circumstances of each of the young men involved. While panic, anxiety, and criminal incompetence offer the closest explanation I have to understanding what fuelled this murder, no definitive interpretive rationale exists, simply making this matter all the more unbelievable.

Meeting at the local high school, Henry and Ben quickly bonded over their shared interest in becoming professional chefs. In respective interviews, their parents continued to question the corrupting influence of the friendship against the (appropriate) values they had instilled in their own child.

> To me it's wrong place, wrong time, wrong *friend*. So yeah and [he's] got 20 years from that mistake.
>
> (Bianca, Ben's mother)

> He met him through [i.e., names school]; that's the other reason it was a mistake to send him there. Had we not have put him there, those two wouldn't have met and there's a pretty good chance this wouldn't have happened.
>
> (Colin, Henry's father)

However, any objections to the relationship appear to have crystallized somewhere along the court process, as both Ben's and Henry's parents supported their sons' decision to leave school and enrol in technical college together shortly before completing Year 11. Prior to this, both boys had been average students, well-liked by others, and they engaged in a diverse range of recreational interests, which included, ironically, Henry's attendance at Neighbourhood Watch meetings with his policeman father. In fact, other than when Henry was suspended twice for truancy in Year Nine – behaviour he put down to boredom ('I just got over [school] like most people did') – there were no disciplinary problems reported at home or at school for either boy. Courteous and polite, each had also taken significant steps to enhance their prospects of working in a commercial kitchen; Henry did volunteer work with a non-profit organization, while Ben washed dishes at a popular hotel. The joint decision to leave school, however, was an ill-fated one, as the technical college was still in its infancy and failed to deliver on either promises or expectations: 'They'd only bought cookery in that year so they were vastly underprepared, so ultimately, we just got all the curriculum we could . . . finished it in six months and left' (Henry). Briefly returning to school, Ben and Henry left once more after securing apprentice chef positions with respected businesses around town. In full-time employment and with money in hand, the boys reported partaking in the usual teenage pastimes: learning to drive, dating girls, and experimenting mildly to moderately with alcohol and marijuana in the context of social gatherings with friends.

But this is where things take a strange turn. Less than six months before the victim was killed, the boys began involving themselves in another, far less conventional activity: 'We started breaking into houses. Whenever we drove past a house we thought was empty, we'd come back, go in, take whatever we thought was worth it and go and sell it or sometimes trade it' (Henry). Aggrieved by the termination of his apprenticeship, Henry spoke of a brief period between jobs as providing him with both the opportunity (i.e. boredom) and the incentive to steal: 'I lost the job just before my offence. So at that stage, we were breaking into houses and just taking whatever we could to sell and [I was] using that to pay for [things].' There was an obvious mismatch, however, between their accounts of property crime as a financially rewarding exercise versus an exciting, presumably victimless game of cat and mouse for 'sneaky thrills' (see Katz, 1988). In relation to this, Ben said the following:

> I never cared for anything [in the houses] . . . I'd go along [but] . . . it was never [about the money]. Realistically, I was never short of cash 'cause . . . I was getting paid and I was getting paid enough so I could live my life how I wanted to.
>
> (Ben)

To this extent, even Henry concedes that his antisocial behaviour did not, in any way, spring from financial *necessity*:

> I wouldn't say that I was forced into it. . . . There were other things I could have done. . . . I could have [got another job] as soon as I could or I could have borrowed money from my parents.

First published in 1988, Jack Katz's *Seductions of Crime* has had a major impact on the research literature and history of criminological studies into deviance. The idea of asking 'what it means, feels, sounds, tastes, or looks like to commit a particular crime' (p. 3) yields a detailed analysis as to the attractiveness, or seductive qualities, of behaving badly. A key concept to emerge here has been that for young people inclined to 'break in and exit successfully but [who] do not try to take anything', housebreaking captures a form of property crime 'in which getting away with something . . . is more important than keeping anything or getting anywhere in particular' (Katz, 1988, p. 52). Certainly, there was a distinct prankster flavour about Ben and Henry's trespasses, as the pair would dress in camouflage ('I think I was trying to pretend to be more harder than I was, which really didn't work for me' [Ben]), then set about rearranging furniture in hopes to confound the unsuspecting residents when they returned home. Why anybody would feel the impulse to enter a house, move tables and chairs around, and leave them for an unwitting victim remains a puzzling question. How could somebody, knowing the potential consequences of a person being home, go through with the crime? If there was an immediate reward, what it was remains unclear. There was no satisfaction from watching the shock on a person's face upon discovering their home has been sabotaged. Typical of many a teenage boy, those projections would be confined to some lively banter during the car ride home. Whatever the precise motives, the plans were not well thought out or executed with any degree of precision. In the following excerpt, I asked Ben how he and Henry knew that the premises were, indeed, unoccupied:

> Well, we didn't. We just looked. No car was usually a give-away that no-one was home. And that was pretty much it: if there was no car, no sort of signs that people were home. Yes I know it was midnight or 1 in the morning or whatever, so it wasn't the smartest plan to start with but that was the idea. . . . [And] nothing [had] ever come of it so it didn't faze me.

But that was all about to change. Switching off the power supply at the meter box and climbing through the bathroom window on the night the victim was killed, Ben was immediately aware that someone was in the house. His natural reaction, quite reasonably, was to run: 'When we got caught, I split.' He told me that he waited in the car, for what seemed like ages, for Henry to join him. Not knowing what was happening to his friend, whether the occupant was male or female, or of what age, Ben eventually decided to return to the property to try and get Henry out:

> [He's] a faster runner than me and more agile; he can get over a fence a lot quicker than I can. . . . [S]o I figured, when he didn't come out, I had to go back in to find out what went wrong. . . . I went [there] to help out one of my mates.

But, as he discovered, Henry was not the one who needed help. Here, Henry offers a concise summary of events:

> My friend went in and then yelled out to me that someone was in the house, so he left through the front door while I waited out the back. [The victim] came out the back yard, I knocked them [*sic*] down, my friend came back with a knife and yeah, [we] made the stupid decision to kill them.
>
> (Henry)

At first glance, this is the archetypal scenario of a homicide that takes place in the course of another crime: a scenario 'in which the victim and the offender act and react to the other's behavior during the course of, first, the [burglary], and then the fatal violence that results' (Polk, 1994, p. 157). The problem here is that the boys could easily have escaped without attacking the victim, as it was manifestly obvious that the elderly woman was no threat to them, nor could she prevent them from leaving the scene. Further, as Henry accepts, there was no realistic prospect the victim could identify them, as (a) it was pitch-black outside and (b) Henry had immediately launched at her, knocking her to the ground, thereby fracturing her nose and a vertebra in her neck. Even when pressed several times, Henry could not shed light on why the two employed lethal violence in the absence of a short-lived episode of rage or passion or the feelings of self-righteousness, humiliation, frustration, fear, self-preservation, and so on that often provokes a slaughter of this kind:

HENRY: I wasn't forced into it, no. . . . I think me and my co-offender, we both just – oh we didn't even really debate it: we were just kind of looking at each other and . . . I don't know. When he came back with the knife and he was holding it as I was holding her down . . . I just grabbed the knife off him and [used it].

SIMONE: Was that because you were worried about getting caught?

HENRY: That's probably the only reason that I could give for it. But then again, you know, she was old and it was in a back yard that was poorly lit, so I doubt she would have seen us anyway, so I couldn't really give you a reason for why I did it.

Arising from the following excerpt, it is difficult not to give Henry some credit for refusing a perfect opportunity to displace blame onto Ben, given Ben's introduction of the knife into the scene. But any benefit has to be significantly tempered by Henry's singular resolve to kill the victim, ending any speculation as to the possibility of a different outcome that night:

> [Even] if he hadn't have come back there was still a chance that I might have gone back into the house and found [a knife] or I might have gone back to

> the car, grabbed it and gone back. . . . I think both of us at some stage – when we realised that there was someone there – I think something just happened in our heads and we just decided that that's what was going to happen. It's not like he came out and said, 'Here, kill her,' or I told him, 'Go get the knife because she has to die.' . . . No-one said anything but I think something just clicked.
>
> (Henry)

Viewing the scenario through the lens of Goffman's (1976) character contest, in which acts are directed towards the goal of establishing evidence of strong character, similarly fails to make any real inroads here. As Athens (2005, p. 637) rightfully argues, 'when people resort to physical force to prove their dominance, they may demonstrate either a strong or weak character rather than always a stronger one'. As he continues, 'when a large adult male physically attacks a smaller adult female, young child, or frail senior citizen, he can prove his sheer physical superiority over them but at the risk of demonstrating a weaker, more twisted character'. Ben lamented this situation, remarking, 'Because mine was [the murder of] an elderly lady . . . they figured that . . . we must be like druggies or something of [that] description because no normal, no sane person does what we did.' Critiques became significantly less 'generous' as local and national media outlets took a rolling interest in the case:

> I've been called a 'thrill killer': they've said that I wanted to kill her for the thrill of it. There have been people who said it was premeditated because we wanted to know what it was like to have someone die. One of the [TV] channels even said something along the lines . . . that [we] slit her throat and then put their [*sic*] hands over it to feel the life force flow out of her.
>
> (Henry)

In such circumstances, it is easy to understand how young people at the centre of high-profile offending fail to engage with the very systems designed, in theory, to reflect their relative youth and the premise that they still have the capacity to succeed in life. Put differently, participants were keenly aware of how 'killer kids' figure in the credibility stakes:

> I couldn't do anything. What do you want me to do? Stand up and say, 'That's wrong,' and 'Liar!'? I'm just going to look like a dick. . . . I just wanted it to be over. . . . Just tell me how long I'm doing. Tell me my time and stop bringing me to court.
>
> (Ben)

This should not be taken to mean that each is somehow innocent of their crimes or that each is a good candidate for release into the community. That, quite clearly, is a decision for the Parole Board. Rather, I want to suggest that mythologies of the 'super-predator' are deeply implicated in how juveniles receive and respond to opportunities in both judicial and correctional settings, with special emphasis on the role of the media in shaping the availability of outcomes at the end. In large measure, I adopt the summary of Halsey and Deegan (2014, p. 2), as they observe the vexed world inhabited by female intimates of (ex-)prisoners, remarking that 'where they remain silent . . . they risk the ongoing marginalization of their needs and experiences . . . [whereas] the decision to "speak up" carries with it the very real risk of public condemnation'. This, of course, is another reflection of the significant barriers facing studies of victim–offender relationships in homicide cases.

In sum

It is difficult, in the context of the current research, to avoid grappling with the rather distasteful and potentially insensitive task of ranking murders from the lowest to the highest end of the scale of seriousness. I am not so naive as to argue that victims' family members will take *any* comfort from the suggestion that theirs was one of the 'good' ones. However, to say that the crimes committed by the youths in this chapter were serious is not to say enough. Assuming most adolescents would have an aversive reaction to the sight of blood or to other people suffering, with regard to this cohort, it was not enough to deter them from taking their violent plan of action to a lethal and tragic conclusion: 'The strange thing is I don't see him as an overly cruel person although he's committed a heinous act' (Vincent, Aaron's father).

Of course, the court hears many situations where the particular reason for the murder is clear and sometimes the gravity of even the most serious of crimes can be, at least to some degree, leavened by the circumstances. It could be a fight gone wrong or a drug deal gone wrong. In these scenarios, both parties have knowingly exposed themselves to risk, 'since there is always the known danger of losing a fight and being physically beaten' (Polk, 1994, p. 93), while violence is accepted as an occupational hazard of the illicit drug trade. But here we are confronted by something quite different. While Polk (1994, p. 93) rightly reminds us that these killings result 'from events which are initially about something else', as time went on, initial motives seem to have little relevance to the brutal treatment meted out to victims. There was also an unpredictable aspect to these murders in that most juveniles had no connection to the victims, with their resort to violence seemingly rooted in the underlying anger and frustration the juveniles carried with them day to day. This confirms earlier research that youth high in *alienation* (i.e. estranged from society, significant others and themselves) are prone to act aggressively (the 'outcast-lash-out effect') (Reijntjes et al., 2010; Warburton et al., 2006) and points to the importance of certainty regarding the physical or emotional availability of the parent/s and to meaningful, close relationships with one's peers.

While there was one example of a young person setting out to commit murder, the general view expressed by participants was that the decision to kill the victim was made in fear of the latter reporting behaviour that had recently occurred. Thus, there are valuable lessons to be learned from the interaction between the offender and victim or, in an extension of Athens' (1980) original thinking, between the *offenders themselves* (i.e. 'He/she will attack *me* if I *don't* do it.') Such enquiries are critical in the context of understanding how, for example, an offence of dishonesty can so quickly and definitively shift into the crime of murder. And, as such, it is not a matter of saying that such acts are purely spontaneous and do not involve a string of decisions made on behalf of the offender(s). Conversely, it is a call to recognize the following:

> Violent engagements do not occur instantaneously. Instead, they occur over a process that unfolds over series of stages and, therefore, over time. Of course, the amount of time needed to complete the stages of this process may range anywhere from a matter of seconds or minutes to weeks or even months.
>
> (Athens, 2005, pp. 651–652)

Of course, the accumulation of various forms of deprivation (broken homes, poor child-rearing practices, behavioural issues, traumatic life events, exposure to domestic violence, substance abuse, etc.) and the absence of protective factors to mitigate these risks will profoundly affect how some individuals respond to adversity. I have tried to show that these are all circumstances apt to promote an inclination towards violence and/or how a lack of empathy and callous indifference regarding others can arise. For those in this chapter, the impact of being cast into prison at such a young age and for such a prolonged period – surely exacerbating their emotional deprivation – makes it difficult to divine exactly what will happen in their future. Perhaps, on this last count, I should leave the last word to Aaron:

> I thought [the crime] would make me a tough person but it just, fucking, proved how weak I was, really. . . . Destroyed everything. Fucking it pushed family members away, fucking, drove my friends off, fucking, I struggle to talk to people in gaol now. Everyone's heard these [amazing] stories of when they were kids and that, and I've got fucking misery and depression. I've just fucking shut myself off from everyone. I just go into my cell, watch telly and come out for dinner. . . . Hopefully [my release] goes well but there's a lot of family members, distant family members and stepfamily members that would happily see me die in gaol.

References

Agnew, R. (2006). *Pressured into crime: An overview of general strain theory*. Los Angeles, CA: Roxbury.

American Psychological Association Task Force on Violent Media. (2015). *Technical report on the review of the violent video game literature*. Retrieved from www.apa.org/pi/families/violent-media.aspx

Athens, L. (1980). *Violent criminal acts and actors*. Boston, MA: Routledge & Keegan Paul.

Athens, L. (1997). *Violent criminal acts and actors revisited*. Urbana, IL: University of Illinois Press.

Athens, L. (2005). Violent encounters: Violent engagements, skirmishes, and tiffs. *Journal of Contemporary Ethnography, 34*(6), 631–678. DOI:10.1177/0891241605280570

Australian Government Department of Health. National Drug and Alcohol Research Centre. (2017). *"Party Drugs"/MDMA/ECSTASY: What you need to know*. Retrieved from http://positivechoices.org.au/documents/P6DrTI1KTM/party-drugsmdma-ecstasy-detailed-resource-for-parentsteachers

Bastian, B., & Haslam, N. (2010). Excluded from humanity: The dehumanizing effects of social ostracism. *Journal of Experimental Psychology, 46*(1), 107–113. DOI:10.1016/j.jesp.2009.06.022

Blumer, H. (1962). Society as symbolic interaction. In A. Rose (Ed.), *Human behavior and social processes* (pp. 179–92). Boston, MA: Houghton Mifflin.

Buckley, K. E., Winkel, R. E., & Leary, M. R. (2004). Reactions to acceptance and rejection: Effects of level and sequence of relational evaluation. *Journal of Experimental Social Psychology, 40*(1), 14–28. DOI:10.1016/S0022-1031(03)00064-7

Chow, R. M., Tiedens, L. Z., & Govan, C. L. (2008). Excluded emotions: The role of anger in antisocial responses to ostracism. *Journal of Experimental Social Psychology, 44*(3), 896–903.

Cornell, D. G. (1993). Juvenile homicide: A growing national problem. *Behavioural Sciences and the Law, 11*(4), 389–396. DOI:10.1002/bsl.2370110406

Cornell, D. G., Benedek, E. P., & Benedek, D. M. (1987). Juvenile homicide: Prior adjustment and a proposed typology. *American Journal of Orthopsychiatry, 57*(3), 383–393. DOI:10.1111/j.1939-0025.1987.tb03547.x

Darby, P. J., Allan, W. D., Kashani, J. H., Hartke, K. L., & Reid, J. C. (1998). Analysis of 112 juveniles who committed homicide: Characteristics and a closer look at family abuse. *Journal of Family Violence, 13*(4), 365–375. DOI:10.1023/A:1022823219276

DeWall, C. N., Twenge, J. M., Gitter, S. A., & Baumeister, R. F. (2009). It's the thought that counts: The role of hostile cognition in shaping aggressive responses to social exclusion. *Journal of Personality and Social Psychology, 96*(1), 45–59. DOI:10.1037/a0013196

Dickerson, S. S., & Kemeny, M. E. (2004). Acute stressors and cortisol responses: A theoretical integration and synthesis of laboratory research. *Psychological Bulletin, 130*(3), 355–391. DOI:10.1037/0033-2909.130.3.355

Drinkaware. (2016). *Alcohol and illegal drugs*. Retrieved from www.drinkaware.co.uk/alcohol-facts/health-effects-of-alcohol/effects-on-the-body/alcohol-and-illegal-drugs

Eisenberger, N. I., Lieberman, M. D., & Williams, K. D. (2003). Does rejection hurt? An fMRI study of social exclusion. *Science, 302*(5643), 290–292. DOI:10.1126/sciemce.1089134

Fiddes, D. O. (1981). Scotland in the seventies – Adolescents in care and custody: A survey of adolescent murder in Scotland. *Journal of Adolescence, 4*(1), 47–65. DOI:10.1016/S0140-1971(81)80005-X

Goffman, E. (1976). *Interaction ritual: Essays in face-to-face behavior*. Chicago, IL: Aldine.

Goldman, L., & Hogg, M. A. (2016). Going to extremes for one's group: The role of prototypicality and group acceptance. *Journal of Applied Social Psychology, 46*(9), 544–533. DOI:10.1111/jasp.12382

Gunnar, M. R., Sebanc, A. M., Tout, K., Donzella, B., & van Dulmen, M. M. H. (2003). Peer rejection, temperament, and cortisol activity in preschoolers. *Developmental Psychology, 43*(4), 346–358. DOI:10.1002/dev.10144

Halsey, M. (2007). On confinement: Resident and inmate perspectives of secure care and imprisonment. *Probation Journal, 54*(4), 338–367. DOI:10.1177/0264550507083535

Halsey, M. (2008). Assembling recidivism: The promise and contingencies of post-release life. *The Journal of Criminal Law and Criminology*, *97*(4), 1209–1260. Retrieved from https://jclc.law.northwestern.edu

Halsey, M., & Deegan, S. (2012). Father and son: Two generations through prison. *Punishment and Society*, *14*(3), 338–367. DOI:10.1177/1462474512442315

Halsey, M., & Deegan, S. (2014). "Picking up the pieces": Female significant others in the lives of young (ex) incarcerated males. *Criminology and Criminal Justice*. Retrieved from http://crj.sagepub.com/content/early/2014/03/12/1748895814526725.ref.html. DOI:10.1177/1748895814526725

Hardwick, P. J., & Rowton-Lee, M. A. (1996). Adolescent homicide: Towards assessment of risk. *Journal of Adolescence*, *19*(3), 263–276. DOI:10.1006/jado.1996.0024

Hollingdale, J., & Greitemeyer, T. (2014). The effect of online violent video games on levels of aggression. *PLoS One*, *9*(11), e111790. DOI:10.1371/journal.pone.0111790

Katz, J. (1988). *Seductions of crime: Moral and sensual attractions of doing evil*. New York: Basic Books.

Loeber, R., & Farrington, D. (2011). *Young homicide offenders and victims: Risk factors, prediction, and prevention from childhood*. New York: Springer.

Myers, W. C., & Kemph, J. P. (1990). DSM-III – R classification of homicidal youth- Help or hindrance. *Journal of Clinical Psychiatry*, *51*(6), 239–242. Retrieved from www.psychiatrist.com/jcp/Pages/home.aspx

Peterson, C. K., Gravens, L. C., & Harmon-Jones, E. (2011). Asymmetric frontal cortical activity and negative affective responses to ostracism. *Social Cognitive and Affective Neuroscience*, *6*(3), 277–285. DOI:10.1093/scan/nsq027

Polk, K. (1994). *When men kill: Scenarios of masculine violence*. New York: Cambridge University Press.

Reijntjes, A., Thomaes, S., Bushman, B., Boelen, P., Orobio de Castro, B., & Telch, M. J. (2010). The outcast-lash-out effect in youth: Alienation increases aggression following peer rejection. *Psychological Science*, *21*(10), 1394–1398. DOI:10.1177/0956797610381509

Ren, D., Wesselmann, E. D., & Williams, K. D. (2018). Hurt people hurt people: Ostracism and aggression. *Current Opinion in Psychology*, *19*, 34–38. DOI:10.1016/j.copsyc.2017.03.026

Roe-Sepowitz, D. E. (2009). Comparing male and female juveniles charged with homicide: Child maltreatment, substance abuse, and crime details. *The Journal of Interpersonal Violence*, *24*, 601–617. DOI:10.1177/0886260508317201

Sprinkle, J. E. (2007). Domestic violence, gun ownership, and parental educational attainment: How do they affect the aggressive beliefs and behaviors of children? *Child and Adolescent Social Work Journal*, *24*(2), 133–151. DOI:10.1007/s10560-006-0071-8

Twenge, J. M., Baumeister, R. F., Tice, D. M., & Stucke, T. S. (2001). If you can't join them, beat them: Effects of social exclusion on aggressive behavior. *Journal of Personality and Social Psychology*, *81*(6), 1058–1069. DOI:10.1037/0022-3514.81.6.1058

Warburton, W. A., Williams, K. D., & Cairns, D. R. (2006). When ostracism leads to aggression: The moderating effects of control deprivation. *Journal of Experimental Social Psychology*, *42*(2), 213–220. DOI:10.1016/j.jesp.2005.03.005

Wesselmann, E. D., Butler, F. A., Williams, K. D., & Pickett, C. L. (2010). Adding injury to insult: Unexpected rejection leads to more aggressive responses. *Aggressive Behavior*, *36*(4), 232–237. DOI:10.1002/ab.20347

Wesselmann, E. D., Grzybowski, M. R., Steakley-Freeman, D. M., DeSouza, E. R., Nezlek, J. B., & Williams, K. D. (2016a). Social exclusion in everyday life. In P. Riva & J. Eck

(Eds.), *Social exclusion: Psychological approaches to understanding and reducing its impact* (pp. 3–23). New York: Springer.

Wesselmann, E. D., Ren, D., & Williams, K. D. (2016b). Ostracism and aggression. In B. J. Bushman (Ed.), *Aggression and violence: A Social Psychological Perspective* (pp. 155–168). New York: Routledge.

Westermann, S., Rief, W., Euteneuer, F., & Kohlmann, S. (2015). Social exclusion and shame in obesity. *Eating Behaviors*, *17*, 74–76. DOI:10.1016/j.eatbeh.2015.01.001

Wike, T. L., & Fraser, M. W. (2009). School shootings: Making sense of the senseless. *Aggression and Violent Behavior*, *14*(3), 162–169. DOI:10.1016/j.avb.2009.01.005

Woodworth, M., Agar, A. D., & Coupland, R. B. (2013). Characteristics of Canadian youth-perpetrated homicides. *Criminal Justice and Behaviour*, *40*(9), 1009–1026. DOI:10.1177/0093854813482390

5 Making sense of murder

Significant others in the lives of young homicide offenders

> When [it] came on the news that they'd found a young lady, a young girl, dead at Marion, the first thing [I thought of] was Lucy, you know? And in some ways in the beginning I wished it was . . . that she had died . . . because it was just horrendous, absolutely horrendous. It would probably be better to have gone through the grieving than go through everything that's been thrown at us because there's been some *major* things.
>
> (Vanessa, mother)

The question of who is more or less likely to suffer the indirect consequences of juvenile homicide offending remains largely unanswered, despite recognition of (life) 'imprisonment as a (gendered) family ordeal as opposed to an individual experience' (Halsey & Deegan, 2014, p. 2). As previously discussed, a large amount of literature has 'identified the family as the key explanatory site of homicide, citing various forms of poor parenting and bad familial socialization as dominant factors' (May, 2000, p. 203). But despite or perhaps because of significant others (parents, siblings, grandparents, partners, and the like) being suspected of toxicity, the post-homicide experiences of these people remain largely hidden. This is also despite the pioneering work by Hazel May (1999, 2000). This chapter goes beyond the primarily negative childhood experiences that best illustrate the pathways to lethal violence. Rather, this chapter underscores the litany of problems that arise for significant others when a juvenile is connected to a deliberate and violent death. It focuses on how these individuals confront the precise nature of their child's criminality, while simultaneously defending themselves against blame and condemnation from a variety of intra- and extra-familial sources. A major conclusion of the chapter is that the lives of young murderers' relatives are a vortex of shame, anger, and guilt with little, if any, formal or informal support as a means to manage or recover from the debilitating stigma and strain.

In total, seven mothers, five fathers, four grandparents, and four siblings were interviewed about their struggles and their views regarding the crimes, punishments, and futures of their incarcerated loved ones. Six core themes emerged from my conversations with these relatives that touch, more or less directly, on the issue of 'secondary prisonization' (Comfort, 2003, 2007, 2008). This term refers to the 'restricted rights, diminished resources, social marginalization, and other consequences of penal confinement' for women whose loved ones and close friends are imprisoned (Comfort, 2003, p. 79). These six core themes from my interviews also relate to parental/familial responsibility for their relatives' homicidal offending. Said themes overlap with the majority of May's (2000) and Armour's (2002) key observations of the post-homicide experience and include the following: confronting the truth; confronting mixed feelings; confronting friends and family; confronting the courtroom; confronting custodial settings; and confronting the future. At the same time, the post-homicide experience often plays out in much messier and more complicated ways than have hitherto been acknowledged. Armour (2002) neatly captures this sentiment:

> [T]here is no order to [the] emergence [of themes]. Rather, any one theme may be present at any point in the experience of a family member of a homicide victim. Moreover, the themes interacted with each other so that the presence of one theme could stimulate the occurrence of another.
>
> (p. 374)

Without doubt, this is still only a small fraction of the larger world of significant others who 'play centrally important roles' in the lives of serious offenders 'at substantive personal and social (not to mention psychological) cost' (Halsey & Deegan, 2015, p. 133). Much, of course, has been written about the impact of pro-social family members on positive prison adjustment and favourable parole outcomes for serious young offenders (McShane & Williams, 1989). My contention is that murderers' relatives remain neglected, despised, and marginalized despite the heavy lifting they ultimately perform in terms of prisoner rehabilitation and post-release life.

Confronting the truth

> Sitting home here as usual, phone rings, [my son's] on the phone. . . . He said, 'You'd better get over here. You're not going to see your grandson for a while.' I said, 'Why? What are you talking about?' He says, 'He's been charged with murder.'
>
> (Brian, grandfather)

> They said, 'Your son has been charged with that murder.' And I went, 'Bullshit!' That was the first thing I said: 'Bullshit!' And they said, 'No, unfortunately it's true and we need to come in and talk to you.' And that was it. From then on my life totally changed.
>
> (Karen, mother)

One of the most emotive issues canvassed during interviews proved to be the moment participants learned that their child was implicated in a murder. For mothers, fathers, and grandparents, this was a defining moment in the waking nightmare that continues, in one form or another, to the present day: 'There's no winners from this, you know; nobody gets to walk away except for maybe the lawyers who made lots of money out of it' (Colin, father). While their youth and naivety appeared to shield teenagers from the seemingly obvious implications of a homicide investigation, significant others were keenly aware that the stakes were high: 'I don't think he realised how bad it was until those handcuffs hit his hands. That's where I think it all sunk in' (Bianca, mother).

> Murder. What the fuck? Like, that's *murder*. That's one word and that's one of the biggest words that could ever be said. . . . [And] I did tell him. I said, 'If the verdict comes back fucking guilty, *you are* going to gaol. There's no ifs, buts, anything. So prepare yourself to go to gaol!' And he cried. He cried. He's going to big boy gaol.
>
> (Dean, father)

> He knew that something was going to happen because he wasn't shocked when they [i.e., the police] showed up. But, you know, being the grandmother, you don't know how to deal with it at the time. . . . All I can remember [is] I was screaming and the parents of . . . [another] boy were at my place and they grabbed me as I went down.
>
> (Dorothy, grandmother)

At that moment, Dorothy, immediately above, was narrating an account of her grandson's arrest. In hindsight, however, it was prophetic of how she would be forced to endure Leo's trial, subsequent conviction, and the imposition of a life sentence upon him: 'It changed his life. It changed everybody's. . . . It's ripped a part of my heart away. And when he went in [to custody] I felt like I had died. *I felt like I had died.*'

While the sequences were not necessarily linear, news that children or grandchildren were named in connection with murder provoked emotional responses not unlike the five stages of grief described by Kubler-Ross (1969): denial, anger, bargaining, depression, and acceptance. The experiences of the parents provide a clear case in point:

> They took his shoes and I thought, 'Oh well, this will clear him.' And then they came back and I was thinking, 'They're just coming to give us the shoes back; they're all clean.' Huh. Wasn't the case. They arrested him then and there and I just [thought], this is unbelievable. . . . But, if I had of known he'd done it two or three days [earlier] I would have dragged him to the fucking police station myself: I'm not letting him get away with shit like that. It's not like stealing a lolly.
>
> (Vincent, father)

> I was just sitting on the sofa looking at Sonny as they were reading the charges [and] it just hit me. Because I would have thought I would look at Sonny and him say, 'No, it wasn't me. I don't know why they're here,' but he was just sitting there in acceptance. And that's when it hit me: that it can't be

> true, but it is. It was such a huge impact. It was almost like a physical impact as well as mental, emotional. . . . I went on anti-depressants. I couldn't sleep. I couldn't function. It was just a feeling of shock.
>
> (Lorraine, mother)

The issue of secondary trauma is important because it goes to the 'vexed world' inhabited by the intimates of (ex-)prisoners. Halsey and Deegan (2014) explain this complexity in terms of the tendency for mothers, whose children live against their own morals or what they know to be right, to avoid people who might hold up mirrors. It was certainly not the case that significant others were ignorant of or unresponsive to the critical need to step in and protect their child from a crisis of epic proportions:

> I heard Henry talking, so I came out and this [cop] is engaging him in conversation and asking him, you know, 'What time do you knock off work?' and 'What sort of shoes do you wear?' and all that stuff.
>
> And I said, 'No! Stop!' . . . He even tried pumping *me* for information at one stage. . . . And I said, 'What do you want to know for?'
>
> 'We're just concerned about him.'
>
> Oh, fuck off. . . . So I went through and read all the legislation and I'm sure they didn't comply with it.
>
> (Colin, father)

But these reactions were weighted against the parents'/grandparents' own distress regarding events surrounding the victim's death, their child's (alleged) role in it, and their resulting incarceration, especially in light of the (appropriate) values they had instilled in their child. Following the dictates of these competing feelings, parents, in particular, were desperate for answers. Their first visit to the juvenile justice centre was instructive:

> I went straight up there and I just looked at him and I said, 'Toby, did you do it?' And he goes, 'Mum, I didn't do it.' But there was a lot going on with the 'Yes I did', 'No, I didn't', 'Yes I did', 'No I didn't.' And I just said, 'Look. No matter what, you're my son. I'm going to support you. But whatever you do, tell the truth.' . . . And that was it. I just burst into tears and I thought, 'That's it. His life's ruined. My life's ruined. Everybody's life is ruined. The [victim's] life.' . . . I thought about all of those, all within a split second of a couple of minutes, and everything just hit me.
>
> (Karen, mother)

> The majority of the cops [were] undercover. One of them talked to me and he said, 'We need that gun.' . . . [My son] was in the Magill prison for youth because this situation happened . . . [and] when I met him . . . I said, 'Please, I'm your dad. Tell me where is the gun?' He said, 'Dad, don't trust the cops: this one, that one' because the majority of young people don't have respect

> for the cops. . . . I said, 'No, please, tell me. Where is it? Otherwise never, *ever*, will I come in here to visit you or whatever happens in the future.'
>
> (Gerard, father)

> Point blank I said to him, 'I want the truth. I don't care what it is [but] I want the truth. If you tell me the truth, I will help you every single way we can help you. But if I find out you lied, that's it: you're cut off.' Like I pretty much blackmailed him. . . . [And] we could have gone in there and said, 'He's got a mental illness,' and he probably would have got off, you know, but again, we don't lie. We tell the truth.
>
> (Bianca, mother)

Confronting (mixed) feelings

> I have to admit I didn't like him. *I didn't like him*, you know, what he'd become.
>
> (Desiree, mother)

For significant others, *needing* to know the truth about their child's involvement in the murder and *wanting* to hear about the victim's last moments in forensic detail were two different things. On this front, mothers told of employing the psychological defence of projection to avoid experiencing the more distressing effects of their situation:

> I became frightened of groups of teenage boys and places where there were lots of teenage boys; I used to have panic attacks after. It felt like [I] was having a heart attack . . . so I stopped going to public places. I was [so] frightened of teenage boys, of groups of teenage boys, large groups . . . because I never thought that teenage boys could be so violent.
>
> (Lorraine, mother)

> I haven't [worked] in neonates for [ages] as I couldn't handle the babies. I felt, you know, *babies*; this is what happens: you have these kids and they become these animals.
>
> (Desiree, mother)

Even for relatives who pledged their ongoing support, I found a hierarchy of 'selective moralising', whereby relatives 'extended various degrees of respect – and therefore various degrees of "normal" engagement – to prisoners . . . dependent on the perceived depravity/cruelty' (Halsey & Deegan, 2017, p. 58) of their criminal conduct:

> We'd seen the thing on the news about the old lady getting stabbed in the head and on our next visit, Leo goes, 'Oh, did you see that old lady that got stabbed? Yeah well *he's* in here.' And I said, '[Are] you serious, lad? Fucking give him a hiding mate 'cause that's an old lady, you know, like he's killed

an old lady.' And Leo's like, 'I can't, Dad; like, we can't do that here.' I said, 'Bullshit. Fucking make a wall in front of the camera and give the prick a hiding. He's just belted an old lady.'

(Dean, father)

Without doubt, the most extreme example of acceptable versus unacceptable criminality was provided by Vincent Larsen, whose life, essentially, has been bookmarked by murder. He is the child of a murdered mother and, in more recent years, finds himself the father of a convicted murderer son. Like others who were interviewed, Vincent was acutely aware that he had choices about how to respond to his son's offending. As he remarked, drawing a line around the limits of care was the only way to suspend feelings of betrayal and resentment about the precise nature of his son's criminality:

> The only way I can deal with Aaron is that I don't read the full police report and the witness statements. Because if I would have done that, I wouldn't be talking to Aaron at all; it would be over and done with. . . . I just want to know that he's committed this crime. I don't want to know the *sickness* [of it] because then I'm angry at him even more than I'm already angry at him. He's not forgiven by any stretch of the imagination. And I love him. But I don't know that I *like* him.
>
> There was a lot of times we [went without speaking], you know, he didn't talk to me for six weeks and to me that was fucking great. I didn't have to try and . . . make up stuff to keep the conversation going because I really had nothing to say: 'What have you been up to?'
>
> 'Just work. Just battling on . . .'
>
> What I actually wanted to say was, 'Just battling on with what you've fucking done. I'm sick of being looked at by the community for what you've done.' That's what I wanted to say. But you don't. And what I wanted to do was flog him within an inch of his life, give him the belting he probably deserves. Look, I was on the other end of it because my mum was murdered when I was 21 and now he's doing it again to me and I'm thinking, 'What have I done? Killed a Chinaman in past lifetime or something?'

Some openly questioned whether their child's current situation was de facto punishment for their own failure to 'be a 'pacifier', a 'civilizer', a 'good mother' and [to] provide the appropriate, non-criminal home atmosphere' (Peelo, Stewart, & Prior, 1991, p. 313). One mother lamented the nomadic lifestyle her son experienced as a result of her successive domestic violence relationships and eventual resort to prostitution:

> Toby was great at school. He liked it, or, he still tells me he enjoyed it. Unfortunately, because of us moving around, he went to too many so he didn't actually get to make solid friends. . . . That didn't sort of pan out all that well for

> him, which was my fault. I think it was me – my instability – up and moving around all the time, that affected him.
>
> (Karen, mother)

Predictably, significant others were often ensconced in managing an adolescent's problematic behaviour long before he or she was arrested for murder. While plenty of kids act up, these scenarios threatened the integrity of the family unit, sometimes necessitating the young person's removal from the home. Certainly, the theme of mental health problems and substance misuse run consistently through many accounts of adolescent-to-parent violence (Miles & Condry, 2015). Jake was estranged from his parents for almost a year due to his ice-fuelled behaviour towards them, which was as appalling as it was unrestrained. In fact, his physical, verbal, psychological, and emotional aggression escalated to the point where an apprehended violence intervention order was on foot at the time of his arrest and prevented him from attending the premises and harassing members of his family. I should add here that a number of different approaches, including (multiple) drug diversions, family therapy, parenting support, and individual counselling sessions failed miserably to affect a wide range of behavioural and vocational issues related to Jake's heavy drug use. In fact, it is clear that due to their experiences with drug-abusing juveniles, many significant others sought but were unable to find any meaningful assistance from any support service. And so it was with Jake:

> Family counselling: . . . he didn't want to have a bar of it and . . . and they'd come back every time and [say] he was fine. . . . Every time they said, 'Oh there's nothing wrong with him. He's just a youth.' He went with me voluntarily but I had to literally drag him. It was only a . . . five, ten minutes' walk [from our house] . . . [and] I remember one day he hit every letterbox on the way down. He just couldn't be fucked and that's when I gave up. . . . [And] the police said the same thing: 'There's nothing wrong with him. He's just a youth and a lot of kids are like that,' you know? And we just thought, 'Hang on a minute: you don't live with him.'
>
> (Desiree, mother)

> We've had to call the police a couple of times because of his . . . violent, threatening behaviour and [his] actual physical violence and all the police would do, well, they'd take him away for a little while, put him in a cell and let him cool down and he'd be released in the afternoon. . . . And I asked several times, 'Look, can you just take him to the hospital and get him seen? Do a quick drug test?' Blah blah blah.
>
> 'Oh no, no, no, we can't do that.'
>
> (Desiree, mother)

Beyond the pain of incarceration, this mother's real angst came from the guilt so many parents have felt regarding what they did, did not do, or wished to have done in the lead-up to the crime. By way of questions such as 'How could we not have known?', 'Surely we could have done something to stop them?' or 'How could we have been a good parent and not prevented this?', mothers and fathers queried the extent to which their own failings were unhappily visited on their children. Despite providing a stable family upbringing, devoid of abuse or trauma, Jake's mother was left to wrestle with the anti-Oedipal conclusion that her son's crime was as much about her own annihilation as it was about the destruction of the victim:

> We had that restraining order out [when the murder happened] . . . [and] until that point . . . I was so angry with him and so upset that it was really hard for me as a mum. . . . And I often think, 'What have I done? Or what could I have done? How should I have managed it better? Why has my child – even, even without like, you know, the murder, before that – what have I done? And have I been a good mother to him? What have I done? What have I done to make it appear that he hates me so much?'
>
> (Desiree, mother)

It was a powerful experience to sit with family members as they recounted the depth of the damage their child had caused to others, 'making attributions about why [the] event occurred . . . [and searching to find] redeeming or transcendent features in the tragedy' (Armour, 2002, p. 373). Weighed down by guilt, remorse, and the impossible situation they found themselves in, some family members used alcohol to attempt to blot out the anguish they continued to experience and, as a result, had been alcoholic for many years. Others were still to fully come to terms with what happened at a time when children were in middle adolescence and, conflicting with life cycle expectations, children experienced events 'as the death of the [their] future dreams as well as creating a profound change in their present roles and functioning' (Christ, Bonanno, Malkinson, & Rubin, 2003, p. 554):

> It [i.e., long-term imprisonment] is [like a death] because that person ceases to exist. . . . I don't know if Sonny will ever be the same again. He's basically a shell of a person; they've destroyed him. The system has destroyed him. And it's been long and cruel. I just feel like . . . we've both lost. We've all lost our sons.
>
> (Lorraine, mother)

> My son went in as a 17-year-old *boy*. I missed all of that, he missed all of that growing up and he has come out [of prison] as a man who doesn't know much. He's actually said it: he's still a 17-year-old in a lot of respects.
>
> (Karen, mother)

> I think of the past, I suppose, before he went in. I [still] kind of see him like that; I don't see him where he is now. I just, I just see him as a 17-year-old. . . . [And] if anyone asks where Ben is, we just say he lives on the other side of the city and he works on the other side of the city, which is a fact, so

> it's not really lying: it's just bending the truth a little bit. Just so I don't have to bring out the truth about where he is and why he's there.
>
> (Bianca, mother)

It is impossible to say whether parents exaggerated their own sense of integrity and obligation to tell the truth for the sake of good copy in an interview. Notwithstanding that, most relatives appeared to arrive at sufficient insight into the meaning of the young person's behaviour to understand that avoiding their relative's crime was of little benefit. Rather, to establish a meaningful and positive life for themselves, the family members needed to make a clean breast of what had occurred. As such, the majority of significant others emphasized the importance of the young person being accountable, despite the resounding view that the murder was an aberration, as opposed to a reflection of entrenched criminality. In fact, one father was quite unforgiving in his advice to those minded to explain away their child's actions against the manifest weight of the evidence:

> [Some parents are] like, 'My son did nothing.' Fuck off. There's a reason your son's there [i.e., in prison]. Fucking own it. That's how naive some people are. Your son's there because *he did* do something wrong, whether that's not [stopping] something or actually doing it and that's the bottom line. . . . Everyone keeps blaming these people, blaming those people. 'Mate, your son could have fucking stood up and [acted differently]. He chose not to. Blame your son. I blame my son.'
>
> (Dean, father)

Confronting friends and family

> I didn't do it but I was the one that suffered the consequences as well. . . . I wasn't 100% a great mother but I didn't do [the crime].
>
> (Karen, mother)

> It's a very . . . shameful or embarrassing thing [to happen] to your son [or] to you. I was supposed to be a doctor: not be in gaol for murder or shootings or whatnot.
>
> (Floyd, juvenile lifer)

Consistent with the post-homicide experience reported by Armour (2002), the participants in my research made it clear that 'the news of the murder was only one in a succession of onslaughts that appeared without warning, thwarted the ability of family members to regain a firm footing, and left them feeling deflated' (p. 374). While significant others knew better than to expect sympathy from the media or general public, the most hurtful attacks were those stemming from an unexpected quarter – their wider network of family and friends: 'No help. No-one contacts you. No-one does nothing. Basically, you're like the black sheep of the family and you're just outcast' (Simon, father). Mothers and fathers waited for support to come, but it never did. On the contrary, people appeared at pains to dissociate themselves from the familial toxicity or 'stain' attached to allegations of serious deviance (see Lefley, 1987; May, 2000). While some of the developments were, upon reflection, viewed positively, the decisions of others to re-evaluate and/or repudiate intimate relationships occurred frequently, were well beyond the control of each participant, and affected them in profoundly negative ways:

> Family dumped me. [My mum] wanted to read all of the police statements; she wanted to know exactly what was going on. And all she said to me after she read it was, 'Good job, Karen.'
>
> And I was like, 'What does that mean?'
>
> And she goes, 'You didn't do a very good job of raising Toby. . . . That's what I meant. Take it any way you want.'
>
> And I didn't see Mum much after that. . . . [Then] my auntie turned around and said to me one day, she goes, 'You've just bred a murderer.'
>
> . . . And none of them at all would come anywhere near me. None.
>
> (Karen, mother)

> [The police] told my partner that he shouldn't have anything to do with me so I had to go through the whole court process by myself. . . . He vanished. He gave me no emotional support whatsoever. [He] said he didn't want to have contact with me, wouldn't speak to me on the phone. . . . He just said, 'Look, Lorraine, I want to have a break.' . . . He told me after that the CIB [i.e., Criminal Investigation Branch] told him to do that: to cut off from me.
>
> (Lorraine, mother)

For families already under strain, high-profile cases enabled members to validate an elevated sense of social standing. In other words, wider family members took the opportunity to look down on the immediate family of the offender. Dorothy's account is illustrative. She raised her grandson from infancy, with no contact from his maternal grandparents to enquire about his whereabouts, activities, or welfare: 'He was treated like a leper as far as I'm concerned.' Ultimately, the maternal grandparents' attention could no longer be denied when Leo was arrested for murder:

> When this happened, I received a message from his other grandparents saying, 'This is what happens with the way *you* brought him up. You did a great job bringing him up, didn't you?' And that hurt. That *really* hurt.
>
> (Dorothy, grandmother)

This point is taken up strongly by Condry (2006, 2007; but see also Gavazzi, Yarcheck, Rhine, & Partridge, 2003; Halsey & Deegan, 2014), who identifies the tendency for females, in particular, to be blamed as discrete causal factors in the wayward behaviour of their sons or partners. Crucially, for my purposes here, Armour (2002) does not overlook the way in which 'the stigma attached to murder resulted in blame from others for the way the victim died, or even for the way the [offender] lived, as well as self-castigation for not having prevented the victim's death' (pp. 372–3). Coming to grips with their new social reality as murderers' relatives, while attempting to navigate the court process, plunged significant others deeper into a sea of helplessness and despair. Against this backdrop, abandonment by extended family was a ball and chain, if not an anchor:

> The amount of stress and the amount of heartache and the amount of embarrassment I had was just too much. I attempted to commit suicide . . . when he got his sentence. I couldn't cope . . . and I just OD'd full on with sleeping tablets. . . . Even though I knew there was no-one else there for Toby other than me, I still couldn't cope. I got put in [psychiatric detention] for 21 days.
>
> (Karen, mother)

Just as participants struggled to salvage the last vestiges of their own personal relationships, modest attempts to reconnect the prisoner to a former support system proved an onerous (if all-too-familiar) exercise in futility. One mother commented, 'He had probably two guys that he was really, really, close to and one of them just said, "Can you please tell him not to ring me anymore?"' (Jacqui, mother). Those who were supposed to care resisted even the most basic of rituals, compounding relatives' sense of betrayal and adding 'to the already significant burden of supporting (financially and/or emotionally) their incarcerated loved one' (Halsey & Deegan, 2014, p. 15), as the following quote demonstrates:

> It's my family that really hurt. Just to get them to send him a Christmas card or a birthday card was *so* hard. And in the end I just stopped; it was such hard work to get them to [do it]. I just thought, 'For God sake, I'll write it myself.' And so I used to buy the card, write it all myself and I'd say, 'Just sign your name on the bottom of it, *please*!' . . . [And Sonny] doesn't understand it; he doesn't really comprehend it. It would hurt him too much to tell him how bad they are. He doesn't know how hard I had to work to get a signature on the bottom of a birthday card or Christmas card. In the end I just stopped. He still has this delusion that they're okay [with him] and that they're caring but they're not.
>
> (Lorraine, mother)

Confronting the courtroom

> Aaron plead guilty so there's no court case; there's just the sentencing. And then his lawyers tried to basically blame it all on me . . . like the way I brought him up: . . . that I condone violence and that is nowhere near what I said.
>
> (Vincent, father)

> [There's] lawyers talking to lawyers or lawyers talking to judges [but] there's no [provision for us]. Yeah, they've got Victim Impact Statements but what about families of the accused? They should have had something [from us], you know,

just to see where this child has grown up and where he's come from and that this is his very first mistake. . . . That could have been something [useful].

(Bianca, mother)

For murderers' relatives, the criminal justice system's inability to respond to their needs and experiences in sensitive and nuanced ways was a particular source of heartache. Somewhat counter-intuitively, the overwhelming majority of juveniles charged with murder came before the Supreme Court as first-time offenders: 'I'd never been in trouble with the police, hadn't had a history of offending or anything like that. . . . It was my first and only offence. So yeah, I really kind of went all out, didn't I?' (Lucy, juvenile lifer). While family members (generally) had praise for lawyers and tipstaff, court hearings were a haven for bewilderment and anxiety, as such processes were largely foreign to family members. All family members felt powerless to challenge prosecutors' versions of events:

> It was so hard not to yell out, you know, when things were being said. Even the jury, they looked at you like, you know, these boys had done what they did, they had killed somebody and . . . you were a part of *that*.
>
> (Dorothy, grandmother)

More specifically, the question of *who* was on trial loomed large both in and around the court precincts:

> [The prosecutor] said, basically, that I'm this single mother, you know, that's got a colourful private life, that's economically disadvantaged or whatever: socioeconomically disadvantaged. . . . [So] do I have to be a nun in order to be okay, morally okay? . . . They assassinate your character and you have to endure that and survive that along with everything else.
>
> (Lorraine, mother)

> The judge turned around and says, 'Oh, they're all from dysfunctional families.' I thought, 'Hang on: Lucy came from a family that was a family unit.' We were the only ones that *were* in a family unit. . . . I was so cross with that because he judged everybody [like] they all came from broken relationships . . . [and] how dare [he] categorise everybody in the one boat.
>
> (Vanessa, mother)

> We've walked out and we had all the cameras there and I've tried to walk away – we made the decision we weren't talking to the press – and the stupid bloody reporter's going, 'How do you feel? How do you feel about this?' And I just wanted to stop and go, 'Well, I'm really proud of him. We've never had a murderer in our family before so we're really excited about the prospect, you fucking idiot.'
>
> (Colin, father)

It is fairly well expected that there will be something seriously wrong with the relatives of people who have murdered, 'perceived by others to be intimately and causally connected with the violence itself' (May, 2000, p. 203). Or, as one father succinctly put it, 'The kids are shit; therefore, *we're* shit' (Colin, father).

These experiences echo what May (2000) calls the 'normative assumption' surrounding the 'symbolic toxic relationship' between an offender and their kinfolk. As Gilmore (1994, p. 354) observes in relation to this:

> Anybody who has emerged from a family that yielded a murderer must also be formed by the same causes, the same evil, must in some way be responsible for the violence that resulted, must also bear the mark of a frightening and shameful heritage.

Although underage defendants' identities were (generally) suppressed, these orders were powerless to mitigate against tremendous invasions of privacy and how family members were portrayed in print, TV, and web-based media. Vanessa was caught in the crosshairs on several occasions, which included her daughter's conviction, sentence, and eventual deportation:

> Everybody used to look at me, 'Oh, there's that mother of the murderer,' you know? And I'm thinking, 'You don't even know the story.' . . . And I took it on board that I was a bad parent for years and years and years.
>
> (Vanessa, mother)

There are a multitude of issues raised by media saturation of high-profile cases, ranging from whether a truly fair trial can be achieved, to the secondary victimization of those trying, vainly, to live with crimes for which they are not responsible and which they do not properly understand. As mentioned previously, Aaron, at the age of 14, killed his victim in circumstances that were particularly troubling (i.e. a frenzied and unprovoked attack on an elderly victim). From custody, Aaron voiced concern (and annoyance) that he remains a cause célèbre of sorts as a symbol for so-called killer kids almost 10 years following his crime:

> I'm always on the news when there's another teen fucking murder and that: 'Oh, another teen at it again; we'll show this one.' . . . I'm the poster child basically for teen murderers. Every time there is one, I'm on the fucking news too.
>
> (Aaron, juvenile lifer)

As with all of my participants, Aaron's father queried the public interest in getting such mileage from a murder, particularly given the devastating impact the murder has had on so many people. Putting the issue of his own discomfort aside, there was also a sense that the true crime genre implicitly contributes to a culture that dishonours the memory of victims and glosses over the suffering of those left behind to pick up the pieces:

> And the media, once a year, will rehash this murder. And that pisses me off because it's not only, it's not just me: it's the victim's family that have to read the fucking newspaper *again* about their poor sister, poor auntie, or poor whatever. They're the ones that have to [relive] this every time it's brought up on *A Current Affair*. And you can watch *A Current Affair* for 10 years and the storyline each year doesn't change: petrol prices will be brought up, food prices will be brought up, how to save a hundred dollars a fortnight on your groceries and some messed-up shit of society like [my son]. . . . So, no, I don't respect any of those fuckers.
>
> (Vincent, father)

Before sentencing was complete, the courtroom had one final 'degradation ceremony' (Garfinkel, 1956) for significant others to undergo: an interface with the family and friends of the deceased. Detectives, prosecutors, social workers, witness assistance officers, and the Victims of Crime Commissioner himself, quite rightfully, surrounded the victim's family members at every hearing. Here, participants knew of and spoke to the shame, embarrassment, and loneliness experienced in situ on the defendants' side of the public gallery. Anxiously floating in the liminal space between so-called good and evil, parents felt 'marked as an object lesson in the community about what can go wrong in someone's life' (Armour, 2002, p. 375). In these very circumstances, one mother was mindful to avert her eyes:

> [It's] very confronting . . . going into a courtroom where *that* side of the court is totally full of . . . the victim's relatives and friends and so forth. And you feel bad enough as it is without having all these people there, you know, sort of looking over at you thinking [you're the cause of it]. You just try and look towards the judge or towards your own son or whatever but you just feel these eyes just peering at you the whole time.
>
> (Jacqui, mother)

While there were examples of the victim's family going out of their way to acknowledge the dual status of murderers' relatives, the general view participants expressed was that they possessed the lived experience but lacked the virtue required as *bona fide* victims of crime. Already wrestling with guilt and blame, this translated into their reluctance (or refusal) to seek help from agencies whose specific remit was to offer support:

> I'm sure if we went in there, Mick O'Connell [i.e., the Commissioner for Victims' Rights] would say, 'You're a victim of this crime' – I think we are – and would make their services available. But I don't think that would be embraced by some of the people there. . . . You'd just get, 'What do *you* want?' You know, 'If he's like that, *you* must have made him like that.' . . . You're just in a no-win situation.
>
> (Colin, father)

I am certainly not wishing to portray those I have spoken with as claiming equivalence with those permanently robbed of a loved one by the intentional and abhorrent act of another. All – with the possible exception of those convicted under accessorial liability – accepted the guilt of their loved one and the requirement that they be punished for what they had done. On the other hand, as one mother was quick to clarify, turning her son's mandatory life sentence or social death into a festivity was a bridge completely too far:

> From the minute we rolled up it was just that everyone that side was completely staring at us. . . . And when it was all over, what did we hear? Someone go, 'Oh, let's go have a drink now and celebrate that.'
>
> (Desiree, mother)

Confronting the future

It is always momentous when a young person pleads guilty to a murder charge, thereby committing themselves to a lengthy period of imprisonment, while saving a number of persons from having to give evidence about distressing events. As such, it is often said that sentencing can provide a degree of closure and certainty about the future for all of the parties concerned. However, the notion of denouement had far less relevance for the families of young killers, who generally arrived at sentencing 'completely drained of both financial resources and emotional energy' (Schwartz & Weintraub, 1974, p. 21), as the following quotes from participants illustrate:

> The first lot of hearings came up to $30,000. I paid that. And [the lawyer] turned around and said that if I could come up with $100,000, Leo wouldn't see the inside of a cell. And I couldn't. Like I didn't have that kind of money laying around.
>
> (Dean, father)

> I don't even know what the costs are now but I know we're in debt. We're still in debt and it's four years down the track. So the lawyer's all paid for: it's just, yeah, our debt.
>
> (Bianca, mother)

> I ended up having a breakdown. I couldn't cope anymore. I didn't even go and see Lucy for a while at that stage 'cause I didn't know how to deal with it. . . . It [was] always at the back of my mind, 'What's going to happen [next]?' . . . [And] after the sentence, somewhere in-between there, [my husband] and I separated.
>
> (Vanessa, mother)

As a result of the financial pressures involved, interviewees often had to re-enter the workplace much sooner than they had anticipated or felt ready to do. In fact, most of those interviewed expressed that their return to work came at a critical time in their child's incarceration and served to intensify the emotional distress they experienced as parents or guardians. This made for particularly challenging times when participants were employed in traditional caregiver or law enforcement roles, as described by the nurse and police officer:

> At work, I was unable to function at full capacity. . . . I just couldn't cope with people. I couldn't cope with – this sounds horrible – moaning, groaning patients, you know? Trying to put a smile on my face. Christ, my whole world's falling apart and my son just killed someone. Just, 'Fuck! Leave me alone!'
>
> (Desiree, mother)

> [Mine] is a very small station: everybody knows everybody and coppers can be very judgmental. . . . The day I came back to work there was no-one in the office area and I walked in and sat down and there was a pair of crime scene gloves sitting on my keyboard. Someone said to me later on that they reckon the cleaner might have just put them there accidentally but I don't think so. I think it was someone at work.
>
> (Colin, father)

In rare instances, colleagues expressed the socially acceptable level of shock and sympathy. And they delivered the usual quota of chicken casseroles and lasagne: 'They found out, as you do. I don't know who told them. I can't remember. So they all came over with their sorrowful gifts and we had a get-together' (Desiree, mother). But as time went by, it became very clear that in most cases, murder was not something people felt comfortable talking about: 'Six months later it all died off and that was it . . . [I] got no support from no-one. No-one said, 'Do you need anything?' (Simon, father). In other cases, co-workers were decidedly less generous:

> I got ostracised so bad that I was sabotaged in my work and I got sacked. . . . That was horrendous because I needed that job. I had to have that job because I was still supporting Toby.
>
> (Karen, mother)

> The staff in [one department] apparently were really bad. I never got to experience them because my supervisor went to the bosses and said under no circumstances was I allowed to work in [that area]. . . . And she said that three-quarters of the staff [there] were talking like that.
>
> (Jacqui, mother)

To make matters worse, significant others quickly discovered that the most frightening attacks against them occurred outside of the public domain. Like the family members interviewed in May's (2000) work, 'at times their safe havens were invaded by abusive telephone calls, damage to property, or passersby who peered into their homes' (p. 208). Here, social media provided the perfect channel for antagonists to avoid even the miniscule amount of personal courage required to make a phone call:

> People were writing on my Facebook page . . . [and] the daggers came out. Oh, it was shocking. . . . It was not polite language in any way and it was out for revenge . . . you know, 'You deserve everything you get.'
>
> (Simon, father)

Sometimes, family members expected retribution from the victim's group or gang, but naturally, they did not know the timing or the circumstances. This, of course, 'strengthened their perception that "out there" was a world of danger and that their private safety needed to be physically reinforced: closing curtains, changing telephone numbers, and, in one case, changing residences enabled the continued avoidance of public space' (May, 2000, p. 208). In the current study, one migrant family was forced to flee interstate after the home they built from scratch repeatedly came under siege from pipe bombs, bricks, and crowds of angry young men:

> Our house got attacked time and time again. My dad's car and the taxi parked in front of the house; that was egged. There was bricks thrown into . . . windows at the front of the house . . . sensor lights were smashed. . . . At one stage 30 people jumped – we were probably the fourth house down – and there was reports of people jumping all four [fences] to get into our house and there was people in our back yard saying my name, my brother's name . . . [until] the neighbours contacted police.
>
> (André, brother)

Having already lost the home in which they had invested so much, things were about to unravel in more serious fashion for this family. André watched as his brother's incarceration took a dramatic toll on his parents' health and daily routine. Increasingly reclusive, his mother began to experience psychotic episodes, culminating in a diagnosis of major depressive disorder:

> Mum wasn't talking. . . . She couldn't communicate with us. She was in a seizure type of state. . . . She's still in a state now where she's depressed. . . . She's constantly in pain, you know, constantly crying and in tears.
>
> (André, brother)

Coupled with that, as the eldest son, André felt pressure to abandon his university studies so that he could support the family by working as a security guard. Thirteen years into Floyd's imprisonment, André started to reflect on the collateral costs of his brother being locked up. In particular, André appeared highly cognizant that 'by producing changes and disruption in the personal, domestic, and social worlds of people who are not themselves sentenced to confinement, secondary prisonization ultimately extends the reach and intensity of the transformative effects of the correctional facility' (Comfort, 2007, p. 297). André reflects the truth of this concept:

> It's like they've locked themselves in. . . . Prior to [the incident], my dad was working and my mum was very active. On top of everything, my younger brother, after this happened, my mum wasn't able to look after him . . . [so] we ended up moving here for my mum's health. I had to start all over again. I've been through a lot of hardships. Starting long hours working security, dealing with drunks. We had a nice house, you know, and it's just, yeah, when someone gets incarcerated, [people] think . . . it's just Floyd in there but it's just all of us together: everyone gets stuck.
>
> (André, brother)

Confronting custodial settings

> They're idiots: the whole lot of them are fucking idiots. If they're not wearing a flower power shirt trying to be hippies and understanding the youth of today, they're trying to play hardball. Give it up.
>
> (Vincent, father)

When a child is convicted of murder, as Macleod (1982) accurately points out, 'a decision [has] also to be made about the amount of energy to be invested in the imprisoned youth' (p. 200). Despite occasional threats to do the opposite, the significant others in my study tended overwhelmingly to support loved ones with regular visits, phone calls, and the subsidy of institutional commissary accounts. They spoke, as family members often do, of prisoners' limited insights into the physically, emotionally, and financially draining aspects of maintaining such a commitment day in and day out:

> I was a real bitch to him one day; I was just so angry. Over the phone he asked me for some money for something, I don't even know what it was; it was something stupid, you know, and I [had] nothing left to pawn. . . . And I said, 'Toby, look. I've added it all up. You already owe me over $60,000. Please, give it a rest.'
>
> And then he goes, 'Yes, Mum, I do realise that and I'm sorry.'
>
> It's like yeah, yeah, yeah, whatever. And of course I got him the money.
>
> (Karen, mother)

> A little while ago he asked us if we'd start bringing some guy's dad up for visits and we were like, 'No. No, [we] don't want to be involved with anybody else.'
>
> But he couldn't see that, you know, he's just going, 'Oh, it's really hard for him to get up here,' and it's like, 'Yeah, and it's very hard for us to get up there too.'
>
> (Colin, father)

It is also clear from talking to significant others that 'knowledge of the physiology, psychology, and culture [of crime and incarceration] . . . led to deep-seated anxieties surrounding their [child's] circumstances' (Halsey & Deegan, 2012, p. 344). Sporadic reports of youth suicide and/or serious assaults in custodial settings reminded relatives that young people occupied 'a unique position in the social hierarchy of prison and [of] the vulnerability which accompanies their low status' (Forst, Fagan, & Vivona, 1989, p. 11). At minimum, this meant acknowledging that 'real friendships among prison inmates did not exist, but that juveniles found 'tactical friendships' in order to survive prison' (van der Laan & Eichelsheim, 2013, p. 438), as the following quote reveals:

> It's 'birds of a feather' [flock together]. Of course they're going to be friends in there because most of them have been downtrodden kids: school of hard knocks, whether it's happening at home or at school. . . . And some of them were really tight with Aaron and Aaron would go, 'Oh they're my mates,' and I'm thinking, 'How do you know what they are?' You know, are they using you for their own personal gain? Because I didn't think Aaron was smart enough to comprehend that they could manipulate [him. . . . In any event,] Aaron couldn't take that support . . . into, like, the general population; he'd still get flogged and I reckon his mates would roll on him. . . . They're supposedly his friends [but] they'd roll on him. Especially when you've got some big bikie [that's] going to smash your teeth in.
>
> (Vincent, father)

It also meant noting, with regret, the subjugation of their parental rights and limited capacity to control or manage juveniles' personal security and well-being – a key pain of imprisonment described by Sykes (1999 [1958]). Aaron's father, Vincent, exemplifies this pain:

> They ring you up [from juvie] – this is the irony of it all – to ask you if they could give the child a Panadol [i.e., paracetamol]. But when it comes to everything else, 'Nah, we're in full control.' Well, stop ringing me to give him a Panadol. Give him a frigging Panadol. . . . [And now he's] in the big house, he's no longer my responsibility *at all*: they don't have to ring me up and tell me he's in solitary confinement. If he is in solitary confinement, 'You don't need to fucking know.' . . . [So] I can either be supportive of Aaron and talk to Aaron and hear his woes or I can say, 'You committed a shitful act and I don't want to know you.' I took the first option. But as far as parenting, there is nothing there at all.
>
> (Vincent, father)

Perceptions that prison staff were allowing and concealing dangerous conditions rather than investigating and responding to complaints made the risk of abuse even more pronounced and the possibility of rehabilitation even more illusory. The most devastating example involved the mother who described being kept ignorant about her son being drugged, raped, and turned into a sexual chattel until emergency surgical and psychiatric intervention was required for him:

> A renowned pedophile didn't just rape [Toby]. . . . He totally abused him; totally abused him with utensils and God only knows what else and he's destroyed him. [Toby's] had bowel operations; he can't have kids. . . . The mental anguish that he has been through – and I think is still going through – is just wrong. And nobody's been held accountable for it. . . . I didn't [even] find out until the operations started. . . . [So] there he was, going through horrendous things . . . and I'm here not being able to do anything. . . . I got no information at all . . . [and] they didn't do nothing about the rape. Nothing. And I'm sure, I can bet my life, that Toby wasn't the only one.
>
> (Karen, mother)

Understandably, parents' fears concerning rape dominated the conversation about sexuality and violence against young people in prison. For juveniles in protective custody, the implications of living in close proximity to convicted sex offenders were especially obvious and rarely incorporated into bed space management and support strategies. From time to time, concerns about the capacity of correctional administrators to provide discrete accommodation to special management cohorts were legitimized by reports of sexualized coercion and grooming by older, more experienced prisoners:

> If you want to stay out of politics . . . you either have to have money, be an incredibly staunch person or do other acts: gay things. . . . A lot of people . . . will prey on younger people here.
>
> (Henry, juvenile lifer)

Such a scenario is tragic because it leaves open only one inference: that further incarceration will probably intensify the anger, distress, and despair that are already prominent themes presented by these young people. There is also no running away from the fact that for juveniles yet to develop a wide repertoire of coping styles, 'prisons may actually encourage the development and continual use of strategies that, if employed outside such a setting, would generally be considered ineffective' (Ireland, 2005, p. 419), as the following examples demonstrate.

> We found out he'd been cutting himself. . . . Somebody who worked at [the prison] told [us].
>
> (Colin, father)

> The amount of suicide attempts he tried was ridiculous, totally ridiculous. I used to be so scared to answer my phone in case they said yes: he's succeeded in one of them.
>
> (Karen, mother)

> I don't care what anyone says, I'm in here, I know what it is, and young guys will never survive in here unless they have someone that looks over them . . . like they never, never survive in here. They'll either end up in [protective custody] or, you know, getting attacked, assaulted or some other things, you know what I mean?
>
> (Marcus, brother)

Consequently, most relatives subscribed to the view of violent behaviour as a necessary and reasoned act in certain situations. At the same time, they acknowledged 'that such defensive actions risk the victim (not just the aggressor) being labelled 'violent', 'high risk', or 'dangerous'' (Halsey & Deegan, 2012, p. 348), a perilous state for a convicted murderer and lifetime parolee.

> He's going to be a hardened motherfucker when he comes out . . . because you just can't tolerate [nonsense] in there. . . . Something's going to piss him off and he's going to react [and] that is all it's going to take for him to go back [to prison] *for life*. That is my biggest fear . . . because from my understanding, if he even gets caught spitting on the sidewalk, he can look at breaching his parole.
>
> (Dean, father)

While it is not new, it is also concerning that significant others continue to express profound cynicism and resignation about the ability of correctional settings to realize their rehabilitative ideals. Whereas the youth training centre was generally seen (by parents and juveniles alike) to promote remedial goals and give residents every opportunity to pursue a law-abiding existence, the adult prison was characterized by deprivation, retribution, and control: 'He's just a number. That's the bottom line. He's a number, fucking, "Do as you're told, shut the fuck up . . . otherwise we'll flip ya!"' (Dean, father). One juvenile lifer roundly captured this perspective: 'Everything that I've done with rehabilitation . . . it's all self-taught. They haven't done nothing for me. I'm not trying to be rude or nothing but what have they done?' (Floyd, juvenile lifer). Like the fathers in Halsey and Deegan's (2012) ethnography, participants were 'concerned to recover the son [or daughter] they knew prior to the onset of crime and incarceration' (p. 350). Having said as much, many were convinced that the vast and varied range of psychological changes that prisoners are forced to undergo to survive a life sentence would combine to make this a tall order:

> I was sat down at [the Juvenile Training Centre] and they told me what would happen when she goes to the Women's Prison. And [they] said, you know, chances are she will become bisexual by then because it's such a long time she'll have [to serve]. . . . They told me that my 17-year-old daughter was going to be a gay girl and it's not by birth or anything like that; it's because of circumstances, because there's a need.
>
> (Vanessa, mother)

> I just like him as a person; I just like who he is. Especially before he became incarcerated. Before he was like harmed or damaged by any of those experiences that he had in there. . . . When they come out [of prison] I think they come out completely different. But I think, *I think*, he's still got the things that I used to see: the intelligence, the sensitivity and the empathy: I think that's still there. I [hope] that we can resurrect that when he comes out.
>
> (Lorraine, mother)

Here, enduring and supporting a teenager through a life sentence was just one aspect of the task facing significant others. The hardest part was knowing that all of their child's adult life to date has been lived within an institutional setting, which was seen to augment and reinforce the problems that had produced the admission to the setting in the first place: 'He doesn't know life yet. *He does not know life yet*. He knows gaol. He knows Home Detention' (Dean, father). While sentence length was a key grievance, the efficacy of the carceral environment to foster aggression and bond criminals together was viewed as the most significant obstacle to juveniles' rehabilitation. The fact that several had continued to use drugs in prison, notwithstanding that these participants had completed drug rehabilitation courses, really brought the problems of the prison community into focus. Time and again, parents questioned how effectively juveniles would be able to break out of that system of thinking, if, and when, their children are eventually released on parole:

> After a period of time, as with any job, you'll be inducted. And whether it's a formal induction or whether it's just a process that takes place over a period of time, you're going to be affected by it: it's going to become normal for you. . . . It's just a matter of whether he chooses to use that [antisocial] knowledge or whether he chooses to go back to what he used to be like, which was a hard-working young kid going somewhere.
>
> (Colin, father)

> What we get out the other side remains to be seen. [But] he doesn't get another chance with me. He goes back in [to prison], that's it. I wash my hands of him. I don't turn up to his court appearances. I don't do anything. He doesn't have my phone number; I'll change that. It will be that cut-and-dry. . . . And if he commits another crime like *that* again, I don't think he'll make a court appearance. But let's hope – *I hope* – that he comes out and he's just happy to be out. His mum seems to think that he'll be a good, honest citizen. I'll always be, 'I'm watching ya.'
>
> (Vincent, father)

As mentioned at the outset, evidence indicates that 'consistent role models and continued family contact are of critical importance' (Bailey, 1996, p. 34) for juveniles convicted of murder. In relation to my significant other interviewees, however, prison visits were difficult matters, 'complicated by insufficient information regarding visiting procedures and protocols' (Sheehy, 2010, p. 143; see also Codd, 1998, 2007; Condry, 2007; Loucks, 2005; Halsey & Deegan, 2014) and the belief that officers prefer power over finesse to achieve their goals:

> [Visits are] a nightmare, *a bloody nightmare*. I think the guards, all the guards need to go back and say or know the rules because every guard is different, every set of rules is different.
>
> (Vanessa, mother)

> When you go visit him you actually feel like the prisoner as well. I don't know, it's just the way they just look at you. . . . [And] having my kids with me, you know, on Sunday they checked my son's top, his pockets, his hood, and it's hard for an eight-year-old to know why this grown man wearing gloves is checking all [his] pockets, you know?
>
> (Manny, brother)

Of course, there is substantial literature dealing with the potential for visitation, intended as a 'straightforward, positive opportunity for families . . . [to] become a difficult and contested aspect of prison life' (Bortner, 2002, p. 264). Due to fear of repercussions for the prisoner, relatives in the current study felt powerless to complain in situations where they perceived themselves to be persecuted or unfairly treated:

> Many a time . . . I've got there late because of traffic . . . and they're just opening the gates and walking [the visitors] down and they've seen me but they won't come back. . . . [Sometimes I've] had dinner with me and everything, you know, 'I've just wasted 30 odd dollars, 40 dollars, to come up here and now you're turning me away?' [And] I said, 'You're just so unfair,' but they just weren't going to let it go. . . . But I've had to learn to shut up. I don't say anything anymore. I'm very polite because, at the end of the day, it gets repercussions on Lucy. And I just, yeah, it's just not worth the effort.
>
> (Vanessa, mother)

And as one father quipped, he was afraid of perpetuating a self-fulfilling prophecy:

> Going into the adult system . . . [where] those glorified security guards look down at the parents, like we're the criminals. And you feel like saying, 'Hey. Fuck you, Jack. You don't know what we've been through. I'm no meth head. I don't smoke drugs. I don't do any of that shit. My son's done all this. I'm a highly educated person and you're looking down at me because you think you have some power, some authority over me.' Well they don't. I'm there to visit my son. And if I had my way, I'd grab one of them by the throat and say, 'You're a fuckhead.' But then I'm just proving the point, proving that they may be right [laughs].
>
> (Vincent, father)

In sum

> 'I think my parents took it harder than I did.'
>
> (Ben, juvenile lifer)

Homicides are complex events, rarely reducible to any single factor or one underlying cause. Physical abuse; sexual abuse; exposure to repetitive or extreme violence; neurological abnormalities; conduct disorder; substance abuse; mental illness; and the intricate interplay between victims, peers, or co-offenders are among the many reasons why people kill. In this book, of course, I 'deal with guilty children and, in some cases, with parents who have grossly erred' (Solomon, 2012, para. 4). Perhaps, on this last count, it is well to admit that each significant other – having regard to the duration over which juveniles struggled with a wide range of problematic behaviours – queried whether the course of events that preceded the victim's death could in any way have been altered for the better. In this sense, authors argue that 'to be or to produce a schizophrenic or a child with Down syndrome is generally deemed a misfortune [whereas] to be or produce a criminal is often deemed a failure' (Solomon, 2012, para. 1). In more pointed fashion, when a child's legacy is murder, blame comes full circle through the activation of a lifelong process of self-scrutiny and the struggle to reconcile the 'offenders' status as murderers with their own understanding of the offenders as good people (Kelly & Totten, 2002, p. 171). I stress that fact because it distinguishes relatives of juvenile murderers from distortions (or assumptions) about who the relatives are and how they feel about their child's behaviour. To those who say 'It's all the parent's fault,' it is also worthwhile observing that most of the parents' comments were in one way or another related to a lack of appropriate responsiveness from key agencies across successive crisis points with their child.

> It was getting really difficult when he was about 14; it was a really difficult age. . . . And I would be on the phone trying to find help for Sonny and there was nothing. There were no services. Nobody had time and nobody was interested.
>
> (Lorraine, mother)

> Some bright spark counsellor said [to my daughter Lucy], 'Oh, you've got the right to go and live away from home if you don't like the rules rah, rah, rah and we can give you a living away from home allowance.' . . . I come home and Lucy wasn't there after that.
>
> (Vanessa, mother)

Unfortunately for significant others, abandonment, stigmatization, and condemnation proved recurrent themes for them between their juvenile's arrest, (intended) trial, and sentence of imprisonment. More specifically, the view that 'they had done it because they belonged to "them" – the poor, the unemployed, the disadvantaged, the people who drink, the people who do not know how to look after their homes and their children' (Sereny, 1996, p. 22) captures the dynamic underpinning each relative's interactions with a wide audience in the aftermath of the murder: 'It's just "us" as a unit: we're just no good' (Lorraine, mother). The unfairness of this message seems to have resonated with this son:

> I knew behind all those smiles [Mum] was fucking doing it hard. She wasn't doing it easy. . . . [The rest of the community] were dissing her and shit. That's why it makes me even more angry 'cause she didn't do fuck all. I did the fucking crime. She shouldn't be treated like that: you know what I mean? It's not her fault I was running amok. . . . [My family] had nothing to do with it. They didn't know I was fucking going to stab someone.
>
> (Will, juvenile lifer)

In spite of these agonizing experiences, all of which they have undergone against their choosing, significant others were typically unwavering in their provision of financial, emotional, and social support to juvenile lifers: '[We visit] religiously 'cause no other bugger does. And I'm not being facetious or a smart-arse: that's a fact' (Brian, grandfather). This is in spite of these people '[feeling] heavily depleted of the energy and resources needed for making a real difference in such circumstances' (Halsey & Deegan, 2015, p. 173).

> Personally I feel like I don't do enough. You know? I leave there every month feeling like I shouldn't be leaving. I want to stay there. I just want to sit there and hold my baby.
>
> (Desiree, mother)

> People think it's just so easy: 'They're in prison, and all you have to do is visit them.' No you don't. . . . I've got a life sentence too. I had a life sentence as well. I haven't bought myself a new item of clothing for 20 years. I have only just now, in the last five months, been accepted back into the family. It's not over. Even though he's out on parole, it's still not over.
>
> (Karen, mother)

Clearly, there is no guaranteed 'happily ever after' for the relatives and young homicide offenders featured in this chapter. But, these findings align with previous research suggesting that 'family members must be recognized as legitimate crime victims and accorded a higher status by the institutions that influence their lives' (Armour, 2002, p. 381). As argued, relatives are literally 'the last line of defence between further condemnation of their loved one and the belief in their capacity for 'making good' (Halsey & Deegan, 2015, p. 138). At the very least, this means investing in, and taking the time to build and/or maintain parent-family connectedness in the lives of today's (imprisoned) youths. Without this element, as indicated by the following excerpt, a life beyond crime and imprisonment appears highly unlikely for those life-sentenced prisoners making their re-entry into the community when they are well into their adult years:

> For him, the people in [prison] will be what's normal when he gets out. Our job I guess is to try and keep him in touch with the real world because the real world is very, *very* different.
>
> (Colin, father)

Again, and perhaps more pertinently, parents understood their children cannot undo the harm they have caused. Perhaps the final word should go to this father, who reflected on his journey through murder, justice, and forgiveness:

> Can he make it up? I don't know. . . . [He'll] always be the *murderer* that's now done [X, Y, Z]. . . . That will always be first, you know: your worst act . . . will always be the one that precedes you. . . . If he got out [of prison], got himself a decent job, bought himself a house, had a family, brought the family up well, stayed off any form of drug, that would please me and then I'd probably say that I'm proud of him. [But] I don't think the family – the victim's family – needs to forgive him. . . . It took me a long time to get over the anger of what happened to my mum. And that guy had been dead for years and years and years and years and I still wanted to unbury the fucker and kill him again. And it wasn't a healthy thing. It's not healthy. So if they're angry, I hope that they lose that anger. They don't have to forgive him. I just hope that they get some peace at some stage.
>
> (Vincent, father)

Acknowledgements

This chapter is adapted from the following work:

Simone Jessica Deegan, The Meaning of Murder: Family Members in the Lives of Juvenile Homicide Offenders, *The British Journal of Criminology*, 2020, azaa055, https://doi.org/10.1093/bjc/azaa055, by permission of Oxford University Press.

I am thankful to the publishers for their permission.

References

Armour, M. P. (2002). Journey of family members of homicide victims: A qualitative study of their posthomicide experience. *American Journal of Orthopsychiatry*, *72*(3), 373–382. DOI:10.1037/0002-9432.72.3.372

Bailey, S. (1996). Adolescents who murder. *Journal of Adolescence, 19*(1), 19–39. DOI:10.1006/jado.1996.0003

Bortner, M. A. (2002). Controlled and excluded: Reproduction and motherhood among poor and imprisoned women. In J. Figueira-McDonough & R. C. Sarri (Eds.), *Women at the Margins: Neglect, punishment and resistance* (pp. 253–271). New York: The Haworth Press.

Christ, G. H., Bonanno, G. A., Malkinson, R., & Rubin, S. S. (2003). Appendix E: Bereavement experiences after the death of a child. In M. J. Field & R. E. Behrman (Eds.), *When children die: Improving palliative and end-of life care for children and their families.*

Washington, DC: National Academies Press (US). Retrieved from www.researchgate.net/publication/253725159

Codd, H. (1998). Prisoners families: The "forgotten victims". *Probation Journal, 45*(3), 148–154. DOI:10.1177/026455059804500305

Codd, H. (2007). Prisoners' families and resettlement: A critical analysis. *The Howard Journal of Criminal Justice, 46*(3), 255–263. DOI:10.1111/j.1468-2311.2007.00472.x

Comfort, M. (2003). In the tube at San Quentin: The "secondary prisonization" of women visiting inmates. *Journal of Contemporary Ethnography, 32*(1), 77–107. DOI:10.1177/0891241602238939

Comfort, M. (2007). Punishment beyond the legal offender. *Annual Review of Law and Social Science, 3*(1), 271–296. DOI:10.1146/annurev.lawsocsci.3.081806.112829

Comfort, M. (2008). *Doing time together: Love and family in the shadow of the prison.* Chicago, IL: University of Chicago Press.

Condry, R. (2006). Stigmatised women: Relatives of serious offenders and the broader impact of crime. In F. Heidensohn (Ed.), *Gender and justice: New concepts and approaches* (pp. 96–120). Cullompton: Willan Publishing.

Condry, R. (2007). *Families shamed: The consequences of crime for relatives of serious offenders.* Cullompton: Willan Publishing.

Forst, M., Fagan, J., & Vivona, T. S. (1989). Youths in prisons and training schools: Perceptions and consequences of the treatment-custody dichotomy. *Juvenile and Family Court Journal, 40*(1), 1–15. DOI:10.1111/j.1755-6988.1989.tb00634.x

Garfinkel, H. (1956). Conditions of successful degradation ceremonies. *American Journal of Sociology, 61*(5), 420–424. DOI:10.1086/221800

Gavazzi, S., Yarcheck, M., Rhine, E., & Partridge, C. (2003). Building bridges between the parole officer and the families of serious juvenile offenders: A preliminary report on a family based parole program. *International Journal of Offender Therapy and Comparative Criminology, 47*(3), 291–308. DOI:10.1177/0306624X03047003004

Gilmore, M. (1994). *Shot in the heart: One family's history in murder.* New York: Viking.

Halsey, M., & Deegan, S. (2012). Father and son: Two generations through prison. *Punishment and Society, 14*(3), 338–367. DOI:10.1177/1462474512442315

Halsey, M., & Deegan, S. (2014). "Picking up the pieces": Female significant others in the lives of young (ex) incarcerated males. *Criminology and Criminal Justice.* Retrieved from http://crj.sagepub.com/content/early/2014/03/12/1748895814526725.ref.html. DOI:10.1177/1748895814526725

Halsey, M., & Deegan, S. (2015). *Young offenders: Crime, prison and struggles for desistance.* London: Palgrave Macmillan.

Halsey, M., & Deegan, S. (2017). In search of generativity in prison officer work: Balancing care and control in custodial settings. *The Prison Journal, 97*(1), 52–78. DOI:10.1177/0032885516679380

Ireland, J. L. (2005). Psychological health and bullying behaviour among young and juvenile offenders. *Journal of Adolescent Health, 36*(3), 236–243. DOI:10.1016/j.jadohealth.2004.02.026

Kelly, K., & Totten, M. (2002). *When children kill: A social-psychological study of youth homicide.* Ontario: University of Toronto Press.

Kubler-Ross, E. (1969). *On death and dying.* New York: The Macmillan Company.

Lefley, H. P. (1987). Family burden and family stigma in major mental illness. *American Psychologist, 44*(3), 556–560. DOI:10.1037/0003-066X.44.3.556

Loucks, N. (2005). *Keeping in touch: The case for family support work in prison.* London: The Prison Reform Trust.

MacLeod, R. J. (1982). A child is charged with homicide. His family responds. *British Journal of Psychiatry, 141*(2), 199–201. Retrieved from www.cambridge.org/core/journals/the-british-journal-of-psychiatry

May, H. (1999). Who killed whom? Victimization and culpability in the social construction of murder. *British Journal of Sociology, 50*(3), 489–506. DOI:10.1111/j.1468-4446.1999.00489.x

May, H. (2000). "Murderers' relatives": Managing stigma, negotiating identity. *Journal for Contemporary Ethnography, 29*(2), 198–221. DOI:10.1177/089124100129023873

McShane, M., & Williams, F. (1989). The prison adjustment of juvenile offenders. *Crime and Delinquency, 35*(2), 254–269. DOI:10.1177/0011128789035002005

Miles, C., & Condry, R. (2015). Responding to adolescent to parent violence: Challenges for policy and practice. *The British Journal of Criminology, 55*(6), 1076–1095. DOI:10.1093/bcj/azv095

Peelo, M., Stewart, J., & Prior, A. (1991). Women partners of prisoners. *Howard Journal, 30*(4), 311–327. DOI:10.111/j.1468-2311.1991.tb00719.x

Schwartz, M., & Weintraub, J. (1974). The prisoner's wife: A study in crisis. *Federal Probation, 38*, 20–26. Retrieved from https://home.heinonline.org/titles/Law-Journal-Library/Federal-Probation/?letter=F

Sereny, G. (1996). Children who kill. In P. Cavadino (Ed.), *Children who kill* (pp. 20–24). Winchester: Waterside Press.

Sheehy, D. (2010). "Staying connected": Families' experiences of visiting an imprisoned relative and implications for social work practice. *Critical Social Thinking: Policy and Practice, 2*, 140–156. Retrieved from www.ucc.ie/en/media/academic/appliedsocialstudies/docs/DanielleSheehy.pdf

Solomon, A. (2012, December 21). When your child kills: The parents of criminals. *The Daily Beast*. Retrieved from www.thedailybeast.com/when-your-child-kills-the-parents-of-criminals

Sykes, G. (1999 [1958]). *Society of captives*. Princeton, NJ: Princeton University Press.

van der Laan, A., & Eichelsheim, V. (2013). Juvenile adaptation to imprisonment: Feelings of safety, autonomy and well-being, and behaviour in prison. *European Journal of Criminology, 10*(4), 424–443. DOI:10.1177/1477370812473530

6 Killing time

Life as a career prisoner

The motivations and routes leading young people to engage in lethal violence all differ from each other in certain important concrete respects, as I have detailed in previous chapters. Where a murder conviction results, these paths ultimately converge in prison through the kind of pain that only a life sentence can levy. Accounts of young lifers, while scarce, consistently describe the indeterminate – or life – sentence as provoking a range of situated choices about the future and their own place in it. Often too, these accounts express how this uncertainty engendered frustration and compounded their anxiety and depression, which, in turn, found expression in the lifers' disruptive behaviour. This chapter does not contest the truth of such descriptions. Rather, it builds on earlier publications suggesting that 'young offenders sentenced to lengthy terms of imprisonment often have a difficult adjustment to prison' (Ruddell & Gileno, 2013, p. 244; see also Kuanliang, Sorensen, & Cunningham, 2008; Tasca, Griffin, & Rodriguez, 2010). More specifically, the aim of this chapter is to explore the nature and meaning(s) of 'life', as narrated by the 19 individuals currently subject to this sanction within the South Australian secure care and prison systems. Do these young people, for example, view the life sentence as just or unjust, as helpful or damaging and, perhaps more significantly, do the implications of growing up in the artificial and punitive environment of an adult prison (rather than in the influence of natural prosocial networks and informal controls) extend beyond the years spent in a prison cell? Or do young lifers essentially see 'life' – as Human Rights Watch (2012, p. 12) suggests – as 'a sentence to be deprived of the potential to become or achieve anything more'?

Prior to the current study, these were questions that had not been asked of life-sentenced prisoners in the Australian context. Presumably this is because, as Russell (2013, p. 498) reminds, after sentence is passed, 'the prisoner is no longer visible, and punishment is imposed behind closed doors . . . [so] the public never has to see the person – and confront the meaning of the time he or she is serving – again'. Rarely, as Garbarino (2018, p. 31) continues, 'does anyone know much about the men [and women] they become, many of them thoughtful, sensitive [adults] . . . who have grown into lives of service and reflection'. It is tempting to fall into the trap of comparing various aspects of the offending with the antecedents, personal circumstances, and beliefs of the offenders to try and identify precisely those factors that support the juveniles' suitability for immediate release. I certainly do not wish to be perceived as arguing that each offender is somehow innocent of their crime, or that each is, in some tone-deaf way, a victim of circumstance or wrongly deserving of punishment in the face of evidence to the contrary. Rather, my much more modest goal is to explore what these offenders' experiences can tell us about harsh punishments, so that 'the public can understand and confront the acts being committed in its name' (Russell, 2013, p. 492). I also want to say something about the human capacity for change through rehabilitation, transformation, and redemption.

Over the wall: joining the society of captives

> The first year inside was all right but after the guilty verdict *everything* changed pretty much overnight and it was like total abandonment. . . . Where there had been understanding, the attitudes changed to be a bit more in line with . . . the general [view] of the media . . . and we became the bad guys so to speak. Everybody's like, 'Yeah, he was this bad devil that everybody thinks he is.'
>
> (Sonny)

> When I first come in they used to beat the living crap out of you, you know. . . . They honestly believed [that] bashing people made them better people; that was the mentality. . . . [And] what they used to do to them kids in the boys' homes. . . . I mean they walked out little bloody animals some of them; they really did. I know some blokes that ended up some right fucking beauties and I mean some *beauties* and they just got smarter [about crime], you know?
>
> (Derek)

There are some circumstances where young people, regrettably, come to see incarceration as 'an occupational hazard made more or less tolerable by access to food, health care, television, video games and recreational facilities' (Halsey & Deegan, 2015, p. 108). When the head sentence is life, however, participants likened the experience to being exiled 'into another world . . . for the same amount of time as you've lived on earth' (Tyson), leaving them depressed, traumatized, and, in some cases, liberated to engage in a rush of criminal activity:

> I felt abandoned. I felt lost. I felt that I had to do this life sentence alone and, yeah, I tried to do everything I could to survive my life sentence by myself and I still stuck with the same people that I did originally before coming to prison. . . . They were into all the drug scenes [on the outside] and they were [supplying] me drugs in gaol. And when you have drugs in gaol . . . you can more or less control most things 'cause most people are motivated by drugs; they will do anything for drugs. And you just get them to do things for you rather than you do it yourself. . . . I started manipulating all the other boys and instead of being against me, they were with me.
>
> (Tyson)

Others began their sentences in less conspicuous style, despite clearly suffering the psychological consequences of their offence, leading to a range of adaptive strategies that similarly made positive adjustment to a difficult proposition:

> I started having nightmares. The same one every time, every night. It was my charge but reversed around, like I was the one dying. And I got to the point that I didn't want to sleep, so I'd stay up and I'd eat and I'd drink and watch TV. . . . And all that time with the eating, I put on a lot of weight, [I got up to] 115 kilos. I came to gaol and I was a mess. I was just going downhill.
>
> (Leo)

> I tried to get rid of things out of my head and I found smack [i.e., heroin] to be the best out of everything to drown out my problems. 'Cause when you've got to start dealing . . . [with things] it fucking hurts. . . . Knowing that you've destroyed – not only that you've taken a life – that you've destroyed a family as well.
>
> (Derek)

> He couldn't sleep. He used to have a lot of nightmares, lots of nightmares and he used to dream a lot about [the victim] . . . especially before he actually got his sentence. I remember him saying, 'I had a dream about [i.e., names victim] and we were playing basketball and he won.' And he goes, 'Oh, I'm going to do a lot of time.' You know, as in, he's telling me something. I go, 'It's a dream' . . . [and] I'm trying to make him feel better, even though in my head I'm thinking, 'Oh shit.' But he did have a lot of nightmares in the beginning. He was scared and I used to think, 'Oh my God!' That's where I used to sometimes look at [his] mum and think, 'I don't get why you're not going [to see him], putting more effort in . . . because he's a young kid.' At the end of it, he's still a young kid that suddenly his whole life has gone from this to that.
>
> (Pamela, teacher)

> I pretty much barred [my family] out of my life for about two years and I just went into a downward spiral from there. . . . I thought they'd be better off without me in their lives because they had to put up with all the media [attention]. The media spotlight, the stigma that comes with being in for the crime that I'm in for, and also generally because I just felt like I had done nothing in their eyes to appease them as a daughter, you know, I had nothing to show for it. I'd fucked up and was doing life in prison.
>
> (Lucy)

This pattern of extreme emotional turbulence, combined with the developmental immaturity of teenagers in general, especially of teenagers with tendencies towards aggression (Garbarino, 2015), made lockup a particularly volatile place for everyone. In fact, secure care (i.e. the juvenile training centre) was consistently earmarked as the place to forge the reputation that would, with any luck, spill over to the adult custodial jurisdiction at age 18:

> There are a lot more [fights] in juvie; it's just the difference lies in the ferocity of the attacks. . . . It doesn't happen as often in gaol but when it does happen, you know about it.
>
> (Sonny)

> When you go into juvie and that – the first time you go in there – you've got to fight. It's like a rule I guess: you've got to fight; otherwise, you get terrorised by everyone. . . . If the person fights, he gets to keep his buy [i.e., commissary]. But if he doesn't, then he either gets his buy taken or he goes to protection. . . . It's bad but, yeah, it happens. . . . [So] juvie gets you prepared. It's just like another step, a stepping-stone. It gets you prepared for the adult system. . . . [S]o as soon as you go up to the adult system you get like welcomed in straight away.
>
> (Luke)

> Everyone is from a dysfunctional family. Everyone comes from a bad upbringing. That's why most people are in there: because they haven't had anyone to teach them [and] they come from poor areas. And when we all mix in the same place . . . full of testosterone, it only takes the slightest insinuation or any remarks or anything, and it would be on.
>
> (Tyson)

Here, there is much in common with the very types of conflict that regularly brought juveniles into custody in the first place. There is aggressive posturing, a fight breaks out, the action breaks off, and one (or more) of the parties departs to fetch weapons or reinforcements (see Polk, 1994). Reflecting on this irony, Floyd remained pragmatic: 'Unfortunately in the environment we live in, violence is rewarded with respect.' It was not all one-way traffic though. Conditions at one youth 'rehabilitation' centre were strongly criticized by United Nations representatives as among the worst of its kind, leading to its eventual closure and demolition in 2012 ("Magill Training Centre 'child abuse,'" 2009). Those unfortunate enough to have been detained there during the 1970s, 1980s, and mid-1990s recounted a disturbing pattern of abuse, punishment, and austere confinement conditions:

> [The juvenile training centre?] They bash you there too: don't worry about that.
>
> (Floyd)

> I've been chained, tied up (hands, feet), had [my] food [thrown] on the ground. I've been humiliated, degraded, all sorts of stuff. They made me do some funny poses. . . . I'm not sure if it's for their amusement . . . to make me feel lower but . . . they wanted [me] to do some poses that don't feel natural when you're naked. . . . It scarred me forever. . . . They stripped me naked, left me lying bound, gagged. They were saying it was for my own safety . . . but I had never made any attempts to hurt myself whatsoever or cause myself any harm and, yeah, that's [just some of] the things they did to me.
>
> (Tyson)

> It's not like the average kid just like growing up in like a decent household and getting a good education. . . . It's a pretty regimented regime you've got going there and a lot of the staff there are ex-army. . . . They love dragging you back to your cell by the neck: . . . first sign of trouble, oh yeah, they're straight over your back. I've seen guys pass out on the way to their cell in those headlocks.
>
> (Sonny)

> Horrendous. Getting bashed on a regular basis. Being mentally tormented. Violence by the officers on a regular basis. . . . In one way you could say that [the juvenile training centre] helped me to adjust into the adult institutions because I found it easier to go from a place like that into the gaol, where I wasn't being bashed on a regular basis or anything. So I was pretty happy to end up there even though it wasn't great. It wasn't great at all.
>
> (Cody)

Remarks such as these suggest it is not surprising that five young lifers were motivated to escape from custody during the initial years of their sentences. Across his 25 years of correctional history, Cody Webb has escaped more than once. In keeping with his age and life experience, none of his attempts involved a degree of ingenuity or sophisticated planning. Similar to the young killers depicted in Heide's (1999) research, Cody did not see lockup as a 'rehabilitating force' (p. 224). Naturally, the life sentence that was imposed raised a question as to what an effective model for treating adolescent murderers such as Cody would entail. As with others I interviewed, Cody felt that his needs, as complex as they were on one hand, were actually quite straightforward on the other. Firstly, he stated quite emphatically the need for an opportunity to demonstrate, from a supported position, his capacity for change and his desire to rebuild the relationships that had suffered as a result of his offending and imprisonment. Secondly, he did not need to be brutalized and to have his worthlessness reinforced in yet another area of his life (see Wright, 2004, p. 196). Thirdly, what he needed was relief from 'the sheer boredom of custody [that] weighed heavily and constantly on all participants' (Halsey, 2007, p. 352). As Ben declared at interview, 'That's all gaol is: it's the punishment of being bored.' These considerations would seemingly be all the more acute in a case such as Cody, a youth who already had a history that included highly unstable personal circumstances, limited insight, involvement with drugs, and problematic behavioural response patterns. If any credence is to be given to concerns about promoting successful re-entry and reducing recidivism, there was a need for Cody to be placed in an environment where violence was less likely and not *more likely*. The idea that the training centre (circa 1985) could have provided that environment appears incredible, bearing in mind the following extended excerpt:

CODY: I did escape from the boys' home at the end of 1985. . . . Me and these other kids . . . just waited for the right opportunity and just went up and over the wall and we just went our own way afterwards.

SIMONE: And what were you trying to escape from?

CODY: Just all the pain and the torment I guess.

SIMONE: What was the hardest part about being locked up?

CODY: Everything generally I think. Just to go from being out and free to being treated like an animal instantly. . . . I was being tormented by the officers there heaps and heaps. Yeah, they were coming into the room at all hours of the night . . . [and] they would pick you up and throw you against a wall and just try to hurt you as much as they could. . . . I've [actually] tried to go over the wall a few times . . . which I thought at the time was normal in one way because everybody was thinking about doing it. . . . That sort of made my time go a little bit more [easy], a little bit faster: . . . the plan [to escape], it just like made the time go.

Tyson was adamant that, as Garbarino (2015) articulates, 'he learned how to fight, how to lie, how to intimidate, how to manipulate, how to protect himself from exploitation [and] how to exploit others' (p. 149) following a series of traumatic incidents in juvenile custody. In a strange twist of fate, around 15 years after his initial incarceration at Magill Training Centre, Tyson formed part of the small offsite workgroup tasked to dismantle the centre. Here, he describes being caught off guard by the strength of his feelings over a decade after first engaging with the juvenile justice process and says destroying it was the only appropriate response:

> When I went back there to work . . . already a period of time had passed; I've grown, I've matured. I liked to think that I was [different] from that little brat that I was. . . . [But when] I went in to the units where I used to be positioned, the table where the staff used to sit [was there]; the whole building was empty but they still had the tables, the carpet and everything. And a childlike side of me came out and I urinated on their table. . . . This was only three years ago when I was already a grown, mature man, and that hatred inside of me was still there.

The trouble with 'life': prison as the grave of the living

> Yeah, it's called the 'Department of Corrections'. I understand that but, no, if you want to survive in mainstream for a long time, there are rules you have to abide by and these do not coincide with those of mainstream society, I'm sorry to say. . . . You just have to adapt to this other way of life. Like the longer you're doing, right, the more ingratiated you become just by default, just by living in it for so long. I mean these are hard facts. It's just the way it is. . . . When you're doing a really long time, you don't worry about the screws' rules: it's just the gaol rules. That's the only way that you can [do it].
>
> (Sonny)

In his influential work *Miller's Children*, Garbarino (2018, p. 37) speculates that the mire of prison life might compel life-sentence adolescents to make a critical choice: 'Will I become a savage barbarian or a cloistered monk?' Or, as Sonny reflected, '[Some] went with the drugs game; [others] went with the Christian game.' But, according to the young people in my research, answering this question had more to do with physical security considerations and distance from release and much less to do with the idea of lifers as a homogeneous group:

> Life sentences are so long these days and possible release is that far in the future, that [you] don't really care about [getting caught with contraband]. . . . When I'm sitting here for 16 years, I've got more important things to worry about than what somebody might think of me or something. Like, come on . . . the average murderers these days, right, you're talking like 23, 24 years; that's a long way away . . . to be worrying about [parole] when [you're] doing it hard *now*. Back in the days they used to have single cells; these days you're doubled up, doubled up for 20 odd years, you know what I mean? I'm doing my head in, so I'm going to take the edge off *now*.
>
> (Sonny)

Mike, subject to one of the lowest non-parole periods (six years) among the cohort, summed up the situation in this way:

> If I got 15 years or something, I think it would have damaged me more, you know. Because if I had that long, I wouldn't care. *I would not care*. I would just be a different person because this is it. *This* is your home for 20 years. . . . Whatever you've learnt on the outside doesn't really mean anything in here. . . . You've kind of got to learn how to be a prisoner.

On the flip side, Sonny *did* get a 15-year sentence (and will soon mark his 21st year in custody). Aged 17 at the time of sentence, he made sense of the tariff in the following terms:

> I knew the numbers but it had not really dawned on me yet. . . . It's hard at that age to be able to perceive that kind of time span. . . . All you see in front of you is this white light, like this block of nothing, right? There's nothing there for eternity.
>
> You haven't really yet grasped how long that actually is but you've got a number: 15 years, all right? So it's a long time but at least you can look forward to the halfway point, you know what I mean: 'If I can do the first half then I can do the second half, surely?' [But] on the other side of it, once you've done half, well that's *half*. The truth of it is you get to that half-way point and . . . it's like, 'So, as long as I've done – and it already feels like an eternity – I've got to do again,' you know, and that's when [the bomb] drops. You're like, 'Oh, deadset.' You're in the thick of it. Yeah. That's hard. That is very tough.

When asked, in his early 30s, whether the life sentence has changed him as a person, he responded as follows:

> It has, yeah. Irrevocably. It's meant that I have had to become a prisoner, a long-serving prisoner. Something I tried my hardest never to be because if you want to get out and re-enter society and be able to do your best, you don't want to be an institutionalised long-serving prisoner, do you? You know what I mean? You want to be somebody. My mentality was, while I'm in here I want to do as much as possible . . . to give myself the best opportunities once I'm out. So while I'm in here I've been working towards my release. But what happened, after I was left waiting so long to be let out, well, I no longer have anything to work towards, right? This eventual release date is looking more and more like it's never going to happen, so I was forced to just become the prisoner. You put that much effort into not becoming institutionalised and [not] getting involved in [prison] politics and all that and then in the end you're forced to 'cause they won't let you out.

In the same interview, I asked him how such a lengthy sentence affected what his future could be. Nearly five years over his non-parole period, he projected a *fatalistic outlook*; namely, in the absence of tangible 'hooks for change' (see Giordano, Cernkovich, & Rudolph, 2002, p. 992), Sonny was neither willing nor able to commit to a future beyond crime and punishment:

> I will never fit back in to society. The best I will ever be able to do is *act* like I'm fitting in, which I'm very good at. . . . Obviously, if I make one false move I'll come back for the rest of my life. That's obvious. I realised that a long time ago: I'm a life-sentenced prisoner.
>
> It's a big part of my life – *it's the majority of my life* – I've spent more time in gaol than out. . . . At the end of the day [my peers] are all in gaol – you have to remember that – so you learn more from their mistakes than their successes. [And] if a criminal gets out and he's homeless, like I hate to sound like a bad person, but look . . . I'd rather go rob a hotel than sleep on the street.

Still, Sonny remains philosophical. With reference to the case of Christopher Lane, the promising Australian athlete gunned down as he jogged along an Oklahoma street, Sonny drew a sharp distinction between his predicament and the life *without* parole sentences on offer for youth in the United States:

> I know there's a lot worse. You only have to go over to the States and most guys like myself, they never get out, you know what I mean? Only just recently [they] had another 15-year-old done for killing that Aussie baseballer. You heard about that? Out the window with the rifle: 22 or something. Shot him in the back. Life without parole. Never to be released. Jesus Christ that's rough, isn't it? Imagine the monster that bloke's going to become in gaol.

Having said as much, it simply cannot be said that Australia has avoided controversy about whether its youth sentencing practices are compatible with human rights. As with Cody, Derek was found guilty of murder prior to 12 May 1988, and the sentence of the Court, passed pursuant to s55 of the *Juvenile Courts Act* (SA) 1971, was that Derek be detained at the Governor's pleasure, the mandatory equivalent of an indeterminate life sentence. Theoretically speaking, by providing a power to the Governor, on the recommendation of the Parole Board, to discharge the offender at any time on licence, the underlying purpose of s55 was to permit the release of a person convicted as a juvenile at an earlier, rather than later, time. In effect, however, Derek had no guarantee of *ever* being released. I asked both Derek and Cody about how having no non-parole period to speak of manifested itself in their day-to-day lives in the adult prison system. Rebellious and unable to cope effectively with both an adult institution and the uncertainty of an indeterminate sentence, Derek spent approximately two-and-a-half of his first three years in solitary confinement. Both men articulated feelings of hopelessness and the inability to set specific goals contemporaneous with disciplinary infractions and police charges for their involvement in prison riots, beatings, escapes and long-standing issues with excessive prescription and illicit drug use. Both men also reported making serious attempts to kill themselves and said that they did this because they could see no future for themselves and periodically thought that life was not worth living:

> [I was] handed GP back then, which is Governor's Pleasure . . . [so I] didn't have any sort of release date at all, which made my gaol absolutely crazy. Everyone else in gaol knew exactly when they were getting out . . . [whereas nobody knew] where I would end up or how much time in gaol [I would have to serve]. . . . It just really didn't look as if I was heading anywhere . . . [and] I probably would have been the youngest bloke in gaol, just being surrounded by some of the most evilest types of people.
>
> (Cody)

> It's like me when I front the Parole Board and I get knocked back for another year. Now when you say 'one year' it rolls out the mouth pretty quick but when you're doing it day by day it's a long time and especially in places like this, it's a fucking hell of a long time, you know? Because not only are you dealing with yourself, you're dealing with everybody else . . . [and] we are not in the easiest place on the planet. . . . It's a whole different fucking ball game here. . . . When you come into a system as a kid, you've got to learn to survive . . . [and] I've seen some horrible things, you know. As a kid I was raped in this system. I've been bashed in this system. I've been stabbed in this system and I've seen blokes being put into comas and [ending] up in hospital on bloody life support machines. Some come out of it, some of them don't.
>
> (Derek)

In a different vein but to similar effect is Tyson's position. Despite (or probably due to) being universally liked and well-respected by his peers, to say that Tyson has assumed the role of management's own *enfant terrible* is probably a generous summation. Imprisoned since the late 1990s without any indication of making parole (despite endorsement by the Board), he has regularly faced disciplinary action for disrupting the 'security, management and good order' of the prison, something he attributes directly to the imposition of the life sentence itself. Reflecting on almost 20 years of defiance, Tyson had this to say:

> [A life sentence] is like being dead. Everything dies. Sometimes your mind dies; everything's numb. Everything just dies out: you don't want to think; you don't want to live; you don't have the strength; you don't want to go on; . . . relationships [die], everything. Like sometimes you just don't want to do it [anymore]; it's just too hard. . . . There's been a few that's commit suicide . . . and the other lifers don't really care; they just indulge themselves with stuff that will kill them anyway. . . . But [for me] getting into trouble, it's like a stimulant. It makes you feel alive, like I'm alive again. I'm feeling an emotion that I'm supposed to feel as a human being. I feel hurt. I feel pain. I feel anger. I feel this and that. If I had a [lesser] sentence, at least I know that [when I get out] I will still be young. I could set goals: 'This is what I am going to achieve in [the future]' . . . and I could see hope . . . at the end of that tunnel. . . . [But] because everything was so far away, I didn't want to grab reach of anything. I didn't want to do anything. And I wanted to get in as much trouble as I [could] to pass time . . . and that's [exactly] how I behaved myself.

He openly attested to the fact that this behaviour also provided him with the opportunity to experience a few of the normal things in life, such as a direct line to the outside world through the possession of a mobile phone:

> I've been to [segregation] many times . . . for suspicion of having a mobile phone. . . . Having a phone in prison changes everything; it just makes everything a lot easier. You can discuss the things you want to discuss without them hearing your phone calls. You can plan a lot of [ways] to get up to no good and it just feels normal when someone calls *you* rather than you [always] calling them.

A series of incidents and regular appearances in the 'hard' cells (i.e. punishment units) brought Floyd similar notoriety from a young age. He is currently nearing the end of his non-parole period but remains guarded about his prospects of a seamless release: 'I don't want to sound like a pessimist but, until I see it, I won't believe it's real.' Whilst it would be difficult to say that Floyd was ever a model prisoner, it is certainly clear that towards the end of his time in prison, he has shown a much more responsible and mature attitude to life than he had previously exhibited. Entering prison with a 15-year minimum sentence, he experienced the 'life-lagging' – his period of penal servitude – as both a challenge and an opportunity to survive and become stronger in the face of adversity, temptation, and the acquisition of power. Floyd quoted an old saying that 'the same boiling water that softens the potato, hardens the egg. It's about what you're made of, not the circumstances.' For a young man given to action, living out this philosophy meant clashing heavily with authority over perceived injustices and negative intentions of staff, while embracing any and all of the (many) consequences that came his way. Floyd remarked at interview in relation to this:

> As hard as it is, as bullshit as it is, as unfair as it is, or whatever the scenario is, the status quo is not going to change: I'm still going to get up and train, I'm still going to care about my family, I'm still going to not care [about what you do to me]. . . . Regardless of rain, hail, or shine . . . I'll still do what I gotta do. You're not going to break me and you're not going to change me. I don't care. I'm not here to be friends with screws: you're my oppressors; you turn the key on me. I don't *hate* you. I know this is a job and you're paying your mortgage and you're feeding your kids, [but] when you go out of your way not to help [me], to ruin [me], well how can [I] have love for that? How can [I] respect that? I'll go the other way: I don't want to see that; I don't want to talk to that.
>
> If you've got nothing, what have they got to take off you? I would rather just hand it over myself, destroy it with my own hands, than let you take it off me [and] let you think that whatever that was, that . . . luxury, was something you've got over me. You *don't* have anything [over me]. I know the rules. I follow the rules. I have no issue with conforming to 'What's right is right; what's wrong is wrong.' The only time I make waves is if I feel like I'm sticking up for myself, as a human being, not as an animal.

With the better part of two decades in gaol, Floyd recounted spending the majority of his days heavily invested in the 'convict code': the set of social conventions administered by prisoners that has as its main objective, 'the hope of bolstering or maintaining their credibility or place in the prison hierarchy' (Halsey, 2017, p. 634). Suffice to say that 'those who follow the code believe it is important to violently defend their honor in the face of disrespect and to avoid talking (or "snitching") to the authorities (i.e., police or prison officers) for any reason' (Copes, Brookman, & Brown, 2013, p. 841). In practical terms, as Copes et al. (2013, p. 841) describe, 'those who can live by these rules are deemed "real hustlers" or "good cons" and develop reputations that carry certain advantages, not least of which is protection from being victimized'. Certainly, the masculinity that virtually defined all of Floyd's interviews also indicated a strong adherence to a culture of loyalty towards and protection of those who were supportive of those attitudes, such as the general prisoner crowd that agreed with his behaviours at the time:

> If you do the 'Yes sir, no sir, three bags full' sort of [approach] . . . if you dob on people, if you're a dog, if you're an informant . . . or you buddy on with *them* [i.e., correctional services officers], you get rewarded [by the system]. . . . So if you like swimming with the tide, you get to your destination, but if you go against it, you drown. And I'd rather drown because I don't

> want to jeopardise my integrity or be bought with incentives because I'm not a prostitute, you know: you can't buy me by saying, 'If you tell us this da da da, we'll give you this and give you that.' Keep it. I don't want it. Because I know, at the end of the day, I've done my time and I did it real and I remember every single day of it. I didn't need to be on drugs. I didn't need to, like, have it easy. I know I done it real. Because, my family, they're doing it real out there. My mum and dad, my brothers . . . [I know] the anguish they're going through. They're the ones incarcerated in their head so I can't cheat them out of it. I've got to do it as real as I can. That's how I feel.

As he closes in on 16 years in a maximum-security prison, it is clear that Floyd has worked hard to reflect on the factors that led to his current situation. Considered a leader amongst his peers, he spoke of himself as a young man possessed of exceptional self-confidence and potential who, tragically, chose to use his personal power destructively. Over the years, he has been haunted by thoughts of his actions as a youth and, upon much contemplation, spoke in favour of the prosocial values that he described as being held by his parents:

> When I look back now, everything went wrong in high school. . . . I mean if I hanged around nerds I wouldn't be *here* I guess, you know. And all credit to [them] because they're the ones that are laughing now. I mean we're sleeping next to the toilet, you know, so . . . I take my hat off to them. . . . They persisted through it and they, you know, kept studying and . . . they listened to their parents and they're successful now, probably married with kids and have got a future. . . . And that's when you sort of see: what the fuck was all this shit for? It was a mug's game. That's when you sort of see it because everyone used to tell you: your parents would tell you; your family would tell you; other people that would care about you would say, 'You're going down the wrong path', 'These people aren't your friends', 'It's not what you think.'

Floyd often referred to his sense of having let his family down and the need to compensate for this by making the most of his incarceration and those (limited) opportunities he perceived to be offered in custodial settings. Through self-motivated study and personal reflection in tandem with natural maturation, otherwise known as ontogenetic processes (see Glueck & Glueck, 1968; Gottfredson & Hirschi, 1990; Moffitt, 1993), it is fair to say that Floyd felt rehabilitated 'in *spite* of prison, not because of it' (Unkovic & Albini, 1969, p. 160). He conceived of his transformation in the following terms:

> I see myself as someone who has been a criminal or who has done criminal offences. It's not like Ned Kelly, where you say, 'Yeah, I'm an outlaw' or 'Yeah, I'm a [murderer].' I say that I'm different to that 16-, 17-year-old kid that [I was]. I'm 30 years old now and my responsibilities are different and the things that I covet from life are totally different from what they were when [I was] 16, 17. . . . Whether that would be status or whether that would

> be materialistic things . . . or whether that would be what I'm focused on today, they *are* two different people. I'm the same person but . . . your goals change, your responsibilities change, your objectives change; you change as a person. Time does that to you. And that's not necessarily because of gaol. It happens to people living on the outside too.
>
> (Floyd)

Even Garbarino's (2018, p. 37) participants – the 'Miller's Children' – eventually wanted out of the 'gangsta' lifestyle they were, at one time, prepared to kill or die for. Muhammed – a juvenile lifer in that work – remarked that 'I'm not attached to the things I was attached to before. I've changed in what I value.' Like the Floyd of today, Muhammed has changed positively. He completed his General Educational Development (GED) and is considered an asset to his community in the prison, displaying empathy towards other prisoners and offering peer support. And this from the violent, gangbanging teenager who first witnessed, at just the age of 9, someone being shot. Generous with his limited possessions, such as commissary, and demonstrating excellent input and leadership skills within programmes, Floyd even appeared to have an appreciation of his previous lack of strategies – or lack of *implementation* of strategies – to de-escalate conflict. Asked if he was 'rehabilitated', he responded this way:

> I was different yesterday and I was more different two years ago and I was [even] more different 10 years ago. . . . I can be reserved now and think about something before I react or talk or [argue]. Even with 'Boss' – if they said something [provocative], I used to *have* to go out of my way to say something back. 'Cause I hated them. And I [felt] they were in the wrong. Now I just say 'Whatever' and walk off. . . . I try to interact less. I try to not be in the spotlight. I try to do things smarter and better. I'm focused more on home [whereas at the start] this [place] becomes everything. Like, 'That's *my* table', 'That's *my* phone', 'That's *my* gym', you know, 'That's *my* soccer ball.' Now I look at it like, 'It's not mine, it's not yours. It [belongs to] these guys and they can keep it. I don't want it.' This [place] is just a dot on the map . . . and it used to be [my] everything. Everything used to be so focused and revolved around *this* world, on this side of the fence. . . . Now, I see this place . . . as just a waste of time.

The shepherds and the sheep: (most) lifers as not like us

> Just because a guy's done 15 years doesn't mean he's not an idiot, doesn't mean he's not a dickhead. And just because he's a lifer doesn't mean he's one of the boys, you know. There's other people: there's armed robbers; there's bank robbers; there's other people that have done a life-lagging but in installments, you see, so they've done the G Division, they've done the riots, they've done the bashing of the protectees to get them out of the [mainstream units]. They've done all the politics, they've done their tour of duty so to speak so they've got an opinion now too. And

> you can't just, if you have that opinion of, 'Oh, he's a lifer, he gets. . . .' Nah. You'll learn quickly that that's not how it is.
>
> (Floyd)

> You're talking about totally different people, right, [and] most of them are just scums. . . . The [only] ones that I half-pie respect are the guys that got touched as kids and that, so they go kill a pedophile, you know what I mean? That's fair enough.
>
> (Sonny)

Across each of the narratives drawn on in this research, I found that understanding what it meant to be a life-sentenced prisoner, again, hinged on the lived experience of the pains of imprisonment, as opposed to the idea of lifers as a cohesive group. One comes to know one's contemporaries in the prison world over time, as in any other quasi-domestic sphere. Predictably, great disdain was reserved for sex offenders (particularly pedophiles), who were seen as deserving of extra-legal punishment should they stray into mainstream units. Entering prison as a particularly young person, Will was strongly advised to consider all living arrangements available to him. But, as he explained, for those of 'normal criminal ethos', protective custody was quickly ruled out as a legitimate option:

> I told them straight away, 'I don't want to go into fucking protection . . . no fucking way. I'm not going in with no protectees.' . . . That's a brand. [Once] you have that, you're fucked, mate. . . . You can't go anywhere after that. . . . People will just talk shit to you all day. Cunts will try and fuck you up; they'll stab you if they get the chance to. Fuck you right up 'cause you're a dog. . . . Pedophiles are usually protectees. People who fucking bash little kids are usually protectees. People who have dobbed on their mate and, you know, got him like 20, 40 years in prison, they're usually dogs. So when you have that brand you can't get it off. I don't want to have that brand. I didn't do that shit. I don't deserve that shit.
>
> (Will)

But elsewhere in the prison, participants were also scathing of the general attitude (and tendency to ruin things) demonstrated by habitual low-level offenders (known as 'backpackers') when prison resources are low and opportunities few and far between. Riding waves or creating them, this type of prisoner threw lifers into an abyss of continuous change, randomness, and chaos, when what mattered was giving purpose and direction to their living:

> [Short-termers] don't care. They just do whatever. They don't appreciate what anyone does for them. Like even today, we had a [fitness] course and they had gloves for boxing and five pairs went missing. And it's just stupid stuff like that that's going to get that course taken away from us because some dickhead wants to steal from it.
>
> (Leo)

> The ones that have only got like six months [are] the ones that are going to throw a computer across the room just because they didn't get their own way. They don't care that the prisoners have to pay for it [from their own wages]. . . . If a prisoner who's only got six weeks goes in and doesn't like the way the toastie [i.e., sandwich press] cooks and throws it against the wall, that makes it hard for everybody else.
>
> (Toby)

> This is *our* home sort of thing and everything that we've got, we've fought for all the way, through the years. And then when you see the young people come along and wreck it all – so everything we've fought for, they've lost for us – yeah, it puts us back to square one.
>
> (James)

For others, like Sonny, it was the kind of systemic (and personal) insanity that allowed prison to become such a revolving door for so many recidivist offenders, which had a particularly destabilizing effect:

> To be surrounded by a bunch of guys – repeat offenders – doing very short sentences . . . it's their third or fourth time: they're getting out, coming back, getting out, coming back. This is my first time in and I haven't been let out yet and these scumbags are repeatedly getting let out. . . . It's a total contrast, right. Most of them that I was doubled up with, [were charged] with AVOs – breaching AVOs – for banging up their missus, right? Now, I've done 16 years mate: I can't even have a missus and you're battering yours. You know what I mean? *And there was that many of them*, so it's not just the act itself that grates on you, right, it's the *personality* of someone who would commit such an act and then having to spend so much time in a locked box with them.
>
> (Sonny)

It has also been argued that, for life-sentenced juveniles ultimately transferred to the adult system, 'the seriousness of their commitment offense may obscure the fact that they are adolescents, who want and need programs to help them gain employment and social skills to avoid future criminal activities' (Forst, Fagan, & Vivona, 1989, p. 11). Again, it was sentence length itself that proved the key obstacle preventing young lifers from accessing all sorts of intensive programmes at the prison. Expressed differently, 'those with the longer sentences are not going to get the same programming as someone who is closer to leaving prison. It's a question of resources' (Human Rights Watch, 2012, p. 32). Most participants described being eligible for courses (and the low-security settings in which to complete them) only in the ultimate and penultimate years of their sentence: 'If you're a lifer you're not eligible for any of them. . . . It's all for people who are on their way home' (Luke). However, as Floyd explained, it was not just about teaching him certain skills but about giving him time to implement them within a structured environment that would give him the best chance of success when he eventually comes out of gaol. For someone seriously wrestling with how to reframe his life away from the prison scene, Floyd's sense of frustration was particularly demoralizing:

> There's a construction course going on but I can't do it. . . . We all put our names up for it, to enrol to do this course and we would [really] benefit from it, [but] then you've got some crack-head that's going to do it and he'll get on it because he's only doing six months. He'll fuck it up as soon as he gets out because he's a junkie; he's got no hope at all because he chooses not to change: it's in his nature . . . to be that way. People have tried to help before and he doesn't listen and [he] comes back and forward, back and forward, back and forward. And then when you *know* what to do – what's right – you've got your game plan, you're ready to go and you're just waiting like a mug. Just waiting . . . [to] be a productive member of society and these people have held [me] back . . . and so that damages [my] hopes; that damages [my] enthusiasm. . . . It's more detrimental than it is helpful.

Backpackers. Wife beaters. Informants. Junkies. Pedophiles. There was just one more category of inmate: other lifers. And the problem, for most of those interviewed, was that – with one notable exception already mentioned – these *were not* mutually exclusive concepts:

> Most of the prison hates them [because] most . . . are in for killing a woman or killing a child.
>
> (Tyson)

> The majority of them? I think that they're weak. In the sense, like, you might think, 'Oh yeah, 'cause they're lifers, they're murderers or they're killers, they're going to be tough.' Nah, it's not [like that]. 'Cause a lot of them were . . . like in a crime of passion – [they] killed their wife – or, you know, it was spousal abuse or something. 'So you killed a woman: Is that your claim to fame?' It's not something to be proud of. . . . How are you going to have *them* as activists to fight for our rights? . . . [So] the charge is the same I guess but the calibre is a bit different.
>
> (Floyd)

By the same token, participants unquestionably rejected the idea that respect or standing could be conferred by sheer sentence length alone:

> People don't seem to give two fucks about how long you've done. They might say they respect you for it but I don't know anyone that actually does. As far as I'm concerned . . . this place doesn't demand respect at all. Even if you are in my position, people don't respect who you are: they don't give a fuck. I like to think respect is earned but unfortunately in here it's fear of retribution that really drives people and they'll be friends with those ['persuasive']

> people. . . . So violence seems to get [prisoners] through gaol. Or drugs. So the polar opposite of what people think motivates this place is really essentially what gets you through it.
>
> (Lucy)

What is more, as Sonny pointed out, serving a life sentence could actually *promote* the types of behaviour frowned upon by old-school prisoners, thus bringing the term *lifer* into disrepute over time:

> Lately, because of these tough laws . . . it's been very hard for lifers to get parole. . . . [They've been] knocked back for years waiting for [the Executive Council] and all that. So a lot of them have become like friendly with the authorities in the hopes that may get them out, because informers are afforded special privileges so to speak and they do tend to get looked after a bit better than a staunch crook who's going to say nothing. . . . And that's what's been happening a lot, right, and it has eroded the reputation of the lifer. . . . Like talking to the Boss and all that: . . . it's classed as a dog act, mate. You can't do that and they're doing it. So these days you can't say, 'Oh, I'm a lifer' and everybody just respects you for it, nah, because a lot of them have sort of turned . . . [whereas] the lifers – being that they're here for the longest and all that – they used to run the joint.
>
> (Sonny)

But, more importantly, most young lifers had incredible difficulty accepting the nomenclature used by the Department for Correctional Services (e.g. 'Serious Violent Offenders') and the way this affected their security classifications, placements, and case management in the same way as their nihilistic and/or sadistic counterparts:

> When I look back on my life now I know where I went wrong and from that time to the time I got arrested, yes, I did engage in violent acts and there was a pattern of escalating violence. . . . Not that the piece of paper says it the right way or defines it [accurately].
>
> (Floyd)

> Serious Offenders Committee: . . . that [should be] for sick shit, you know what I mean? You can tell a sick, sick murderer when you see one. . . . They've just got that look about them and . . . I think, 'That's a fucking serious offender.' . . . Blokes don't murder their fucking wife and kids and shit like that: that's fucked up. . . . It's fucking disgusting, mate. I'd never put myself in the same fucking category as that.
>
> (Nick)

Whereas Wright (2004) has noted a tendency for prison 'staff [to] see prisoners through the rear-view mirror of their crimes' (p. 202), so-called stand-up lifers were equally dedicated to regulating those life-sentenced prisoners who had crossed the lines of accepted criminal and prison mores. Throughout his incarceration, Floyd went to great lengths to demonstrate that even among the condemned, moral distinctions are made:

> It depends on what they've done, but [generally] it's 'Pack your shit. Get the fuck out. Fuck off. You're not fucking welcome.' Now it's getting too hard [to do much more] because there's cameras everywhere or Boss is always looking at you. So you're like, 'Listen. We know what you did. You can stay for the weekend but Monday morning you're out of here.' . . . So I give them a week's amnesty but, you know, that's the best they're going to get: 'Listen. No-one's gonna touch you but you're not welcome here. Get the fuck out.' You know, that's the politest way.
>
> (Floyd)

Of course, as certain lifers experienced first-hand, this was most likely to happen to those whose offence was a murder of a sexual nature or a crime involving a defenceless or otherwise vulnerable victim:

> I went to mainstream. Fourteen hours later [I was in] protection and I've been in protection ever since. . . . I was just told to leave 'cause when they found out who I was, it was like, 'Yep. Leave cunt. Now!' . . . They were like, 'Leave now or you're going to get hurt.'
>
> (Aaron)

In such circumstances, authors have noted that 'prisoners become the sum total of what they have done, and what they have done is very often taken to predict what they are more likely to do' (Halsey & Deegan, 2014, p. 57). But more than that, as Trammell (2012) discovered, taking part in structured arrangements to assault 'dirty inmates' allowed prisoners to take 'pride' in their own non-deviant status and 'united' them (p. 113). All of Trammell's participants – the Californian inmates serving time for various offences ranging from drug possession to attempted murder – understood prison violence as an important currency and a legitimate mechanism of social control. Anthony, a participant in that work, serving time for parole violation and assault, spoke in the following terms:

> The boys have a code: you take out your own. This proves that we're all on the same page with this shit. The boys come together over this and we all know who's dirty.

As Trammell continues, 'to maintain a worthy identity, violence was necessary' (2012, p. 113). So with the young men in my study. And as their prison capital grew, so did the pressures upon them to perform violence to prove their allegiance to the mainstream moral community:

> One young bloke who come in, I think he was 19 years old . . . was in for raping an 18 month old . . . and I'm not proud of what I done but I actually

> bashed his head into a wall for every day he was in gaol . . . [and] he was raped by just about every bloke in the bloody system. Yeah, it was a funny place.
>
> (Derek)

> They have to leave, one way or the other. I don't want to be housed with that because that makes me look like I condone it. . . . And who wants to live with a bunch of pedophiles or informers or rapists or granny bashers or something? Who wants to be known as that? Or who wants to be housed there? They're filth even by our books. . . . So sometimes you need a wolf sort of figure, like a shepherd, to put the sheep in line.
>
> (Floyd)

Don't go breaking my heart: isolation and limited opportunities to maintain social and family networks

> I'm scared about a lot of other things as well. I have problems in relationships and things like that. It's hard to explain but I've been brainwashed for so long. I can't see it the way other people see it and I can't even put myself in a relationship with anyone because I can't see a 33-year-old woman being as innocent as I am so there's a bit of emotional mixed feelings there.
>
> (Tyson)

In a hyper-masculine environment with little levity, romantic relationships with people outside the prison, where they occurred, offered prisoners a break from the politics, isolation, and monotony that quickly became their reality. They also afforded – through nights spent ruminating over a partner's dedication (or current whereabouts) – the means to derail the confidence and composure required for young lifers to do 'good' time:

> [A relationship] gives you a bit of excitement for a bit, but in the long run, it has the opposite effect on you: . . . [There's] so much you can't control, especially who she's seeing. I mean, I don't want to control that but when I'm locked up, fucking, you can't help it. . . . [And] it takes [so] much energy out of you . . . especially when you're locked in your room; that's when all the shit kicks in, all the thinking. All these fucking thoughts run through your head.
>
> (Will)

> You're dealing with the scum of the earth in here and it made me a very introverted type of person. . . . One of the first things I realised shortly after getting locked up is that I would have to hide my true self from those around me and I did. [But] in order to have a relationship with a woman you have to . . . open up, which I also did, right? And she then broke my heart and . . . that taught me that I really have to be careful about things. . . . It's important

> that I maintain a level of self-control [in here]. If I lose that control, it can end badly.
>
> (Sonny)

> It's worth it. Yeah it does make it harder, like, you're always thinking, 'What's she doing?', 'Okay, is she all right?', 'I miss her fucking heaps blah, blah, blah,' and yeah you want to ring them all the time and that, but it's worth it just to fucking hear their voice, you know what I mean? I'd rather have that than not talk to them at all.
>
> (Leo)

In the end, though, the benefits of potential relationships really came down to a few short questions. The first was obviously whether it made sense to risk exacerbating the insecurity, anxiety, and despair that were already part of the psychology of each juvenile lifer. The second was whether the prisoner had formed genuine feelings for their partner and, in doing so, turned their mind to the possibility that the individual might want or deserve a different kind of love than they were capable of giving: 'I wouldn't expect too many people to be waiting around. And even if [they] did, what are [they] waiting for, really?' (Cody). The third question was similar but different: In the absence of a likely release date, how long was too long to live in limbo with meagre hope of the basic perks most people expect from a relationship, such as cohabitation or physical intimacy?

> You're kidding yourself. Are you going to sit there and do it hard in relationships? Mate, let her go. Let her live her life. Why are you dragging her down? If you love her, let her go. . . . It's synthetic: it's not a real relationship where they're involved and you can contribute and you can have an input to the extent you want to help or whatnot. . . . You're better off focusing on your gaol – *you're here now* – and just trying [to] lighten the weight of your responsibilities. . . . Who knows: they might get bored in six months or a year; they might find someone better or [someone] that actually *can* be a man for them out there and then what are you going to do? You're back to square one and you're upset. I don't want [that]. I just switch off. I don't put myself through that shit.
>
> (Floyd)

In such circumstances, the only relationships compatible with long prison sentences were those between people who were more interested in the well-being and happiness of the other person than themselves. This was usually only the case with family (particularly mothers) and trusted childhood friends. But even those relationships could be seriously strained and pushed to (and sometimes beyond) breaking point:

> [When] I got locked up . . . the first thing [Mum] did was she wrote a letter and said she was real sorry [for abandoning me]: she had some stuff going

on that she needed to sort out blah blah blah. Okay, whatever, but if [our relationship] is going to happen this time, well make sure it happens, you know what I mean? If something goes on, well talk to me about it. Don't just fucking leave me.

(Leo)

When I talk to my mates and that, the things that's important to them is like materialistic things: the amount of girls they get with; the amount of . . . parties they go to; the amount of money that they spend. And it's hard for me to try and relate to that now 'cause it's been a while, you know? I'm just like, 'Who gives a shit, man? You've still got your basics. What [more] do you need?' . . . The struggles that I have in here as a 20-year-old [are] *a lot* different to the struggles that like a 20-, 23-year-old would have out there.

(Eddie)

My parents . . . reacted badly and we never spoke for years. . . . They never . . . wanted to see me. They never came to my trial. They never wanted to talk to me. I think over a period of time, like years and years later when I think they finally did find it in their heart to some sort of forgive me, they started talking to me and having contact with me again.

(Tyson)

Leaving aside the specific conditions that led to the conflicts, several lifers observed that any relationships they built up were often short-changed by their tendency to present as emotionally blocked – a strategy frequently used by prisoners to flatten the peaks of exposure to persistent overwhelming events (Crewe, Warr, Bennett, & Smith, 2014):

One time [Mum] cried like in front of me, and fuck, I've never felt like that before in my life. . . . Like, my fucking head was going to explode and my heart was in my throat. I've never felt [that] uncomfortable before and I started going off at two other crims [in the visits centre] just 'cause they were looking at [her]. . . . I just snapped. And I've never felt like that before and it fucking made me so – I was scared – that's how sad I felt. . . . And I just told her, you know, I said, 'Just don't do it again. . . . If you've got to cry, go cry in the car or something' . . . [and] I just cruised from [the visit]. I had to go.

(Nick)

Peter pan and the lost boys (and girl)

I don't see myself as a 32-year-old man at all and sometimes when people call me a man I get offended by it because I don't see myself as a man. I see myself as a kid. I'm Peter Pan. I'll always be. . . . My life is frozen and I can't progress or do anything better than what I've done.

(Tyson)

> [My personal development] is not so much on pause: it's pretty much on rewind because your skills are kind of going back to when you were younger; your vocabulary is going back to how you were when you were younger. It's basically that your body is continuing to grow and your mental state is just dropping so much . . . and yeah, it concerns me.
>
> (Henry)

As I have written before (see Halsey & Deegan, 2017, p. 67), I am generally sceptical of claims that prisoners consciously prefer or freely choose to serve stints behind bars. This is, to be sure, a fundamentally different question than whether custodial facilities can have a stabilizing effect on some people (by providing regular opportunities to detox, sleep, gain weight, etc.). Outside of the oft-cited sentencing goals of retribution, deterrence, rehabilitation, and restoration, participants unequivocally noted the value of the correctional system as a means for short-circuiting cycles of harm:

> If I didn't get arrested for this, it probably would have been [for] something else.
>
> (Leo)

> The whole situation, the whole gaol thing, I see it like maybe this was supposed to happen for me to find direction in my life. And obviously not for murder, but maybe I really did need this time to really think about my life.
>
> (Nick)

> I'd only been out [of home] for a year and in that time I . . . managed to get myself into *so* much shit and cause *so* much trouble and irrevocably fuck my life up completely [to the extent] that I ended up when I am now. . . . [Any longer and] I would have either been dead or in a mental hospital because I wasn't far from both I don't reckon.
>
> (Lucy)

But, for those young people sentenced to life, the fly in this prescription was that long-term incapacitation was an opportunity for personal stagnation to prevail over personal growth:

> I needed [gaol]. I would say that I needed it. But I didn't need this long. I didn't need this long 'cause . . . I learnt my lesson as soon as [claps hands] the impact of 'Fuck! What have I done? I've ruined my life; I've ruined my family's life; I've *taken* someone's life.' Like these are all huge consequences and huge impacts – that's like the wake-up call of a lifetime – you know, and where's this going to lead? Where's this going to go? What do I need to change?
>
> (Floyd)

While the basic 5 R's (reading, writing, arithmetic, right, and wrong) were evident at each prison, many young lifers had completed their high school equivalency in juvenile settings and said that there were only so many paintings one could do behind bars:

> The education programme's *that* basic. . . . It's pointless really. . . . Everything has just been scaled back and dumbed down for everyone. . . . So a lot of people in here will just go, 'Oh stuff it, I'm not doing it. It's pointless. What am I going to learn from that?'
>
> (Marcus)

> It's not rehabilitation for sure. 'Cause they don't do anything for us, you know: they might get us to Grade 7 education but, fuck, what are we going to do with that? So we've got to rehabilitate ourselves and that's if we *choose* to rehabilitate ourselves, so if we don't choose to, we're not going to get anywhere. They don't do fuck all for us.
>
> (Leo)

> I really feel as if I haven't matured. The only time you feel as if you've matured is when you've done something wrong and you've been told off by the Parole Board or something like that. That's about the only time I feel as if I've sort of learnt something. . . . I haven't improved. All I've done is basically aged.
>
> (Cody)

In the latter scenario, despite participants' best efforts, meaningful personal growth processes were impossible to sustain, merely intensifying and then retreating again, only to (hopefully) re-emerge sometime before release:

> I can't even see tomorrow let alone like five years ahead. I have no dreams, no hopes about existence. I live each day as they come along. I've been put in a cage for so long with no directions, no help, no assistance, no nothing, no rehabilitation. No indication of getting out or how to progress forward to achieve the things that I want to achieve. They don't give you a release time or date or any indications. It could be from now until five years or ten years later. One day you'll have some sort of genius idea that I want to be like a rocket scientist and the next day you want to be a bum, so you can't really hold onto your dream long enough. It crushes your spirit. It puts you through mood swings and I think it kills your self-esteem as well when you get treated like a kid and get told what to do and someone is trying to go out of their way to make you miserable. When you do have big plans there's always someone that will destroy them or you can't have the resources to continue further to better yourself. It's very limited. I'd like to be a lot of things but I know I can't be those things because I'm too old.
>
> (Tyson)

For juvenile lifers such as Tyson, mentioned earlier, it was as if all the cognitive behavioural therapy, educational and vocational skills programmes, or 'Making

Changes' courses (if and where available) could only scratch the surface of what Maruna (2001) called a 'Redemption Script'. Such a script assists prisoners to discover their true and better selves, take real responsibility for their offending pasts, perceive personal control over their destinies with optimism, and actively create meaningful futures. To this end, 15 or 20 years *after* participants committed their crimes, the impact of standardized programmatic responses in custodial settings meant very little, if nothing, without foreseeable release dates and the means to practise arranging the basic building blocks for managing in the community:

> You just sort of feel as if you're not really moving on, you know. You're constantly reminded of what you have done if you're in a maximum type of gaol [and] you're constantly reminded that you are like a security risk sort of thing as well.
>
> (Cody)

> It sort of shifts away from you . . . if you've learnt all these things and you got all these . . . certificates and courses and whatnot; your life priorities have changed and you've got a goal and a game plan for life, waiting all this extra time: it's sort of expiring. Now you have to sort of *re-plan* because things change . . . and the damage just gets bigger. It gets bigger from what I see. . . . It's like Demolition Man: you're just waiting to get defrosted just to live your life again, you know, be back to a normal life I guess.
>
> (Floyd)

As with the young men in Halsey and Deegan's (2015, p. 210) work, 'far from embracing or permanently desiring the criminal life, each young [lifer] wanted ultimately to become a good employee, father, student or the like. They wanted, simply, to become better people.' Not only this, but they also needed a means for establishing and strengthening positive relationships with those persons who not only witnessed but helped to validate their changes:

> My [request] has always been, 'House me closer to my family' so I can maintain my family structure and dynamics so I can have some sort of –input, not just a 10-minute phone call. That's not sufficient enough to have an input in my younger brother's life, to guide him or to give him good advice or just to have that family contact, regularly. Why is it, out of all the prisons, I've got to be housed at [a rural and remote]?
>
> (Floyd)

> I haven't had family contact, you know, under the same roof. I haven't had that work opportunity . . . and I like working. I would like to be given an opportunity to prove that, you know, I can just get into that slipstream and do what everybody else does out there from 9 to 5.
>
> (Derek)

> Mentally I was ready to get released a few years ago. Now, I'm getting out of prison with most of my family passed away and probably a lot harder to re-connect with them than it has ever been.
>
> (Cody)

Instead, in virtually all my interviews, the bureaucratic emphasis on *protecting the community* (deferred parole applications, few opportunities for low-security placements, off-site education and training) and the 'primacy of the state's agenda for justice' (Armour, 2002, p. 372) ('truth in sentencing' legislation, negative articles, features, editorials, letters to the editor) was front and centre for each young person:

> [Low-security prisoners] can go what they call 'off centre', right, into the community cleaning up and, I don't know, weeding and stuff. They [also] have . . . a camp way out in the sticks [where] you'll be at some cattle station or something like putting up fences and all that type of stuff, maintenance work. . . . [But you] can't do that stuff as a lifer. . . . I think maybe [because] the community kicked up a stink. Obviously murderers are considered murderers. If you don't know a murderer you just obviously think that's like the baddest person on the planet sort of thing, right. So they're like, 'Oh, nah, we don't want these murderers just traipsing through the community. What happens if one of them has an episode', you know what I mean? 'There could be all kinds of mayhem.' That's their mentality.
>
> (Sonny)

In regard to a number of parolees who, shortly after release, had gone on to commit crimes of horrendous proportions, Lucy noted how high-profile incidents became imbued with greater significance for lifers, only adding to the issues that they had to grapple with:

> Some fucker decided to do the bolt from the Parole Board and everyone suffered as a result. Not everyone is capable of doing that but that's DCS going into overdrive as usual when something happens. So, male or female, whether you're fat, thin, small, fucking can't talk English [or] have one leg, they'll still shackle you and double handcuff you because they're just dogs like that. . . . [When it happened] I said, 'You've got no idea what this is going to do. This just makes us more [notorious].' And, at that stage, my release date was meant to be [that year] and I was thinking, 'That's all I fucking need: photographers and fucking media personnel camping outside the fucking gaol. . . . My family's been hounded down the street and having phone calls and prank calls and acts of violence against them . . . [all] because you guys couldn't do your job properly.'
>
> (Lucy)

Added into that mix was the power of the Governor in Executive Council to veto parole decisions for prisoners sentenced to life. Under the relevant Act, the

Governor in Executive Council is not required to offer any reason for vetoing a parole decision: 'In here you're not obliged to get an answer. If they don't see fit, you will not get one' (Lucy).

In this legislative context, the 'interaction of adversity, temperament, social environment outside the family, substance abuse, and idiosyncratic circumstances that led to the moment when a gun, a knife, a club, or a fist made that juvenile into a juvenile killer' (Garbarino, 2018, pp. 12–13) was lost in its entirety. Lucy was left in a particularly unfortunate position. Her parents took out a loan to (successfully) appeal the length of her sentence, only to have both her new, and then old, non-parole period expire under repeated rejections by the Executive Council:

> My lawyer had said that my length of sentence didn't seem justified . . . [so] my parents spent a fortune on a fucking appeal that didn't even work. It did [work] but it's amounted to nothing: it's 10 grand just wasted. I got a reduction that was the maximum that they could take off . . . and that's now null and void 'cause 15 years have been and gone. . . . That appeal made absolutely fuck all difference because . . . I've now done six years more [than my original sentence].

And to add insult to injury, Lucy did not know why the recommendations of the Parole Board were not accepted or what she might do to change the situation. Naturally, this led to concerns among lifers that government intervention in judicial decisions unfairly politicized the parole process. Mike explained to me that all of this was reinforced by the logical assumption that if decision makers had good reasons to reject a parole application, then surely they would say what they were:

> That Executive Council is just ridiculous. They don't make decisions based on your crime or how you've rehabilitated yourself: it's more a political decision, like, 'We can't be seen as letting murderers out because we'll look bad and we won't get votes.' That makes us all almost political prisoners, you know. It's disgusting. It should go, 'Right. This is the crime that he's been done for. This is how long he's done in gaol. This is what he's done since he's been in gaol. Is he a good prospect for parole? Is he rehabilitated? Is he going to be good in the community? Well yes he is? No worries,' you know. Theirs is just like, 'Nup.' It was something like four people a year they were approving – could be 40 people applying for it – and they were just letting a couple slip out the door that wouldn't get big media attention and stuff.
>
> (Mike)

Amid a 'disempowering' (Miller, 2000) and 'infantilizing' (de Vigianni, 2007) regime that eventually chews prisoners up and spits them out in various stages of disrepair, Sonny, subsequently, became known more for his unhinged antics than any straightforward progression through the system. Whereas he was a bit-part player in the murder itself, he remains incarcerated long after the principal offenders have been released. He explained this by saying that the usual pains of imprisonment paled in significance as his depression and anxiety escalated to a complete mental breakdown. After experiencing psychotic symptoms and regressing to a childlike state (perversely met with a period in solitary confinement), he was diagnosed with bipolar disorder during the later years of his sentence. On that count, the question of whether he had been broken by the implications of living in an 'impoverished environment . . . with little autonomy and [positive] social interaction' (Meijers, Harte, Maynen, Cuijpers, & Scherder, 2018, p. 1) remained central to Sonny's narrative:

> I had a psychotic episode and I had to be sequestered in the hard cells . . . [and] sent down to [another prison] for a month. I've [since] been diagnosed with bipolar disorder and now I'm on medication. . . . In truth, I do not know [whether I really am bipolar]. . . . All right I've been diagnosed with it . . . [but] when you suffer long periods of abuse, could be physical, sexual, could be mental, psychological, and nothing is done about it – you have to cop it – well, what happens? If someone pokes you with a stick your ordinary reaction is to retaliate but if you find yourself in circumstances where you are not allowed to, where you will be punished for defending yourself and you have to cop that abuse, you're going to have it building up, right. And then what usually happens is you snap: a brain snap. That's how in some cases . . . people wind up getting diagnosed with these mental disabilities. . . . But I mean, I think if you *don't* find yourself getting depressed – like it's been hard growing up in gaol – *then* there's something wrong with you.

Certainly, as Garbarino (2015, p. 134) writes, 'the concept of psychological maltreatment often proves useful in understanding how human growth and development becomes emotionally warped'. At the same time, Sonny openly questioned how one can determine what is suitable correction for a child and to bring home to him a personal sense of awareness of his responsibility to society *unless* a significant period of incarceration is taken into account:

> But look, at the end of the day, what's that going to say . . . if they're giving sentences of no longer than five years for murder, right? Well then, it's just like, 'What's five years, mate?' You know what I mean? So you've got to weigh things up.
>
> (Sonny)

Tyson also appeared to understand the complexity of the situation, conceding, 'You can't compare a human life with [any] sentence . . . because if it was my life or my family's life, I'd want blood for blood' (Tyson). But the larger truth is that Sonny knew that he had reached a level of maturity and success in his personal development where further incarceration would probably cause further deterioration in his present state of mind and would be detrimental to his motivation and prospects of rehabilitation. He asked me to bear in mind how difficult it is to get parole and to ascribe the fact that he had not been released due to his difficulties imagining an independent and sound life for himself, rather than deliberate laziness or preoccupation with criminal pursuits. In our final interview, I asked Sonny what advice he would give to a young person starting out on a life sentence today. He offered the following words:

> There's two types of prisoner, right: those that serve out their time and are released and those that *survive* it. . . . It's [the State's] job – in their mind – to crush our soul and destroy our spirit, to break us so to speak as if we're wild animals [and] to take away that part of us that makes us unique. That's what happens to most lifers – most lifers and long-term prisoners. To survive it means you do have to fight, unfortunately.
>
> I would say be yourself. I would say do your best. I'd say take it as it comes as well. Yeah, you don't really want to have expectations . . . [because] they soon get dashed. You have hopes for one eventuality, something good happening [and] more times than not, it doesn't happen and you're left feeling more disappointed. So, yeah, it is what it is: it is gaol and this is tough, but it's supposed to be tough, right? This is the punishment for the most heinous of crimes that we're copping so it's not going to be easy, yeah, but it is character building.

'Different strokes for different blokes': LOPS, SOPS, and the power of the pen

> Trying to get anything in this place, you have to get half a dozen 'yesses' and one 'no' can screw you over.
>
> (Ben)

> If I say to them, 'No, it didn't happen like that,' they say to me, 'Cody, you're lying and you don't want to take responsibility.' So you have to become a liar in here because if you don't own up to things – which half the time [you] haven't even done – it just looks bad for you.
>
> (Cody)

> [Everything] comes down to . . . LOPS and SOPS. LOPS are like Local Operating Procedures . . . [and then] you've got SOPS, which are Standard Operating Procedures that are set down by law and have to be followed. . . . LOPS are subject to change at any given time and usually by management. . . . It chops and changes all the fucking time and it's trying to keep up with them and their attitudes, which really does fuck people up.
>
> (Lucy)

An equally prominent theme to emerge from interviews – and one which can be seen as tied to 'the ascendancy of risk as an organizing principle' (Griffin, 2018, p. 104) – was young lifers' contention that modern penal practices were an incredibly efficient way to destroy their sense of hope in a future beyond bars: 'I can't rely on anyone, I can't have faith in [the system] . . . because it's never been the one rule for all; it's different strokes for different blokes' (Floyd). Crewe's work (2011, p. 512, but see also 2009, 2007) seems to encapsulate, in large degree, the way in which the new penology of case-notes, checklists, criminogenic 'risk-need' instruments, and paperwork of various kinds 'created some new burdens and frustrations that differ from other pains [of imprisonment] in their causes, nature and effects'. For those in my study, the gap between what is required for life-sentence prisoners to obtain parole, as against what is available to support this process, only added to the illegitimacy of their indefinite confinement:

> I'm sitting down one end and right down the other end was [the Chairperson of the Parole Board] and I don't know who the other people were. But the next minute she's launched over the table and she's called me every useless bastard [name] under the sun because I'd been in gaol for X amount of years and I hadn't bothered to educate myself, I never had a trade, I didn't do this and I didn't do that and I walked out of there thinking, 'What just happened in there?'
>
> (Derek)

Returning again to Crewe (2011, p. 514), 'prisoners serving indeterminate sentences, in particular, complain that the things required of them are unclear and unattainable. The sense is of moving targets, which always slip away: [like] "dangling carrots" and "moving goalposts".' More recently, authors such as Halsey and Deegan (2015, p. 125) have observed a fine line between 'assisting' versus 'annoying' (ex-)offenders. By all accounts, the (ex-)prisoners in that work were certainly busy trying to fulfil State-sanctioned requirements for release on parole – reporting, attending programmes, giving urine samples, and the like, yet 'nothing of any real significance was changing. "Jumping through hoops" failed to yield so much as an ID card or bank account' (Halsey & Deegan, 2015, p. 125). And to extend this idea, it was all-too-easy for young lifers to query whether 'the use of risk assessment served purposes beyond actuarial prediction and need identification' (Griffin, 2018, p. 107). Given his designation as a 'Serious Violent Offender', Floyd was perplexed when he was deemed unsuitable for the Violence Prevention Program [VPP] (generally acknowledged as a prerequisite for parole), on grounds that he could pick up bad habits from other, more 'high-risk' inmates:

> Well that contradicts [everything]. I'm living and housed with criminals. I'm celled up with a criminal. I go to the gym with a criminal. Everything in here is *with a criminal* so don't you think I'm learning bad behaviour by living 24 hours a day with the criminals? So what's a course going to do, you know? It doesn't make sense.
>
> (Floyd)

Floyd understood that demonstrably antisocial attitudes must be factored in and guarded against. But at this juncture, custodial-based intervention was seen as 'paying mere lip service to the damage that crime and incarceration was doing not only to his own life but to those he cared about' (Halsey & Deegan, 2015, p. 38) and the wider community as well:

> I've even said it to all of them: 'I'm more than happy to do these courses if it's going to better me, if it's going to give me something to build on . . . as a foundation to be a better person. I'm more than happy to do this course and learn something from it. But why do you have to make me wait until I've finished my time, to say, "Oh we think you're suitable now to do it"?' Obviously I'm suitable. I'm in for a violent offence. Isn't that eligible already?' . . . But these programmes, they're more like a back-up for them: when something *does* go wrong, when they've let someone out that's the fucking retard that gone and fucked it [up], it's like to say, 'Well, we did [our best]. He did complete this course and that course.'
>
> (Floyd)

This was, more or less, a conclusion shared by Hannah-Moffat, Maurutto, and Turnbulls' (2009) interview-based study of Canadian correctional workers, which included probation officers, senior correctional managers, and policy developers. Having described an atmosphere of increased public scrutiny and efforts to decrease recidivism and increase public safety, Hannah-Moffat et al. (2009) describe the following in their findings:

> The embrace of, and pragmatic faith in, risk technologies by practitioners is linked to broader concerns about transparency, accountability, and the crime-control demands of the public. . . . The actuarial illusion created by the risk score mitigates, to some degree, practitioners' responsibility for their judgments of risk and its consequences.
>
> (p. 398)

More tellingly, though, juvenile lifers believed the factors that motivated them to engage in lethal violence were highly unlikely to be affected by the patronizing and unrealistic messages of the CBT (cognitive behavioral therapy) meant to improve them:

> I've done VPP [the Violence Prevention Program, which employs CBT] and it's quite stupid. . . . It's all from a textbook [and] not everyone's situation is exactly the same. . . . And most of the time it doesn't work 'cause they've got things in there like, 'If you're angry, count to 10.' If I was angry, I could count to a million and I'd still be angry. You've got to find other methods to deal with it.
>
> (Tyson)

All told, organizing 'rehabilitation' around the concept of an inevitable sequence of events (i.e. 'traps', 'triggers', and the 'planning' of offences in the vernacular of cognitive behaviouralism) had much less relevance for juveniles typically caught up in scenarios of spontaneous or flashpoint violence than those engaged in ongoing cycles of crime. By this reckoning, many 'individuals felt such programs "distracted" from things more likely to be of benefit. Things like work, training and education' (Halsey & Deegan, 2015, p. 108). For Leo and Mike, it was not necessarily the content but the *timing* of such intense 'concentration' on negative thoughts and behaviours (which may no longer be present) that had the potential to unsettle them during critical moments surrounding their release:

> VPP they want me to do as late as possible [in my sentence plan]; they want me to go over my bottom [i.e., non-parole period] to complete the course . . . and that will take all my time away from going to [the pre-release cottages] and adjusting to the community. Instead I'll be stuck in [a medium-security gaol] doing a course [that's dredging] up all the old shit I've already got over and bringing it all back to life again right before I get out.
>
> (Leo)

> VPP: that's meant to be about violence prevention and if you've been in gaol . . . for nearly seven years, that part of my life I've kind of put it to the back of me and tried to forget about it. And then you have to go through this whole course, this process, *just before* you get released and relive that whole experience again in front of a group of people that you don't even know or trust and expect them not to tell people about it. It doesn't make sense. . . . It could take people from being in the right headspace and then they're talking about their crimes; it might take them to another place.
>
> (Mike)

Meanwhile, 'considerable latitude in how practitioners identify, collect, and interpret information used to assess risks' (Hannah-Moffat et al., 2009, p. 394) was seen to give rise to the potential for 'decision-makers to draw inferences from that data that may not be appropriate or accurate' (Griffin, 2018, p. 113). To this extent, lifers expressed cynicism about the inconsistent and one-dimensional case-note system, which, as they understood it, provides a logical bridge to the larger issue of their ultimate endorsement for parole:

> We're here [in prison]; we're convicted criminals so, in their eyes, we're scum. So imagine the level of how [officers] speak to us, you know what I mean? But *that* doesn't get recorded. Only our response will get recorded [as a case-note] . . . so it's a lose-lose. Everything that comes out of your mouth . . . looks like it came out of nowhere, like, 'Why speak to an officer like that?'
>
> (Marcus)

> These case-notes that they write, they only write the incidents. They don't go and reward you for the good things that you've done and we don't go up and say, 'Oh listen, I did this today. I stopped this or I prevented that. You need to write this down.' That will never happen, so the Parole Board will never get a chance to know about that. . . . So say if you see something is about

> to happen and you go and mediate and say, 'Listen guys, you can just talk it out,' . . . you've prevented an incident. If someone was feeling suicidal and you've talked them out of it and you've got them into training and got them to stimulate their mind differently [from using drugs] and [how they] view life – that there's more for them – have you saved a life?
>
> (Floyd)

It was a good question. But here, more than anywhere perhaps, an opportunity for authorities to interpret the actions of prisoners 'with suspicion or as serving some ulterior motive' (Halsey & Deegan, 2015, p. 195) seemed to present itself. On this score, Floyd worried much about what Halsey (2017, p. 635) identifies as '(whose) *power* and (whose) *knowledge* influences whether people's stories are given "truth" status or not', especially given a preponderance of commentators who believe offenders will say almost anything to get out of prison.

> Because I wear this colour t-shirt and they wear the blue one, their word is what's final and [my] word is what's over-ruled. Theirs is the truth and mine is the lie.
>
> (Floyd)

All of this is important for many reasons. In the context of 'rehabilitation as risk management', offenders are made to 'recognize that their criminal identity . . . constitutes the pivot around which all other aspects of their personality revolve' (Lacombe, 2008, p. 72). As highlighted by this quote, popular perception of violent offenders suggests that recidivism is inevitable and that offenders will almost always repeat their predatory acts in the future, which, in actual truth, may be quite off the mark. It is worth noting here that the very serious long-termer has an 'extra burden to carry because his stigmatizing offence record would be parked at the forefront of his dossier' (Toch, 2010, p. 5). Of course, as Halsey and Deegan (2015, p. 195) remind, 'criticism by offenders of the way things run tends to be quickly recast as an attempt to displace one's own role in creating a life of crime and reincarceration'. Cody and Eddie noted that while being in denial was synonymous with active, repeat offenders, that attitude brought a special kind of hell to the lifer and long-termer communities, inspiring prisoners to engineer their participation in programmes to fit the accepted order of things and 'keep therapists at bay' (Lacombe, 2008, p. 70):

> And that's the way it is now. . . . If I'm ever blamed for like this, this or this, I can't say to them, 'No, that didn't happen.' Now, I have to go and say, 'Yep, that's right. I'm owning up to it. Can we just move on?'
>
> (Cody)

> There was a couple of times where you had to fill out like, it had to be five scenarios of fights [you'd had] at parties. And I could only think of three. And they were like, 'Well how many have you had, Eddie?'

And I'm like, 'Not that much.'

And they're like, *'Well how much*?'

And I'm like, 'Three.'

And they're like, 'Whoa! That's a lot.'

And I'm like, 'Three's fuck all!' So I [wrote down] three and I made the other two up. I had to. I said, 'I've got three and that's all I've got. That's all I've done.'

And they're like, 'Surely there's more. Come on. You need two more or you fail.'

(Eddie)

Crewe (2011) similarly captures this idea by observing that 'few truths or lies are acceptable to the system, leaving many prisoners in performative purgatory – always concerned that the wrong step might entangle them all the more in the carceral net.' Crewe reflects on this dilemma:

> One prisoner – Martin – argued that, to be considered 'honest', he had to play up to a record that portrayed him as 'some violent beast'. Asked in an offending behaviour course how he would react were he to bump into an ex-girlfriend with a new partner, he was disbelieved when he claimed he would simply 'say hello': 'so I just said "all right then, I'd buy him a drink and I'd glass him", and [the tutor said] "that's what I thought you'd do"'.
>
> (p. 516)

However, in McDermott and Kings' (1988, p. 373) terms, how prisoners experience, discern, and interpret penal power also makes us question whether the 'nature of physical confrontations between prisoners and staff may be changing'. As reported by the prisoners in that work, 'they don't beat us anymore – they don't have to. They can win using bits of paper. It's all a mind game now.' Reflecting on the limited array of choices (or places where which to retreat) within correctional settings, participants made several interesting points. Chiefly, they queried the utility or generalizability of themes or behaviours to emerge in the prison context:

> In here, if I don't talk to the screws [i.e., officers], if I don't say good morning to them, that's 'antisocial behaviour'. Why? Why is that antisocial? I talk to my other peers. I talk to you. I talk to him or her. Just because I don't say good morning to *him* because he's fucked me around before – and gone right out of his way to fuck me around – why am *I* the bad guy? . . . [Or] if I've just got my headphones in and I'm just listening to music and I just do my own thing, well they're going to say, 'Something's wrong with him.' They're going to say, 'Send him to the psychiatrist because he's [withdrawn]. He needs medication' . . . [but] if you talk to *everyone*, you're [also] doing something wrong: you're a drug dealer or you're planning something, you're inciting something, or you know [something's] going to happen: you're in the know. So what do you do, Simone? Do you know?
>
> (Floyd)

The answer, according to each of the young people I met, lay in steadfast belief that 'understanding [them] required hearing [their] life story, not just learning which diagnostic label [they] had been assigned' (Garbarino, 2000, p. 70). In spite of this, the final decision as to when and whether young offenders could progress through the system would be up to the Serious Offenders Committee (drawn essentially, from a largely conservative-flavoured corps of Correctional Services employees, including police representatives and victims' rights advocates who meet to decide such things):

> [The Committee] looks at my behaviour, my case notes, my urines, and they just go ['Yay' or 'Nay']. But you can't judge someone by a piece of paper . . . so I'm not getting my hopes up at all. . . . They don't know you – or they [might] have a sense of it – but it's still nothing. . . . We'll get chucked straight in that [serious offender] category until we can prove otherwise.
>
> (Leo)

> They knock you back [for things] . . . and they don't have to tell you why. Well how are you meant to know what to change and what you're doing wrong if you don't know *why* [you're] getting knocked back? It's a stupid system. . . . It's ridiculous how they treat people.
>
> (Mike)

Other lifers had similarly low hopes, given that the Department's decision was final and that no correspondence would be entered into:

> They're all in Head Office somewhere so . . . they just read paperwork about you and then make a decision based on that; they don't have any interaction with you whatsoever. [And] you can't appeal the decision, which is bullshit in my opinion 'cause you can't explain *why* [something has happened]. But I suppose . . . you're a crim and they think all crims are liars and junkies so why the fuck would they want to ask your opinion on something anyway?
>
> (Lucy)

I do not pretend, of course, that all or even many determinations regarding lifers would be altered if prisoner accounts were believed, acknowledged, and/or adopted in more meaningful ways. Nor do I contest the occurrence of 'pockets [within] the prison system in which treatment and conditions [are] more positive and progressive' (Crewe, 2011, p. 511). However, a series of measures deliberately intended to increase the flow of information between lifers and the institutions that influence their lives would nevertheless represent an improved approach to handling these people. Much to lifers' disappointment – although not to their surprise – significant decisions to date had 'effectively bracketed out particular narratives very likely to be of relevance to [their] understanding [of] such events' (Flynn, Halsey, & Lee, 2016, p. 183). Cody expressed this point:

> It's really easy for any sort of gaol to like tell the [Serious Offenders Committee], 'Look, this guy needs time on the outside; yous guys have got the

power to wave a pen and go bang, bang . . . let's get Webb outside of the gaol [for some work experience].' But, at the same time, I can sort of see the gaol wanting me to slowly work my way out. *But explain that to me. Explain that to people.* Don't just make them feel as if they're not going to be getting anything while they're [here]. Explain it. Do some communication.

Almost certainly, Cody is undereducated, but he is no fool and struck me as someone who could have coped much more maturely with the receipt of bad or unwelcome news had official sources not remained so defensive and guarded in what they told him, frequently responding with answers of 'Go and speak to your case manager.' To this extent, juvenile lifers universally agreed that the anxiety they felt regarding 'outcomes that [were] delayed as well as uncertain' (Blackburn & El-Deredy, 2013, p. 16) was most likely worse than the penalty itself.

> Me and Tyson came up to [the front office] last time we were here and they basically said to us the words, 'Fuck off. Don't ask us for anything.' . . . [And] we just wanted to know what we can and can't do here. But we clearly heard the words 'F off. Don't ask us for anything,', as if like, 'Just be happy you're here.'
>
> (Cody)

If this case indeed happened, the outcome – that some young lifers continue to act impulsively without great thought – seems fully predictable, notwithstanding that it is obviously going to cost them a lot in terms of imprisonment as an adult:

> If you get stuck in one place you feel like you're not going anywhere: you think, 'Why am I doing the right thing when I'm not getting anything in return?'
>
> (Luke)

> I've written letters to the Parole Board every year . . . but they don't really seem to explain too much though . . . so I've been writing to MPs [i.e., Members of Parliament] and people like that. *All the time.* [But] I've been told that I can't write to too many people anymore. . . . The [general manager] up there told us, 'Okay. If you *ever* want to get released from gaol, you might want to pull up writing to anyone else.'
>
> (Cody)

> I had not received any indication from the Parole Board as to when I would be released. I felt that I had done all that I could to show the Parole Board that I was worthy of being allowed to return to the community. I received no response from the Parole Board despite all my efforts. I was aware of an escape that was being planned by other prisoners and I foolishly decided to go with them.
>
> (Derek)

In sum

> I believe that the community wants different people. Different from when they first walked in. Isn't that what it's all about? Whatever the problem *was*, or *is*, you go to gaol, you are helped to sort yourself out and you are released. That's what it's meant to be about. Not to go to gaol and to be poked and fucking prodded and called a useless bastard and you're no good for this and you're no good for that.
>
> (Derek)

I began this chapter wishing to say something about the social, psychological, and vocational inertia of the lifer's inherent state and to frame it in terms of a departure from individual, community, and systemic expectations regarding ('serious') young offenders' rehabilitation and reintegration prospects. Part of my argument has been to show that youth who commit homicide fall into many categories and, *while all criminal acts are in a sense wilful*, the motives underlying each act can vary tremendously. And each life discussed has highlighted just how difficult it is to successfully balance the ongoing personal development of dysfunctional, unhappy, traumatized, and/or aggressive teenagers against the realities of growing up in prison with only older, more experienced criminals for constant company:

> People think that you've done something wrong so you come to gaol and you get rehabilitated and that's not the case. You do something wrong, you come to gaol and . . . you sit around with 48 other criminals [and] serve out [your] time.
>
> (Henry)

As noted elsewhere, many of 'these youths tend to interpret the intense messages from the adult criminals *not* as "I am scared of the consequences of my current activities, so I will curtail my delinquent behavior," but rather as "I am going to have to be even more tough to survive prison"' (Garbarino, 2015, p. 256). In recognition of these circumstances, real progress or rehabilitation was not reducible to a random collection of case-notes, programmatic course completions, mouth swabs, urinalysis, or a compilation of the people so-called high-risk offenders converse with or meet. To my mind, it is idle and naive to suggest that any of these goals 'anchor them [offenders] in the positive life of the larger society' (Garbarino, 2000, p. 154). Achieving such an outcome requires getting to know people and, if possible, allowing them to 'tell their story in their own words, using their own sense of time, place, and significance of events' (Halsey, 2017, p. 639). The important question, of course, is whether these young people could have been lawfully dealt with for matters of lethal violence in a different and more effective manner. But there is more to consider than just the conditions of juveniles' confinement. In common with the stories of so many young lifers I interviewed, Sonny 'struggled to make sense of what he did and who he was. And what he would become' (Garbarino, 2015, p. 228) over the course of his 20-odd years of imprisonment:

> The one thing you can become in gaol if you're given a lengthy sentence, is a successful career criminal; that's the only thing, right? You know how they say, 'What do you want to be when you grow up?' and that when you're a kid.
>
> And [you say], 'I want to be the president' and 'I want to be an astronaut.' 'Okay, well work hard enough sir and you do it.'
>
> It's not true though, is it? How many people actually become professional soccer stars or whatever? *But*, if you want to be [a criminal] and you're in gaol for the foreseeable, you can be that with the right amount of application and determination. It's not something that's going to – you're not just going to wake up a super villain, right: you have to apply yourself. But, if that's what you want to be, you can be. That's all I have to say.
>
> (Sonny)

While their demeanours (generally) gave no hints of troubled pasts, life-sentence juveniles were often complicated individuals, being paranoid, rudderless, frustrated, and/or angry. Even their own parents and various prison staff shared this view, believing that the offenders' immature, impulsive, and sometimes irresponsible behaviour was in no way assisted by the implications of their lifer status. Recent research indicating that even a short stay in prison increases risk-taking behaviour and reduces attentional performance (Meijers et al., 2018) reflects the preceding notion. Drug intoxication certainly appears to have habitually constituted the behaviour of those who struggled to cope effectively with the length and uncertainty of their prison terms:

> They just get on whatever they can to make themselves sleep. That's how they do their time.
>
> (Henry)

> I have a drug problem and I need to address it. . . . [It's] only been in the last six months . . . [but] I've been [using] pretty bad. . . . Boredom plays a big part in it. . . . I'm just, yeah, running out of things to do . . . [and] it's very, very easy to get: they come to you or you go and get it.
>
> (Nick)

Undoubtedly, there will be occasions where the public interest *will be* best served by taking the opportunity to sentence a youth to greater, rather than lesser, custodial sentence. On very rare occasions, a youth may remain too dangerous to release at all. However, based on the material before me, it can be said with as much confidence as it will ever be possible to have that imposing particular sentencing considerations on *all* youths convicted of murder, regardless of the seriousness of the offending, their level of involvement in the crime, and their (lack of) embeddedness in criminal networks, 'only compounds the injustice imposed upon them by the world in which they grew up' (Garbarino, 2000, p. 23). As I have previously stated, from mid-2018, the minimum penalty for any such offence is 20 years' imprisonment – *the same as for an adult* – thereby fuelling the argument that in reality society cares little about the interests of troubled, vulnerable children and young people, 'except as potential threats to the community' (Garbarino, 2000, p. 20). When one considers all of that material, and even allowing that it is impossible to say, at this point, whether participants will find their way back into mainstream Australian life, a solely punitive view of these matters has to be rejected. Knowing many juvenile offenders as I do, I find it hard to believe 'that these young people are *inherently* more criminal than their same-age peers' (Guardian for Children and Young People, 2017, p. 7) who partake in 'violent assaults that fail to produce a dead body' (Garbarino, 2000, p. 25). As I say, recent alterations to the *Young Offenders Act* 1993 (SA) and the *Sentencing Act*, 2017 (SA) are clearly in error. The fact that those participants with shorter sentences (say, fewer than ten years non-parole) fared better in terms of positive engagement with the justice system, hope and planning for the future illustrates well that a more medium-range strategy foregrounds better outcomes for both the offender and the community in equal measure.

References

Armour, M. P. (2002). Journey of family members of homicide victims: A qualitative study of their posthomicide experience. *American Journal of Orthopsychiatry, 72*(3), 373–382. DOI:10.1037/0002-9432.72.3.372

Blackburn, M., & El-Deredy, W. (2013). The future is risky: Discounting of delayed and uncertain outcomes. *Behavioural Processes, 94*, 9–19. DOI:10.1016/j.beproc.2012.11.005

Copes, H., Brookman, F., & Brown, A. (2013). Accounting for violations of the convict code. *Deviant Behavior, 34*(10), 841–858. DOI:10.1080/01639625.2013.781444

Crewe, B. (2007). Power, adaptation and resistance in a late-modern men's prison. *British Journal of Criminology, 47*(2), 256–275. DOI:10.1093/bjc/azl044

Crewe, B. (2009). *The prisoner society: Power, adaptation and social life in an English prison*. Oxford: Oxford University Press, Clarendon.

Crewe, B. (2011). Depth, weight, tightness: Revisiting the pains of imprisonment. *Punishment & Society, 13*(5), 509–529. DOI:10.1177/1462474511422172

Crewe, B., Warr, J., Bennett, P., & Smith, A. (2014). The emotional geography of prison life. *Theoretical Criminology, 18*(1), 56–74. DOI:10.1177/1362480613497778

de Vigianni, N. (2007). Unhealthy prisons: Exploring structural determinants of prison health. *Sociology of Health and Illness, 29*(1), 115–135. DOI:10.1111/j.1467-9566.2007.00474.x

Flynn, A., Halsey, M., & Lee, M. (2016). Emblematic violence and aetiological cul-de-sacs: On the discourse of "one-punch" (non)fatalities. *British Journal of Criminology, 56*, 179–195. DOI:10.1093/bjc/azv039

Forst, M., Fagan, J., & Vivona, T. S. (1989). Youths in prisons and training schools: Perceptions and consequences of the treatment-custody dichotomy. *Juvenile and Family Court Journal, 40*(1), 1–15. DOI:10.1111/j.1755-6988.1989.tb00634.x

Garbarino, J. (2000). *Lost boys: Why our sons turn violent and how we can save them*. New York: Anchor Books.

Garbarino, J. (2015). *Listening to killers*. Oakland, CA: University of California Press.

Garbarino, J. (2018). *Miller's children: Why giving teenage killers a second chance matters for all of us*. Oakland, CA: University of California Press.

Giordano, P. C., Cernkovich, S. A., & Rudolph, J. L. (2002). Gender, crime and desistance: Toward a theory of cognitive transformation. *American Journal of Sociology, 107*(4), 990–1064. DOI:10.1086/343191

Glueck, S., & Glueck, E. (1968). *Delinquents and nondelinquents in perspective*. Cambridge, MA: Harvard University Press.

Gottfredson, M. R., & Hirschi, T. (1990). *A general theory of crime*. Stanford, CA: Stanford University Press.

Griffin, D. (2018). *Killing time: Life imprisonment and parole in Ireland*. Cham, Switzerland: Palgrave Macmillan.

Guardian for Children and Young People. (2017). *Looking for balance: A response to the Statutes Amendment (Youths Sentenced as Adults) Bill 2017*. Retrieved from www.gcyp.sa.gov.au/wp-content/uploads/2017/08/GCYP-SUBMISSION-Youth-Sentenced-as-Adults-Bill-2017-29-8-17.pdf

Halsey, M. (2007). On confinement: Resident and inmate perspectives of secure care and imprisonment. *Probation Journal, 54*(4), 338–367. DOI:10.1177/0264550507083535

Halsey, M. (2017). Narrative criminology. In A. Deckert & R. Sarre (Eds.), *The Palgrave handbook of Australian and New Zealand criminology, crime and justice* (pp. 633–647). London: Palgrave.

Halsey, M., & Deegan, S. (2014). "Picking up the pieces": Female significant others in the lives of young (ex) incarcerated males. *Criminology and Criminal Justice*. Retrieved from http://crj.sagepub.com/content/early/2014/03/12/1748895814526725.ref.html. DOI:10.1177/1748895814526725

Halsey, M., & Deegan, S. (2015). *Young offenders: Crime, prison and struggles for desistance*. London: Palgrave Macmillan.

Halsey, M., & Deegan, S. (2017). In search of generativity in prison officer work: Balancing care and control in custodial settings. *The Prison Journal, 97*(1), 52–78. DOI:10.1177/0032885516679380

Hannah-Moffat, K., Maurutto, P., & Turnbull, S. (2009). Negotiated risk: Actuarial illusions and discretion in probation. *Canadian Journal of Law and Society, 24*(3), 391–409. DOI:10.1353/jls.0.0092

Heide, K. M. (1999). *Young killers*. Thousand Oaks, CA: Sage.

Human Rights Watch. (2012). *Against all odds: Prison conditions for youth offenders serving life without parole sentences in the United States*. Retrieved from www.hrw.org/sites/default/files/reports/us0112ForUpload_1.pdf

Juvenile Courts Act 1971 (SA)(Austl.).

Kuanliang, A., Sorensen, J. R., & Cunningham, M. D. (2008). Juvenile inmates in an adult prison system: Rates of disciplinary misconduct and violence. *Criminal Justice and Behavior, 35*(9), 1186–1201. DOI:10.1177/0093854808322744

Lacombe, D. (2008). Consumed with sex: The treatment of sex offenders in risk society. *British Journal of Criminology, 48*(1), 55–74. DOI:10.1093/bjc/azm051

Magill Training Centre "child abuse". (2009, August 31). *ABC News Online*. Retrieved from http://mobile.abc.net.sa/news/2009-08-31/magill-training-centre-child-abuse/1411636

Maruna, S. (2001). *Making good: How ex-convicts reform and rebuild their lives*. Washington, DC: American Psychological Association.

McDermott, K., & King, R. (1988). Mind games: Where the action is in prisons. *British Journal of Criminology, 28*(3), 357–375. DOI:10.1093/oxfordjournals.bjc.a047734

Meijers, J., Harte, J. M., Maynen, G., Cuijpers, P., & Scherder, E. J. A. (2018). Reduced self-control after 3 months of imprisonment: A pilot study. *Frontier Psychology*, *9*(69), 1–7. DOI:10.3389/fpsyg.2018.00069

Miller, T. A. (2000). Surveillance: Gender, privacy, and the sexualisation of power in prison. *GeorgeMason University Civil Rights Law Journal*, *10*(2), 291–356. Retrieved from https://sls.gmu.edu/crlj/

Moffitt, T. (1993). Adolescence-limited and life-course persistent antisocial behaviour: A developmental taxonomy. *Psychological Review*, *100*(4), 674–701. DOI:10.1037/0033- 295X.100.4.674

Polk, K. (1994). *When men kill: Scenarios of masculine violence*. New York, NY: Cambridge University Press.

Ruddell, R., & Gileno, J. (2013). Lifers admitted as juveniles in the Canadian prison population. *Youth Justice*, *13*(3), 234–248. DOI:10.1177/1473225413505386

Russell, S. (2013). A "second look" at lifetime incarceration: Narratives of rehabilitation and Juvenile offenders. *Quinnipiac Law Review*, *31*(3), 489–521. Retrieved from www.quinnipiaclawjournals.com/quinnipiac-law-review.html

Sentencing Act 2017 (SA) (Austl.). Retrieved from www.legislation.sa.gov.au/LZ/C/A/SENTENCING%20ACT%202017/CURRENT/2017.26.AUTH.PDF

Tasca, M., Griffin, M. L., & Rodriguez, N. (2010). The effect of importation and deprivation factors on violent misconduct: An examination of Black and Latino youth in prison. *Youth Violence and Juvenile Justice*, *8*(3), 234–249. DOI:10.1177/1541204010366619

Toch, H. (2010). "I am not now who I used to be then": Risk assessment and the maturation of long-term prison inmates. *The Prison Journal*, *90*(1), 4–11. DOI:10.1177/0032885509356408

Trammell, R. (2012). *Enforcing the convict code: Violence and prison culture*. Boulder, CO: Lynne Rienner Publishers

Unkovic, C. M., & Albini, J. L. (1969). The lifer speaks for himself: An analysis of the assumed homogeneity of life-termers. *Crime and Delinquency*, *15*(1), 156–161. DOI:10.1177/001112876901500114

Wright, R. (2004). Care as the "heart" of prison teaching. *Journal of Correctional Education*, *55*(3), 191–209. Retrieved from www.jstor.org/stable/23292135

Young Offenders Act 1993 (SA) (Austl.). Retrieved from www.legislation.sa.gov.au/LZ/C/A/YOUNG%20OFFENDERS%20ACT%201993/CURRENT/1993.57.AUTH.PDF

7 Going straight . . . or straight back inside?

> When you kill somebody and do all this time in gaol, that [regular] sort of stuff goes out the window – it just does. You can't expect to be normal – you can't. What are people going to say? 'Oh yeah, you're all right.' You know what I mean: 'You've done your time and that.' Nah, very few people are like that in reality. Most people are like, 'Oh jeez, I better be wary of this bloke,' or they're just having as little to do with you as possible.
>
> (Sonny)

In the scholarship of life sentence juveniles, little is understood about the reintegration of these men and women upon their eventual release. What is more, studies that evaluate prisoner re-entry tend to emphasize the risk of reoffending rather than the combination of personal and social factors that impact on recidivism or rule violation (health, housing, relationships, and employment) (Halsey & Deegan, 2015). Of course, juvenile lifers are uniquely placed to contribute to our understanding of how (ex-)prisoners come to interpret and respond to personal and social factors that contribute to what (ex-)prisoners see as success or failure on parole. As is clear from their experiences, achieving a 'survival time' of at least 12 months in the community was highly significant and obliged participants to frequently revise down their goals and expectations around being part of the Australian economy, having conventional relationships, or being accepted back into mainstream society. Realizing that life in the community posed a different set of constraints than life in the prison was frequently a source of consternation and bitterness. At the same time, while many participants were firmly committed to succeeding on parole, they often made some decisions that threatened their future place within society. I will say more about the lead-ups to the breach incidents and the circumstances of the incidents themselves in the course of this chapter. As shall become apparent, when support systems broke down (i.e. when modest attempts to comply no longer worked and a return to custody seemed likely), the most common solution was to engage in further bad decision-making in the hope to undo, neutralize, or outrun the impending breach report. With this is mind, the experiences of those in this chapter speak of incarcerated children, who, as adults, tried with varying levels of success to overcome damage from the past and to 'develop the skills and opportunities needed to interact successfully in the community' (Heide, 1999, p. 235).

Beyond neverland: finding a place in the real world

> I'm glad they did allow [my request for resocialisation] at the Adelaide Pre-release Centre [APC] because I mean, as you saw yourself, I had enough trouble coping with [my release]. It would've been worse if I hadn't had [that time] at the APC . . . [just dealing] with everything at once and wondering whether that person over there is thinking, 'Oh, he used to be a murderer,' or something like that. It's just the little crappy things that all add up.
>
> (Toby)

As noted by Heide (1999, p. 237), '[i]t is unequivocal that society fears the return of young killers to the community. What might be surprising to many is that the young killers also expressed fear about their getting out of prison.' By this, she points to the fear of rejection (from potential employers, prospective partners, free people, and a technologically complex society) as a key anxiety in the lives of life-sentenced youths. This is well demonstrated by the following excerpts:

> I've been in here [so long] and I'm fucking scared about getting out. I know it's going to be hard. . . . Adelaide's a small place: everyone knows everyone. Like *in here*, I'm just a criminal: I'm one of the boys. *Out there*, if they know who I am, then I'm fucking pushed aside: I'll be the outcast again, you know what I mean? It's just I'm scared of that. It's going to be tough to adjust and to get back, settled. . . . I just don't want to get pushed aside and look like the outcast because of my crime and being in gaol.
>
> (Leo)

> I've been pretty steady for three and half, four years, you know. Maybe in the last 12 months or something it's got, it's gone a bit up and down. But I think that's because I'm thinking that I'm getting close to getting out. Maybe I won't get out. Maybe I will get out. What's going to happen when I do get out? Sometimes you can't help but think the worst and that kind of brings you right down.
>
> (Mike)

> You can [use murder for status], like, *in here* you can, but if you get *out there* and try and do something good for yourself, that status is not going to get you nowhere. I mean, the only place it's going to get you – that status – is in a crew, like, a gang: 'Oh fuck, we've got a murderer in here.' You know what I mean? No-one else gives a fuck and they'd probably frown upon it.
>
> (Leo)

In terms of making a good life for themselves, participants' previous 'terms of reference' (i.e. money, cars, thrills and sex) (Garbarino, 2015, p. 149) were quickly identified as inimical to their prospects of success.

> Where I've seen people go wrong is [where] they've done, say, 10 years, and then they get out and they try to fit that 10 years into a month. Like, 'I want to do *that*, I want to do *that*, I want to do *that*.' And that's . . . setting up for failure because you're living too fast again. . . . You're not calm, you're not relaxed, you're not [logical] in your decision-making. . . . You need to just let it go and accept you've lost that [portion of your life]. But, you've got *this* ahead of you and [if] this is what you want to do . . . set yourself a five-year plan and be realistic about it. . . . It will be hard . . . [but] if you try to do it all in a week, how are you going to do that, legitimately?
>
> (Floyd)

> He'll never catch up for lost time. I don't want him to reconnect with his peers because they own their own homes and have families and expensive cars now: the ones he was going to [high school] with. Some of them are buying investment properties, you know. I don't want him to hear all that. Because he can't, [so] it's only going to make him feel bad about himself: it's going to make his present circumstances all the more painful. . . . I just want him to focus on, you know, just humbly: head down and work. And just . . . living with integrity, being a good person, working hard and learning life skills, you know, one small step at a time
>
> (Lorraine, mother)

> [She's] the first person that's paid him attention as a *man*. Yeah, he went in as a child, a young boy, and he's come out as a man so he's grasping at that. And she's paying him a lot of attention as a *man*, yeah. And it's scary. It's scary. . . . He's latched on [to her]. He's latched on to the attention that's being paid to him as a man. But really, I don't think he's matured enough in his mind as a man yet. 'Cause he still, to me, he went in so young and in all those years nothing's turned him into a man, really. I mean, the rape, that hasn't turned him into a man. That's made him revert straight back to being a child.
>
> (Karen, mother)

In fact, most of the participants' comments were in one way or another related to lifers' inexperience navigating even the shallowest of social and financial waters.

> I've taken the proactive approach of saying, 'I want to be shown how to do a tax pack', 'I want to know what a home loan is'. You know, 'I want to know how many points of ID that I need for certain things.' . . . [But] this place refuses to show me or they just don't think like I do. Doesn't mean to say that I'm full of myself, but if you want me to be a responsible person outside of here, give me the reason *to be*. And show us some of the things that normal regular people do. I don't want to be dependent on the dole for the rest of my life.
>
> (Lucy)

And, by all accounts, instantaneous social media connectivity provided fertile ground for all kinds of disasters. The case of Toby (whose experience with an online scammer will be described later in this section) is an example. He was aged 17 when he committed murder, he served nearly 20 years' imprisonment, and he undertook a graduated release from gaol at the age of 36. Just prior to his last release, Toby expressed enthusiasm regarding his apparent progress: day release in the outside community; the ongoing support of his mother; part-time employment; and a positive attitude to a world very different from the one he knew as a teenager:

> I'm scared . . . excited but scared . . . [of] the unknown. It's been so long since I've been amongst any of this and it's just, 'Wow!' . . . When I get out of here it's like, 'Okay, well the last 19 years has not existed. Today starts my new life.' Or you know. I think I said to you once before, 'For all the years that [I've] been standing on the sidelines wishing for right now.' I'll remember that on the 9th of October when I walk out [for good].
>
> (Toby)

Despite his admirable optimism, Toby was also, at that time, plainly struggling with adjustment in the sense contemplated by Heide. Such a conclusion was reinforced by the flurry of text messages I received in the weeks following our interview.

I'm over it.
I wanna go back to Mount Gambier [Prison]. Sorry Simone. At least there I knew who hates me and I don't have to waste time and money on them to find out.
I don't know what else to do.
I'm sorry.
[Me: Hey Toby, what is going on?]
I thought I could handle this but I can't.
Not coping, problems.
I'm sorry.
[Me: What are the problems? I'm sure they are not so bad]
I can't do this.
I have no right to bother you.
I'm sorry.
I can't fix this
[Me: What can't you fix?]
Life
Easier in jail
I wanna go [back]
I've lost

> Everything is so damned crowded and all I want is to be left alone. I can't even go for a walk around the block without mum coming up with some stupid reason to text me. . . . She thinks that she needs to try and make up [for

> lost time] by smothering me but that only makes it worse. How the hell do I cope with this fucked up stupid world? All I want to do right now is go to the Myer Centre [i.e., a high-rise building in Adelaide's CBD] and jump but I can't even do that cause there's too many fucked up do-gooders that think they know what someone who's been alone for 19 years wants. All I want is to be left alone! How hard is that? What do I do? I don't get it and I wish they never released me. Hooray! I'm crying at a bus stop and some stupid girl just stopped and asked if I'm ok. Fuck off!

There were personal losses too. Indeed, life on parole was a steep learning curve for Toby, who made several ill-fated attempts to form romantic connections and gain acceptance from those around him.

> My neighbour . . . moved in next door and I thought she was nice, so I spoke to her. We ended up going for walks and that together. I mentioned one thing once about parole and that was it: she became fascinated again like they seem to. I told her everything and then I got a text from her the next day saying, 'I want to move out because I'm afraid of living next door to you because of what you've done. I'm afraid you're going to hurt me and my daughter,' and I just lost the plot. It's like, 'What the fuck?' I was honest and where does that come from? I'm not going to hurt anybody.' . . . I'd already had so many good reactions, so I trusted her and it went wrong. . . . I can't be honest anymore. I lose everything. I've lost everything.
>
> The biggest problem with being a lifer [is] when you come out of [prison] you don't know how to interact. . . . There's a lot of stuff you [just] don't know. Here's an example. I got an email from someone called 'Gia'. She works [in the city]. Wanted to meet me. She sent me a photo. I thought, 'Yeah she looks pretty cool.' Oh, 'But I need to get your credit card details so that I can realise whether or not you're over 18.' Stupid me put them in there. . . . Shit like that they don't teach you: that you need to experience to learn yourself.

Conflating a Nigerian confidence trickster with a full-blown parole crisis is obviously dangerous territory, but this is what Toby was dealing with on a day-to-day basis. He was not afraid of a structured and disciplined routine; however, sometimes the rigours of being a parolee overwhelmed him. He told me – just as he had described to the Parole Board when he was summonsed on a breach warrant – that one of the biggest challenges of everyday life was how to successfully manage his financial affairs. Earning \$510 dollars a fortnight working (briefly) at a Christian organization dedicated to prisoners and their families, Toby recounted how greatly he valued being able to buy his first car and travel around Adelaide for shopping trips and social engagements. He also attested that these trips provided him with opportunities to experience regular things in life, such as buying a new phone or the latest technical gadget. Evidently, though, Toby did not successfully balance these pursuits against the demands of his parole agreement, which required him to pay $350 a fortnight for room and board to the Pre-release Cottage (at the APC) where he slept at night. I do not, however, regard this as Toby displaying an overt disrespect for his parole, so much as the desire to introduce a degree of normality into his life. Toby's active decision to fall behind in his rent at the APC was, in many ways, a misguided attempt to increase the money available to him for doing other things such as running a household with his new partner and putting fuel in his car. My point here, in line with Halsey (2017, p. 17) and others, is that 'even the best therapeutic work in custodial environments is liable to falter if not matched with concerted efforts to transform the social, economic and cultural milieus to which people return on release'. Of course, I am not suggesting paying room and board to the APC is, of itself, a bad idea. Instead, I would contend that, for those (ex-)prisoners also juggling, say, a private rental agreement, there is a doubling-up of responsibilization that might actually set them on a path towards more harm and more time inside.

Whether the extremely high-interest, short-term credit (i.e. payday loan) Toby took out (to pay off his parole debt) exacerbates or mitigates his financial distress remains to be seen. Toby's mother observed in relation to this:

> He's got no sense of responsibility because everything was always done for him [in prison]. . . . I still pawn [things for him], right up until last week, you know: it's ridiculous. 'Cause he's got no concept of finances. But then again, that's the prison's fault.
>
> (Karen, mother)

I questioned Toby extensively about his reasons for not contacting his parole supervisor when these difficulties first emerged. As with many of the young men in my research, he said it related to feelings of inadequacy, of having already failed: that asking for help or indicating he was not coping would lead to being penalized rather than assisted. Such a conclusion was only reinforced by the knee-jerk punitive response (breach report) that eventuated. In no small measure, Toby's pride was at stake as well. He wanted so badly to succeed on parole and did not wish to admit to feeling out of his depth on occasion. This was particularly so given that his (learned) helplessness (Seligman, 1972) was reinforced on a daily basis:

> I went for a job interview the other day . . . and the interview was completely different. It wasn't a one-on-one. It was just sit around a group and all discuss things and the whole time I was there thinking, 'You've got to be kidding me: every single one of these [applicants] is five to 10 years younger than me and they've done *everything*. This guy's been over in America doing this and this chick's been in charge of some super company and what the hell? I can't even write a resume.' . . . And [the employer] basically asked, he said, 'All right, what I want to do is go around the room: you're going to tell me your name, where you're from, what you've been doing recently, what you've done workwise, what are your interests,' and all this sort of stuff.

So, it was like what you do in school, you know, [when] you've got a new class: it's like, 'Okay kids, introduce yourselves.' That's what it felt like but the other kids were [all] like super intelligent [and] they've been everywhere. . . . I said I'd been working at Second Chances. I didn't really know what else to say after that, so I actually told the truth.

I said, 'Second Chances is a charity that looks after the kids and families of prisoners,' and you could see it, you could just see it: everybody's, 'Whoa!'

Making scenes and flushing keys: the realities of the situation

> You get people going to the [APC], right, people [who] have been locked up for five years and they go, 'Oh jeez, I'm freaking out about bloody going out there and doing this and doing that [in the community]'. Do you know . . . how long *I've* been locked up for?
>
> (Derek)

It is almost inevitable that those who suffer indirectly from homicide will demand that the victim's killer be profoundly punished – if not executed, then separated forever from the rest of us. But reality is not obliging on this score, and all of the individuals in this book must be released at some time from custody. Undoubtedly, there are and will be individuals who are so profoundly damaged as to warrant being classified as psychopaths. Garbarino (2000, p. 26) prefaced this same conclusion by postulating a case of 'pure amorality' when it comes to interpersonal aggression and violence. While these offenders are incredibly rare, it would be wrong to say that society has nothing to worry about when homicide offenders are eventually released. While the literature is unequivocal that very few released homicide offenders (between none and 3.5%) will go on to commit a second homicide (Broadhurst, Maller, Maller, & Bouhours, 2018, p. 399), there is always some risk in parole. And on a basic human level, it is difficult to assess the effect on a person of being returned to society following a decade (or decades) in prison.

Even during the pre-release phase of their sentences, several participants in the current study at times acted impulsively, suggesting to the Parole Board a real risk that they may commit further offences. Lucy went window-shopping en route to her work placement. Will experimented with steroids to boost his confidence. Tyson left a shopping centre pass-out to fraternize with a girlfriend. Again, these were understandable decisions given lifers' limited life experience but they were also, admittedly, careless ones given their knowledge of the likely consequences of such behaviour (cancellation of pre-release and regression to high-security settings). More starkly, there is recent evidence to demonstrate that the rates of *general* reoffending post-homicide range between 50% and 60%, 'with rates of non-violent reoffending usually higher than for violent offending' (Broadhurst et al., 2018, p. 399). Liem, Zahn, and Tichavsky (2014) found that race and being convicted of a financially motivated homicide are the strongest predictors of recidivism. Garbarino (2000, p. 211) noted the case of Jose ('a boy whose seventeenth birthday wish was that he lived to see twenty-five') and how his situation reflects the complexities of release:

> As sweet as he was in the interviews and as sincerely as he insisted that he had learned his lesson, he was back in jail four months after his release. . . . Although Jose completed the program offered by the juvenile detention center where he was housed, he went right back to the world he had come from and soon was back with the same group of drug dealers he associated with before his initial arrest.

Cody and Derek, participants in this study, exemplify this same pattern. With nearly three decades of custodial time between them, it was highly unlikely that either would ever last in the community without considerable social work intervention and support from outside agencies on their release. Derek was at liberty for only five weeks before he was arrested after a spate of robberies he committed with a balaclava, an accomplice, and a sawn-off shotgun. This was 'big crime' (Haigh, 2009, p. 312) and, taken at face value, a significant indicator that Derek had changed little since his arrest for murder some 13 years earlier. I discussed with Derek the circumstances of his most recent offending, and he described a combination of factors as contributing to his demise. The primary one, of course, was his extreme poly-drug abuse, which only served to exacerbate his difficult behavioural and attitudinal presentation, high degree of restlessness, and identification with delinquent peers:

> [When] I was released for the first time . . . I had a full-blown heroin habit. I even had a shot an hour before I walked out of the gaol. . . . My girlfriend at the time, she was heavily into heroin. I was heavily into heroin. We were hitchhiking back to Adelaide once a week with our money . . . and we were buying heroin with it. The girl that we were buying it off of, she introduced me to this bloke who was rather active at the time running around doing whatever and I got involved in a few things with him, which was armed robberies. I was caught and sentenced to a further . . . 24 years with 20 years on the bottom.
>
> (Derek)

It was patently obvious in the way things unravelled between his release and his arrest that there were problems in relation to Derek's rehabilitation, especially when Derek was locked up, but also following release. Academic writing on support people/professionals situated *beyond* custodial environments has approached the parole process in a number of very different ways, ranging from analysing it as a potential means to 'positively influence recidivism rates and desistance from crime' (Halsey & Deegan, 2017, p. 53) to a system 'geared toward policing and capturing the breach, not rewarding and affirming progress' (Halsey & Deegan, 2015, p. 174). Admittedly, in Derek's case, 'progress' appeared to be in seriously short supply. Nevertheless, as with many lifer parolees, his perspective speaks to the important distinction between control and support. Halsey and de Vel-Palumbo (2018, p. 9) have summed up this situation, writing that successful community justice initiatives require actors who 'seek to hear, resolve and/or marginally alleviate the distress in people's lives'. Derek, having tasted heroin in prison and jumping on the bandwagon, reported trying desperately to speak to his caseworker soon after exiting custody in the 1980s. Whether the magnitude of events that followed could have been altered for the better given empathetic counselling does not bear close analysis. The truth is, of course, that Derek – who had been incarcerated at *every* adult correctional institution in South Australia – did not cope *at all* with the pressures of release into the community. He was, like so many of Garbarino's (2018, p. 147) juvenile lifers, 'thoroughly prisonized'. Nevertheless, in the absence of a collective effort for assisting people across successive crisis points, Derek makes a fair point: 'If you don't give people hope and stick with them, shit happens. It does.' He explains further:

> When I got out I was bloody stupid . . . [but] at the time I did cry out for help. . . . I knew I was going downhill and going down quick and I didn't want it to happen. We were living in this town here and I was going back to Adelaide every week to get onto heroin and I said to [my parole officer] one day, 'Please,' I said. 'I've got a major problem here. I need help.'
>
> And she was new, I was her very first lifer parolee, and she went and said to her boss, 'Look, Derek's screaming out for help. What do we do?'
>
> And his response was, 'As long as he signs his card once a week, who cares?' And yeah . . . six weeks after that [I was back] and I've been here ever since.
>
> (Derek)

Cody also came into contact with the law, and frequently that contact was a result of alcohol abuse. Since his first release in 1996, he has been returned to custody on no fewer than five occasions. As distinct from Derek, however, Cody's reincarcerations were not related to major types of offending. Instead, Cody's typical trajectory on release from custody was to get drunk, act in a disorderly manner, and breach his parole conditions. Despite express warnings that he was *not* to consume alcohol, within hours of each release, he did so. Cody's development as an individual with a significant level of intellectual slowness (assessed in the dull to dull-normal range) is helpful in understanding the nature and quality of his acts on parole. For example, eight hours after his first release, Cody was arrested after (drunkenly) making off on a police bicycle. This immature behaviour was tolerated, to some degree, until his later breaches, when the Parole Board started losing patience. Weeks became months and months became years back in prison. Everything, though, came crashing down around Cody when the Governor in Executive Council was given power to veto parole decisions for prisoners serving life in prison. A verbally abusive episode on public transport left him in the order of eight years to sit and contemplate the error of his ways. Like so many (ex-)prisoners, the factors driving Cody's behaviour were complex and required a combination of interventions and support around domestic violence/trauma exposure, substance abuse, mental health, education investment, and employment. Such strategies are often seen as too hard and expensive to meaningfully fund and much harder than the blunt instrument of gaol time. In short, the system was still using inaction to manage these issues away. Cody reflected on and lamented the total custodial time he had served (just short of 30 years):

> Sure I do things and I make bad choices [such] that the end result is the fact that I have breached parole . . . [but] I've been paying for it . . . far too [long] now. Back then, like once your time was up, you were out. But I definitely was a bit naive in the sense that I thought that *once I was out of gaol*, that it would all be over and I definitely had plans of doing this and doing that. But the reality of the whole thing was nothing like it.

Transition, as described by Rossmanith (2013, para. 19), 'is the breezy term used to describe an inmate's re-entry to the outside world'. But as she continues, 'those who invoke it recognise the daily labour that the expression cloaks'. Whether Cody would have been any closer to reintegrating with society *even if* he had been able to comply with his parole conditions – staying off alcohol, living at a designated address, avoiding particular associations, and so on – remains a critical question. To focus on his situation simply as the sum total of his bad choices is to ignore the 'longer and wider view of the social and penal landscape' (Halsey & Deegan, 2015, p. 32). There is a pressing need to remember that 'all choices are made in a particular context, a particular place and time. Who, where, and when you are plays a role in shaping the range of choices open to you' (Garbarino, 2011, p. 158). The extent to which basic human needs (positive relationships, shelter, employment, education, etc.) are often overlooked in custodial and post-custodial 'support' arrangements has been highlighted by several authors (Halsey & Deegan, 2015; McNeill, 2009; Ward & Maruna, 2007). When Cody was released from prison after a long period of institutionalized life, it was always particularly difficult for him to get a job. Like the majority of the cohort, he did not take his education very far and had very little employment since leaving school. Although he had roles in various prison industries, all failed to translate into anything beyond economical labour for the prison estate. Toch (2010, p. 7) has told of this reality in the following terms: 'Sadly, the person who has spent years faithfully stamping licence plates is restricted to practicing his craft if and when he is re-imprisoned – which is usually 6 months after he is released.'

James and Toby encountered similar issues and both remain unemployed three years after their release:

> I got told when I got out that because of my health and my age [i.e., 56 years of age] and everything [else] that I wouldn't find a job, and even the people at Centrelink [i.e., social security] know that. They've given me pension cards and everything . . . even though I'm not [old] enough to go on a pension.
>
> (James)

> I applied for so many [jobs] it's just not funny. . . . I applied for Ingham's [poultry processing] and they said, 'You don't have food handling experience.'
>
> I told my parole officer and she said, 'Well, why didn't you say you worked at the Yatala [Prison] kitchen?'
>
> And it's like, 'Well, *that's* something you don't advertise.' But it's standing there on a conveyor belt throwing chickens at each other. Really, how hard is that?
>
> (Toby)

What is also apparent from interviews with Cody is his ready recourse to flight mode in response to being breached (or the mere threat thereof). When last granted day-release into the community, Cody absconded from his pre-release cottage when confronted with a random breathalyser test. When his prison photograph was circulated widely in the news media, I saw a middle-aged man who was deeply, deeply troubled and for whom, in all likelihood, there was no way out. Cody will kill himself, I thought, as crime-stoppers internet chat rooms were deluged by an outpouring of schadenfreude. Years earlier, Cody's sense of optimism about the future had free fallen as he was left to rue the devastation of a similar setback:

> I used to be a really happy person but in the last few years I feel as if I've really changed. . . . [I'm] just not happy anymore. I used to be like pretty chirpy all the time [but] the last few years, yeah, [I'm] just sad.

Thankfully, Cody did not suicide. Highly agitated and paranoid, he was arrested 24 hours later, sitting out the front of the court precinct, in a dramatic and bizarre cry for help to the State's Parole Board. In past work, I have discussed in detail the way in which the parole officer who decides to consistently overlook or exaggerate a wrongdoing is the one who will bewilder the parolee and make bad situations much worse. In particular – and harking back to an earlier point made about control and support – the result

> is constitutive of what we term the 'fuck it mentality' – a view which stems from parolees' or ex-prisoners' perceptions (often rightly held) that all the good things they had done are about to be entirely discounted by the 'unjust' or overly punitive decision of someone who, in the end, has no real sense of what it is like to have to walk 'in their shoes'.
>
> (Halsey & Deegan, 2015, p. 50)

Remarks by Cody, now aged in his 50s and still in custody three years after the event, demonstrate the way in which 'the blend of bad decision-making mixed with overtly harsh treatment can leave a lasting impression' (Halsey & Deegan, 2015, p. 190). To these were added dozens of similar complaints I had come to expect at such moments:

> [If we] leave gaol with the mentality of 'Oh, if you do anything wrong, you can expect to come back to gaol for maybe 10 years,' . . . I can't see anyone doing the right thing – if they were to do anything wrong – you know what I mean? . . . You'll just want to grab a backpack and take off, go on the run. You don't want to just hang around for something bad.
>
> (Cody)

> I would rather walk out of here in front of like a Mack truck than ask for help. . . . I don't really see the point in asking for help for anything because it just doesn't happen. And their help is, 'Oh, let's just lock him up.'
>
> (Cody)

Derek committed armed robberies. Cody could not pass up a drink, no matter the cost. What their experiences revealed was that both routes were simply alternatives to the same destination, with each man serving more time *after* being released than he had initially served for murder. The weakness of deterrence as a restraining influence on ex-prisoners is writ large here (Bagaric & Alexander, 2012). While their parole status – and/or whether the Board is still invested in the prisoners' futures – is not clear these days, both men have learnt not to over-promise 'around the process of becoming an ex-offender and of leaving that label behind' (Halsey, 2017, p. 638). Their goal each day is only to show an interest in furthering their rehabilitation and to working towards their future release. Derek was pretty clear on that front, fully expecting that next time would be the last time: 'I know if I was ever to stuff up again I'd be taken out the back and a judge would drop the key in the bloody toilet in front of me and flush it' (Derek).

Workers, 'wounded healers', and prisoners of parole: the rest of the story

> 'Civilians' I called yous back then 'cause I was just used to being a prisoner. I almost forget that I'm out sort of thing. Like it's weird, I'll be talking to my friends, talking like I'm still *in*: little things I say and then people look at me and I think to myself, 'Oh, must have been a gaol thing that I said.' More times than not it just felt the same, like I was stuck in time. But I wasn't: a lot has happened, a lot has changed. And I'm sort of seeing all of that stuff now. I suppose I struggle with no routine in my life but I'd rather deal with issues out here than in gaol any day of the week.
>
> (Eddie)

Essentially, as Maruna (2015, p. 320) identified, 'offender rehabilitation research is notorious for its pessimism and the specter of "nothing works" is never far away in the difficult efforts to help repair highly damaged lives'. As far as the current project is concerned, a fatalistic outlook was, at various points, a view widely shared: 'I'm opting not to have children. . . . And it's not that I *don't* want them: it's just simply [that] my life is too majorly fucked up to bring a child into it' (Lucy). But this is not a complete picture of the impact that juvenile lifers can have as employees, neighbours, role models, and, more importantly, as human beings. Recall that Eddie was 16 when he chose to accompany a group of youths to a sports club in Adelaide's western suburbs where a confrontational encounter took a sudden and lethal turn. Prosecuted under extended joint enterprise, it has to be said that Eddie, along with his supporters, was always sceptical of his arrest and conviction for murder:

> I went to the police station and handed myself in. The other thing I will never forget is when they formally charged me with *murder*. And I was confused. I was speechless. I was like, 'Man, these dudes have it all fucking wrong.'
>
> (Eddie)

> It pains me to think that someone who was at an incident, who didn't commit the actual crime, is charged with that crime and serves the time when they actually didn't do that. I know that's the law; I think it's wrong.
>
> (Shane, employer)

A related issue was Eddie's complete disavowal that he should be judged on a single action – or *inaction* – that would determine his legacy. At the same time, in all of his interviews, Eddie possessed several psychological strengths, including hope, gratitude, and spirituality (Guse & Hudson, 2014). As an Indigenous man from South Australia's Ngarrindjeri nation, he strongly identifies with and is proud of his culture. He made the most of whatever opportunities were available to him to further connect with his culture whilst incarcerated and was highly respected by other prisoners, particularly those of Indigenous heritage. In a mini-documentary for NITV (SBS), Eddie presented his story as a well-adjusted, mature, hardworking Indigenous man who was recently granted a second chance at life and is thriving. This, he hoped, would send an important message to other young people struggling to break the cycle of poverty, crime, and incarceration:

> I felt, 'I'm having an impact on their life,' and yeah, they muck up but they're good kids, man. Positive role model, yeah, I'll put my hand up, I'll be that for them. . . . I might as well try to make a change while I'm here. Not a big one, so long as it's a couple of people.

The principle of the 'wounded healer' upon which Eddie's motivations were based reflects 'the notion that people who have faced and overcome adversity might have special sensitivities and skills in helping others experiencing the same adversity' (Whyte, 2000, p. 1). In Guse and Hudson's (2014) exploration of re-entry and desistance, such a sense of post-traumatic growth was evident in the narratives of ex-offenders who had managed to successfully negotiate post-release life in South Africa. When asked, for the documentary, about his plans for the future, Eddie had this to say:

> I made a promise to myself that no matter how long I get, I'll still remain myself: don't be bitter, don't be angry. It's funny, I did grow up in there [i.e., prison], you know, but you come out, you make it right. And, at the end of the day, I can still smile and show them that I'm still me, yeah. I'd like to think that I've made it count as best as I can. I just hope that in the future I can have my own little family, um, well I've already got my car. Probably just [buy] a house and keep my job. That's probably about it. If I can influence people, for the better, yeah, I'd be pretty content with that, eh.
>
> (NITV Television, 2019)

For two and a half years, Eddie has worked full-time at a civil contracting and building maintenance company based in Adelaide. He was recently promoted to the demolition crew and is working towards securing a dogman job (crane operating and rigging) in the near future. It was the routines and attitudes required of the workplace that had a special draw for Eddie, who had often struggled without purposefulness in his life: 'If you have something to do and you know what you're doing – something constant – [it helps].' In recognition of these very circumstances, sociologist Wilson (1996) asks us to look squarely at the devastating effects that joblessness has had in America's inner cities:

> Work is not simply a way to make a living and support one's family. It also constitutes a framework for daily behavior and patterns of interaction because it imposes disciplines and regularities. Thus, in the absence of regular employment, a person lacks not only a place in which to work and the receipt of regular income but also a coherent organization of the present – that is, a system of concrete expectations and goals. Regular employment provides the anchor for the spatial and temporal aspects of daily life. It determines where you are going to be and when you are going to be there. In the absence of regular employment, life, including family life, becomes less coherent.
>
> (p. 73)

The company Eddie works for, which is Indigenous-owned, managed, and controlled, is one of the largest private sector employers of Indigenous personnel in Australia, exceeding 90% across all aspects of their business (Intract Indigenous Contractors, 2019). General Manager, Shane, a proud Yorta Yorta man, has devoted a large portion of his working life sharing his industry experience and working with Indigenous people in his local community and across all states and territories of Australia. Amid the intense focus on the over-imprisonment of Aboriginal and Torres Strait Islanders, Shane has worked with many men post-release and says that the *right* kind of assistance for those trying to change is lacking under current programmes and policies:

> Doing what I'm doing now with these guys is putting runs on the board for me to approach government, to approach Corrections, to approach the

> judicial system and say to them, 'Look, there's better ways of helping these people transition out of prison.'

Shane was among those who indicated that, despite outward appearances, Eddie's reintegration was – and *is* – anything but an overnight success:

> When he first came to work for us, it was an adjustment. . . . It was a massive step for Edward and I didn't know how he'd cope with it. . . . It's all the simple stuff that [he's] still not knowing and [hasn't] grown up with yet.

At times, in fact, Eddie took liberties that, realistically speaking, could have resulted in his sacking. For example, Shane was perplexed when Eddie's perfect work attendance during pre-release waned when he was eventually granted full parole. As Eddie explained, the original motivation for, and attraction to work, was to escape from the boredom and monotony of prison life. When it became an option – weighted against friends, family, and the need for autonomy and space – working was tantamount to being in lockup again:

> On pre-release, it didn't matter if I was sick, tired – whatever the case – it didn't mean nothing when you have the chance to get up and leave the gaol for the day; if I have it, I'm taking it. It's funny, *now I'm out*, yeah, it's like a choice. I do feel obligated to work, but now I work to live – for money – whereas before, the money wasn't a factor 'cause [in the prison] I couldn't even spend it. I just loved being out for the day.
>
> (Eddie)

By virtue of their incarceration experiences, it is not surprising that many young lifers come to resent others' authority when it is (continually) asserted over them. From interviews, there emerged a weariness 'borne through the application of rules to bodies' (Halsey, 2006, p. 153). In the work yard beyond the prison, Eddie felt himself highly visible and vulnerable. From an Indigenous perspective, it was 'shame job'[1] when colleagues knew his entire backstory while remaining virtual strangers to him. In short, Eddie was sick of being Aidos.[2] He wanted to *win* for once.

> What I'll say with Shane and that, yeah, like I thank him. I take my hat off to him for giving me a job but in all honesty, like fucking anyone could have given me a job. You know what I mean? I'm not obligated to this place or anywhere. I'm not, and like other people say, 'Oh, well, at least you've *got* a job.' Like, from where I was at the pre-release centre, I wasn't the only one in the gaol that had a job, so it's not that fucking great. I don't know: maybe sometimes people feel like surprised by my response to that. Sometimes it's like well, sometimes I feel like I don't want to be humble anymore, like some days. Do you know what I mean? 'Cause it's like, well, where does it get you?
>
> (Eddie)

Not far, according to employer Shane, when expectations of parolees vary so drastically from those of regular employees. He spoke extensively about an episode that occurred as Eddie, bedridden (in the prison) with illness, failed to report for work as part of his pre-release programme. A swift (over-)reaction to an appropriate use of sick leave threatened to become a major incident. As Shane explained, while coming down hard on (ex-)prisoners was a long-standing correctional tradition, it rarely served a constructive purpose, instead reinforcing ideas of opposition and fatalism that stood in the way of effecting change through persuasion:

> One morning Eddie didn't show up for work. I was a little concerned as [he] had been on time *every* working day for 10 months. . . . [S]o I rang the number I was given to call if there was a problem. . . . When they answered, they seemed shocked and agitated and not impressed with my questioning of where Eddie was and was he okay. . . . [Then they] rang back later on to say that Eddie was sick and wouldn't be in. The next day I caught up with him at start time to make sure he was at work and that he was okay. He was quite reserved and a little withdrawn and when I asked what was wrong, he went on to explain that he was summonsed to the [manager's] office after my call while he was still in bed and feeling very sick. Eddie didn't move straight away, as he could barely sit up, [so] she kept screaming at him [punctuated with an expletive] over the intercom to get to her office immediately. When he eventually arrived at her office, she went on a tirade about 'he will never make it on the outside', that 'he was letting everyone down', that 'he won't get parole' and more. Eddie took a beating over this psychologically and it seemed to push his confidence right back to where it was [when he first came to us]. After that, I promised Eddie that I would *never* ring them again if he did not show for work. . . . Guys like [him] are testament to what can be achieved . . . in a friendly, supportive environment, not [when they're] spoken to worse than dogs, having their self-esteem stood on.

Eddie's ability to grow and move forward in his career was met with other obstacles. For example, the conditions of his release have, until recently, precluded him from possessing a mobile phone or having access to a work vehicle. Thus, he has been unable to attend the training courses required for working on team site jobs, confining him to general yardman duties, something he performed but wholly detests. Work issues aside, a designated parole condition not to consume alcohol or attend licensed premises gave Eddie further pause to consider how 'the experience of "going straight" can be painful and lead to limited lives' (Nugent & Schinkel, 2016, p. 569). As Halsey (2010, p. 550) argues in relation to this:

> Whether one speaks of the capacity to have a drink with one's friends or the ability to legally drive to or from work, these are more than just minor inconveniences in peoples' lives. Rather, they present to parolees as further reminders of the fact that they are outsiders to mainstream society and that

> the path (back) to becoming an insider is long, frustrating and sometimes downright impossible to contemplate let alone endure.

In no small way, non-attendance at the annual staff Christmas party was the least of Eddie's worries:

> I feel out of place. Say I meet a girl, I can't openly go and take her to a restaurant 'cause that's a licensed premises; I need permission for that. The other week I needed permission to go and sleep at my sister's house and that was almost a problem. And they expect of me to act as a normal member of society, right, but all of these restrictions and stuff is anything but normal. So how am I going to act normal if I can't . . . *live normal?*
>
> I tried to get permission to go to my sister's [house]. . . . And I knew that my brother-in-law (like her partner) like he was a bit of a little shit when he was younger [i.e., 10–15 years ago] but he's never been to prison. But anyways, I just thought, 'They don't have to know that he lives there, so whatever. I'll just tell them it's my sister and her kids.' And yeah, she [the parole officer] typed the address in – my sister's address – and she goes, 'Oh. Who's Terence Michael?'
>
> And I said, 'That's my sister's partner.'
>
> And she goes, 'Oh, there might be a problem 'cause he has a [police] record. He's an offender.'
>
> And I was like, 'Yeah. And?'
>
> And she goes, 'Well that might be seen as a problem that you're going there to that address where he is.'
>
> And then I said to her, I said, 'Why? Just because there's two "offenders" there, what, we're going to meet up and *offend*? Like we can't just be normal and do family things?' . . . Straight out [we] got judged.

Eddie's point was not that he wanted to consume alcohol and/or to associate with active criminals but rather to demonstrate that 'compliance [with one's parole] is not the same thing as (re)integration – that is, becoming a fully functioning and participating citizen' (Halsey & Deegan, 2015, p. 3). In light of the staggering over-representation of Aboriginal and Torres Strait Islander Australians in prison and youth detention,[3] it was almost inevitable that several members of Eddie's inner circle *would* have a police record. For Eddie's part, the key implication of the exchange with his parole officer was to confirm suspicion that 'that's probably all I'll [ever] be to them: just an offender. . . . But it's like, whatever. They're not – they're not my friends. I only show them like the part of me what they need to know, like that's about it' (Eddie).

Even Cody, for all his difficulties associated with sobriety, touched on his belief that parolees 'so often get caught up in a bizarre world of checks and balances that the main goal of reintegration recedes from view' (Halsey & Deegan, 2015, p. 198). As mentioned, Cody's attempts to escape the shadow of his lifer status have generally come to naught:

> The Parole Board or your parole officer, they try to tell you, 'Look, it's up to you to move on with your life, put all that gaol behind you even though we want you to come in here and piss in front of two grown adults every week: that's normal. We want you to take time off of work because we want you to come in early this week; don't worry about next week [yet].' All right. Then next week come by: 'We want you to come in at 10.45 but don't worry about your job.' Because they first tell you, 'Oh, your job's very important and we can work around that.' Then they'll say, 'No, parole's more important,' and you can't argue with that. . . . They want you to have a normal sort of life but with your parole conditions and the way that SAPOL now has a lot more input with everything that you do [it's tough].
>
> (Cody)

There is one further element undermining Eddie's reintegration process. The link between entrenched disadvantage, reincarceration, and indigeneity is not something that emerges only as the European system of parole and conditional release develops; it is right there, in the context of the law and the appropriate use of discretion by various enforcement personnel. The following extended excerpt captures the importance of such:

> Me and my two brother boys . . . were standing right out the front . . . around my car, yarning. . . . We started talking about 9 [pm] 'cause we just come back from the movies and then, yeah, and we just got into deep conversation for like an hour. It did cross my mind. I said, 'It's like 9.30,' but I'm out the front, I'm still *home* . . . so we kept yarning. And shortly after that, yeah, a police car pulled up. And then instantly I was like, fucking, I wasn't nervous, I was just more like, well, they're pulling up for something. Are they going to try and get me for something? Honestly that's what I thought. . . .
>
> So we're looking at each other . . . and then they're like, 'Oh so, what are you boys' names? Do yous live here?'
>
> And I'm like, '*I* live here.'
>
> They asked me for my name. I gave my name.
>
> And they said, 'Do you have any [parole] conditions?'
>
> I said, 'Oh, only just a curfew till 9.'
>
> And he checked it and the one in the passenger seat, he goes, 'Oh well, you better get behind your fence.'
>
> I said, 'Excuse me, Chief?'
>
> And he goes, 'Oh, you better get behind your fence. You're out of bounds.'
>
> And I was like, 'Sorry, Chief, I'm not trying to argue or whatever, but with respect, I'm pretty sure I'm safe here. I'm at the front of my house.'
>
> And he goes, 'No. *You're fucking not!*'
>
> I was like, 'Well, again, I'm not trying to argue but when I was on Home D, I could be across the road and still be in-bounds. So I'm on curfew . . . [but] if this was a check, right here, right now, from where I am right now, I can present to the front of my door and give you a spot check.'

> And he's just like, 'Stop fucking talking and get behind your front gate *now*.'
>
> And I looked at my brothers and they're just like, pissed off, you know what I mean? And I was like, 'Wow.' And in my head I was like, I don't know, like, what the rule is so I'm like, well, I'm just going off what I think is reasonable but, I don't know, I could have been wrong, you know what I mean . . . [but] I don't want them to talk shit to me. I'm not the type to try and prove a point or whatever, like to be right all the time. I don't really care. The only thing I care and thought, 'Well, that was reasonable for me to be there, I wasn't doing anything wrong. I co-operated. I could have lied. I gave them my name.' And yeah, I thought, 'Him saying that, like he could have been reasonable, like, and said, "All right. But go on [inside]."' Not just [demanding] me to get behind my gate. . . . So yeah, instead of saying, 'Well fuck you, cunt, you dog, scumbag,' I just tried to hit him back [with the facts] and stand my ground, you know, and just defend myself but with words and sort of like, you know, know what I'm talking about.
>
> (Eddie)

Was this a breach of curfew? Eddie never quite got his answer, but that's no discredit to him. The role that community corrections officers play in terms of turning such situations around was evidenced by the perceptions of all the parolees in my research. What Eddie needed was culturally relevant support – actual advocacy – at a time when he was most vulnerable. Instead, casual racism took up where hard power stepped off. And this, as he explained, was a fundamental part of what it means to be Eddie:

> That happened on the Wednesday night and then I seen [my parole officer] the Thursday arvo and she goes, 'Anything interesting happen?' Like she asks me every week.
>
> And I didn't *have* to tell her but I felt I did, just so I could know what to say next time. So I said, 'Something did happen last night,' and I explained it to her, like what I said before. And I said, 'Well what do I say?'
>
> And she goes, 'Well, *technically*, you were in the right . . . like if they did do a curfew check, [you were] in a reasonable spot to present to them.' And then she goes, 'But you have to sort of see it from their view.'
>
> And I was like, 'What do you mean? Like can you explain, please?'
>
> And she goes, 'Oh well, like three young Indigenous men.'
>
> I said, 'Yeah, but we're dressed nice.'
>
> She's goes, 'Oh yeah, but you're standing around an expensive car.'
>
> And I was like, 'Yeah but that's mine: I own that. We own our clothes. We all work.'
>
> And she goes, 'Oh yeah but, you know, they're probably like, stereotypical.'
>
> And I was like, 'Wow. Like, fuck.'
>
> And then later she was going on and she said, 'Even though I know that yous aren't like that, that's how the police see it rah rah rah.' . . . And she's like, 'You have a point and it's sad, but it is what it is.'
>
> And I was like, 'Fuck. That's what we – *what I* – have to live with. Not you.'

In sum

That Eddie could not escape the shadow of his prison origins was not a failing on his part. None of the juveniles in this book could, and it is a testament to how encompassing, for a whole cohort, serving a lifetime on parole really is. Through account after account from participants, the role of fatalism in enduring parole was found:

> [They're] tying a noose around our neck, you know what I mean? We're on the pedestal and [they're] tying a noose around our neck: one slip up and we're gone: . . . we're back in; we're not going back out. Even a speeding fine I reckon will almost kill your parole.
>
> (Ben)

> I fucked up but I was 16. I haven't even fucking lived yet . . . and now I'm supposed to spend the rest of my life not living? Yeah, I'm outside but I can't even go to a fucking restaurant or anything like that: I have to ask them and see if they approve it. Can't go on a holiday or nothing.
>
> (Leo)

> I'm already used to being in gaol so that's not a problem . . . if I do six years, eight years, 10 years, you know? But, the 'life' sentence is what hurts . . . because once I get out of gaol, I don't really have a future, you know? My future is signing in at Corrections every week. . . . If I have kids and . . . my kids turn 18, I can't have a beer with [them] you know? Or I can't go to the soccer or the footy or stuff 'cause they serve alcohol [there]. All that crap. I can't do any of that, you know? And not being able to do that for the rest of your life, you kind of just have to live as a hermit.
>
> (Mike)

> Having to hide things from the authorities – whether it's the Parole Board or the police or the judge. Having to hide things rather than if you can be open and honest and say, 'Listen, I need help,' or 'I'm feeling like I'm powerless and I can't do anything.' [Parolees] can't actually go and say these things. They have to hide it and then it builds up like a pressure cooker and then they do something really silly and then they're back to square one. And then [the authorities] say, 'See. We told you so. *That's why you don't let them out.*'
>
> (Floyd)

I strongly agree with Garbarino's impression that 'the ordinariness of their [juvenile homicide offenders'] aspirations and, sometimes, their goodwill, stand alongside the fact that they have taken a human life in a shooting or a brutal knife attack or beating' (2015, p. 257). But the participant earlier statements reflect a crucial problem. Should, as a matter of principle, *all* juvenile lifers be subject to a lifetime on parole? *Especially* where

> their behaviour in the murder appears to be linked to the kind of impulsive and stupid behaviour often demonstrated by adolescents . . . [and] not

> necessarily [indicative] of . . . immutable and deeply ingrained . . . violent and antisocial thinking.
>
> (Garbarino, 2018, p. 35)

Especially given 'a life sentence prisoner committed to prison today can expect to serve a number of years more than his [sic] counterparts committed in the preceding years and substantially longer than those committed a decade ago' (Griffin, 2018, p. 225)? Naturally, the idea of making offenders permanently answerable to the State is very attractive for governments and presumably for many members of the community, as it fits snugly within a broader criminal justice ideology of 'getting tough' on crime, including making the offender 'pay'. As Derek's and Cody's experiences illustrate, juvenile lifers who manage to free themselves from a highly dysfunctional past can be counted on one hand, with fingers to spare. Slowly carving out a modest existence, Toby and James appear to fit somewhere within this category. And then there is Eddie. Whereas 'it is the length of time served in prison that captures the interest of most observers' (Griffin, 2018, pp. 223–224), Eddie reminds us of the truth of Halsey's words:

> In no small way, young [people] subject to [significant] periods of incarceration carry this transgressional sense of self with them because custody confirms – in the most visceral of ways – that they *are* offenders first and foremost and only secondarily (and incidentally) people dealt a rough hand or start to life, or who made bad 'choices' at 'critical' moments, or who could indeed 'make good' given half a chance (given the kinds of support desired by each young person).
>
> (2007, p. 362)

Eddie's complaints turn on norms that are widely shared. His objection is not just about the *length* of time juveniles are liable to serve in prison but how the treatment of (ex-)prisoners in pre- and post-release settings 'has direct repercussions for their own and other people's lives' (Halsey & Deegan, 2017, p. 53). Another one of life's little parallels.

Notes

1 Investigations into Indigenous communication and well-being demonstrate the way in which 'Aboriginal communication often includes use of English words with an altered meaning. . . . Shame has an altered meaning to describe stigma and embarrassment associated with gaining attention through certain behaviours or actions' (Victorian Aboriginal Community Controlled Health Organisation, 2014, p. 8). A *shame job* is a widely used Australian Aboriginal English term to describe 'an event which causes a person shame or embarrassment' (Mental Health First Aid Australia, 2014, p. 2) and can occur 'when a person is singled out or in a circumstance that directly targets a person's dignity' (Mental Health First Aid Australia, 2014, p. 2).

2 Aidos: The Greek Goddess of shame, modesty, respect, and humility. As a quality, 'it is the emotion which focuses on actions and states of affairs which are 'ugly', unseemly, or which are said to excite others' indignation (*nemesis*); in this sense it is normally

translated 'shame'. The range of these categories is wide: it includes personal failure, especially in battle, but also failures in one's obligations to others' (Cairns, 2011, p. 30).

3 In 2018, Aboriginal and Torres Strait Islander people made up just 2% of the Australian adult population and 7% of the general youth population. For the same period, they comprised more than one quarter (27%) of the national adult prison population and over one half (54%) of those in youth detention. (Russell & Cunneen, 2018).

References

Bagaric, M., & Alexander, R. (2012). The capacity of criminal sanctions to shape the behavior of offenders: Specific deterrence doesn't work, rehabilitation might and the implications for sentencing. *Criminal Law Journal, 36*(3), 159–172.

Broadhurst, R., Maller, R., Maller, M., & Bouhours, B. (2018). The recidivism of homicide offenders in Western Australia. *Australian and New Zealand Journal of Criminology, 51*(3), 395–411. DOI:10.1177/0004865817722393

Cairns, D. (2011). Honour and shame: Modern controversies and ancient values. *Critical Quarterly, 53*(1), 23–41. DOI:10.1111/j.1467-8705.2011.01974.x

Garbarino, J. (2000). *Lost boys: Why our sons turn violent and how we can save them.* New York: Anchor Books.

Garbarino, J. (2011). Understanding criminal "choices" in context. *American Journal of Orthopsychiatry, 81*(2), 157–161. DOI:10.1111/j.1939-0025.2011.01083.x

Garbarino, J. (2015). *Listening to killers*. Oakland, CA: University of California Press.

Garbarino, J. (2018). *Miller's children: Why giving teenage killers a second chance matters for all of us*. Oakland, CA: University of California Press.

Griffin, D. (2018). *Killing time: Life imprisonment and parole in Ireland.* Cham, Switzerland: Palgrave Macmillan.

Guse, T., & Hudson, D. (2014). Psychological strengths and posttraumatic growth in the successful reintegration of South African ex-offenders. *International Journal of Offender Therapy and Comparative Criminology, 58*(12), 1449–1465. DOI:10.1177/0306624X13502299

Haigh, Y. (2009). Desistance from crime: Reflections on the transitional experiences of young people with a history of offending. *Journal of Youth Studies, 12*(3), 307–322. DOI:10.1080/13676260902775077

Halsey, M. (2006). Negotiating conditional release: Juvenile narratives of repeat incarceration. *Punishment and Society, 8*(2), 147–181. DOI:10.1177/1462474506062102

Halsey, M. (2007). On confinement: Resident and inmate perspectives of secure care and imprisonment. *Probation Journal, 54*(4), 338–367. DOI:10.1177/0264550507083535

Halsey, M. (2010). Imprisonment and prisoner re-entry in Australia. *Dialectical Anthropology, 34*(4), 545–554. DOI:10.1007/s10624-010-9173-y

Halsey, M. (2017). Narrative criminology. In A. Deckert & R. Sarre (Eds.), *The Palgrave handbook of Australian and New Zealand criminology, crime and justice* (pp. 633–647). London: Palgrave.

Halsey, M., & Deegan, S. (2015). *Young offenders: Crime, prison and struggles for desistance*. London: Palgrave Macmillan.

Halsey, M., & Deegan, S. (2017). In search of generativity in prison officer work: Balancing care and control in custodial settings. *The Prison Journal, 97*(1), 52–78. DOI:10.1177/0032885516679380

Halsey, M., & de Vel-Palumbo, M. (2018). Courts as empathic spaces: Reflections on the Melbourne neighbourhood justice centre. *Griffith Law Review*, 1–20. DOI:10.1080/10383441.2018.1500081

Heide, K. M. (1999). *Young killers*. Thousand Oaks, CA: Sage.

Intract Indigenous Contractors. (2019). *About Intract: The Intract vision*. Retrieved from www.intract.com.au/about-intract/

Liem, M., Zahn, M., & Tichavsky, L. (2014). Criminal recidivism among homicide offenders. *Journal of Interpersonal Violence, 29*(4), 2630–2651. DOI:10.1177/0886260513517302

Maruna, S. (2015). Qualitative research, theory development, and evidence-based corrections: Can success stories be "evidence"? In J. Miller & W. R. Palacios (Eds.), *Qualitative research criminology: Advances in criminological theory* (pp. 311–338). New Brunswick, NJ: Transaction Publishers.

McNeill, F. (2009). What works and what's just? *European Journal of Probation, 1*(1), 21–40. DOI:10.1177/206622030900100103

Mental Health First Aid Australia. (2014). *Communicating with an Aboriginal or Torres Strait Islander adolescent: Guidelines for being culturally appropriate when providing mental health first aid*. Retrieved from https://mhfa.com.au/sites/default/files/Aboriginal-Adolecent-Communication-Guidelines-2016.pdf

NITV Television. (Producer) (2019, January 19). *Our stories: Stuck in time* [Television series episode]. Retrieved from www.sbs.com.au/ondemand/video/1409268803943/our-stories-stuck-in-time

Nugent, B., & Schinkel, M. (2016). The pains of desistance. *Criminology and Criminal Justice, 16*(5), 568–584. DOI:10.1177/1748895816634812

Rossmanith, K. (2013, October). The release plan: What is life on parole like? *The Monthly*, 30–37. Retrieved from www.themonthly.com.au/issue/2013/october/1380549600/kate-rossmanith/out-parole

Russell, S., & Cunneen, C. (2018, December 11). As Indigenous incarceration rates keep rising, justice reinvestment offers a solution. *The Conversation*. Retrieved from https://theconversation.com/as-indigenous-incarceration-rates-keep-rising-justice-reinvestment-offers-a-solution-107610

Seligman, M. E. P. (1972). Learned helplessness. *Annual Review of Medicine, 23*(1), 407–412. DOI:10.1146/annurev.me.23.020172.002203

Toch, H. (2010). "I am not now who I used to be then": Risk assessment and the maturation of long-term prison inmates. *The Prison Journal, 90*(1), 4–11. DOI:10.1177/0032885509356408

Victorian Aboriginal Community Controlled Health Organisation (VACCHO). (2014). *Koorified: Aboriginal communication and well-being*. Fitzroy, Victoria: Adams, K (Ed.). Retrieved from http://www.vaccho.org.au/vcwp/wp-content/uploads/2011/03/Koorified-Aboriginal-Communication-and-Well_Being.pdf

Ward, T., & Maruna, S. (2007). *Rehabilitation: Beyond the risk paradigm*. London: Routledge.

Whyte, W. (2000). The history of recovered people as wounded healers: I: From Native America to the rise of the modern alcoholism movement. *Alcoholism Treatment Quarterly, 18*(1), 1–23. DOI:10.1300/J020v18n01_01

Wilson, W. J. (1996). *When work disappears: The world of the new urban poor*. New York: Alfred Knopf.

Concluding remarks

The Australian courts routinely talk about trends in offending and about young people committing certain types of offences. However, it is not surprising that I have been unable to find any other study dealing with children sentenced for murder under Australian legislation. It is such a rare offence. Notwithstanding that, the crimes in this book are unquestionably grave and extremely violent; some were committed in decisive, short-lived episodes of rage, while others constitute the most horrendous of murders, involving calculated intent over a number of hours. All have attracted a great deal of publicity. Consequently, in South Australia at least, considerations of rehabilitation normally applicable to young offenders (*Young Offenders Act* SA, 1993) give way to the protection of the community, to community revulsion at such shocking crimes, and to the deterrent effect any proposed sanction may have on other youths (see the *Statutes Amendment [Youths Sentenced as Adults] Act* 2017). This book is about the 18 men and one woman sentenced to life imprisonment for crimes committed before their 18th birthdays. These are the voices of the juveniles as they are today, in some cases more than 20 years after the offenders were convicted of murder.

There are three features, it seems to me, that stand out in these case studies. The first is the circumstances of the murders themselves. When a person kills, an outraged public, quite reasonably, will ask what the motive was, and I suggest it is only explicable in the following terms. At times, making sense of murder is a straightforward exercise, with no dispute as to why offenders were at the scene and the nature and extent of their involvement and intentions. On the other hand, as is often the case in criminal trials, we may never know the truth about what exactly underscored these events; we can only look at the facts. Whereas Aaron became fixated on the idea of taking the victim's life, all of the other killings in this book resulted 'from events which initially were about something else' (Polk, 1994, p. 93). Indeed, I have drawn heavily on Polk's (1994) schema for classifying the major patterns whereby people take the lives of others: *confrontational homicide*; *homicide in the course of other crime*; and *homicide as a form of conflict resolution*. In keeping with their age, none of the participants in the current study was living with a de facto partner, much less being in a serious relationship, at the time of the murder. As such, Polk's fourth scenario, *homicide arising out of a sexual relationship*, was a theme notably absent from the data. Of course, as

Polk himself correctly identifies, 'there will be no single theory which accounts for the exceptional diversity of homicides' (1994, p. 211).

Just as there is fluidity about the social dealings of adolescents in general, an adolescent's involvement in a homicide often straddles multiple categories. By all accounts, a side order of an 'all-in brawl' was always a distinct possibility – if not a probability – when groups of (antisocial) young people converged (for a variety of reasons) in time and place. In respect of the current study, the only bearing that motive might have on a juvenile's state of mind would be that if it was a revenge killing or even a robbery or jealousy at, say, having a girlfriend/boyfriend taken away, that might speak to real anger and more an intent to kill than does the confrontational scenario that so often confronts us here (see Chapter 3). These are the cases that revolve around groups of teenagers who were minded to enter an affray with another group and to assault members of that group. Participants described instantly chaotic events with altercations between individuals and small groups within the context of the broader attack. At some point, the principal offender came across the victim and inflicted a single stab wound. As Marcus described, to try and diffuse the situation would have been futile:

> The expectation [of the prosecution] is, 'Oh well, you've got to pull yourself together and fucking make a decision whether you're part of it or you're not or what are you doing?' You know what I mean? But how can you in a situation like that? . . . You've got close to 30 people, [or] over 30 people, running around on a bloody football oval chasing each other and things like that, you know? In that environment – and its seconds – you know what I mean, you're not thinking about anything but . . . feeling vulnerable.
>
> (Marcus)

This passage is important because it denotes the fact that some young people allowed themselves to get involved in a confrontation out of a sense of bravado but were quickly out of their depth and were indeed in real physical danger. It is difficult to imagine how a 15 or 16 year old copes with the impossible situation some participants found themselves in – especially when, in preparing to attend the scene, they never once turned their mind to the possibility that one of their number might use a weapon to kill or seriously hurt someone. On this count, none of the young people spoke in consistently clear terms about what they were *thinking* as much as what they were *feeling* when giving an account of their movements immediately before or after the death had occurred:

> I was unsure of [the situation] with the victim and his friends and it created that fear inside me. . . . If I was confident, I wouldn't have done that to him. . . . But I wasn't confident. I was scared. I had everything going on in my head.
>
> (Tyson)

These hooliganesque events that frequently occur without any sensible or proper motive, according to the material available to us (i.e. 'fighting over trivial things' [Griffiths et al., 2011, p. 61]), are typically reported in the media as 'senseless' acts of violence. Admittedly, 'it is hard to see how these acts are rational in the conventional use of the term. The gains rarely make sense in terms of the harms to the victim and the consequences to the offender' (Bennett & Brookman, 2008, p. 171). It is tempting, at first blush, to put this sudden violence down to groups of undercontrolled young people simply losing the plot. But as Bennett and Brookman (2008) describe, violent street crime is often 'not explained in instrumental terms, but in terms of the buzz or excitement that it generated' (p. 174). A *cultural perspective*, as they observe, denotes how 'acts of violence that appear meaningless or gratuitous might be understood when viewed with respect to the values of the street. These include achieving status among peers, punishing disrespect, managing masculinity, and inflicting informal justice' (Bennett & Brookman, 2008, p. 172). Whether the crime was done in panic and/or out of fear of getting caught at the scene is, of course, another matter. Some murders committed by teenagers bear all the hallmarks of something having gone terribly wrong. As seen in Chapter 4, the actions of Ben and Henry are atypical of individuals with a history of prosocial, non-violent behaviour. At the same time, it is quite possible for juveniles to 'play the role of both victim and offender' (Polk, 1994, p. 58) in incidents that turn lethal. The respective cases of Floyd and Will speak volumes about that. These killings were not pre-planned; indeed, there were opportunities for thought and alternative action which were not taken – a well-established phenomenon in research on adolescent brain development (as seen in Chapter 1).

Whilst juvenile perpetrators acting alone were rare, establishing the true number of offenders involved in an incident presents something of a problem. In Lucy's case, for example, a number of people went to the scene where the victim was being held. Some came and went, stayed, or even left and returned. In fact, many of the juveniles in this research stood trial with other juveniles who were eventually acquitted or given prosecutorial immunity in exchange for providing evidence against the other accused. It is beyond the scope of the present discussion to debate the adequacy of prosecutorial discretion and past/current charge-bargaining practices. But it suffices to say here that I have identified for further investigation a number of areas related to (youth) homicide. For instance, advancing knowledge of the relationship between the victim and the offender should continue to be a core aim of future homicide research. In the present study, distinctions between 'stranger' and 'acquaintance' homicides were not easily made. This creates the potentially treacherous situation that Pampel and Williams describe in *Intimacy and homicide: Compensating for missing data in the Supplementary Homicide Report* as being one in which 'arbitrary classification can produce a distorted image of lethal violence . . . and introduce an unknown degree of bias into any analysis of homicide rate variation' (Pampel & Williams, 2000, p. 677). One way of determining these issues is to firmly decide whether the state of mind required to establish a relationship is victim-centred or offender-centred. That is, establishing *whose* perception and *whose* knowledge influence whether a pre-existing relationship is made out or not. Mutuality and reciprocity in other areas of the relationship also need to be discussed. The following case is illustrative. One participant decided to call a locum doctor service to the house in question for the purpose of robbing the practitioner of drugs and money. The deceased had made a house call there on an earlier occasion and had arrived in a 4WD vehicle that the juvenile had found attractive. The young man intended not just to rob the doctor of drugs and money but also to steal his vehicle. Even this brief account of the crime demonstrates that the violence was not random. However, it does not follow, as a matter of logic or as a matter of the proper exercise of the term contemplated by Wolfgang (1958, p. 205), that someone fulfilling an essential community function would consider every person they fleetingly assist as an 'acquaintance'. Decker (1993, p. 593) has similarly told of the ineffectiveness of using 'personal recognition of the suspect by the victim' (Kapardis, 1990, p. 242; see also Loftin, Kindley, Norris, & Wiersema, 1987; Mouzos, 2002) as a means to distinguish between acquaintance and stranger homicides:

> The acquaintance category may be closest to that of strangers in the attempt to understand homicides. Many acquaintances themselves may have misjudged the nature of the relationship between themselves and the assailant: victims may perceive a degree of insularity in the relationship, a perception not shared by the suspect. Such non-reciprocal relationships may be found most often in the friend or acquaintance category.
>
> (Decker, 1993, p. 593)

The second thing that stands out is the similarity in the lifestyles being led, at the time of the homicides, by all those who were present (often including victims themselves). To this end, several authors have proposed 'that homicide victims and homicide offenders are "chips off the same block" and share many of the same offense characteristics and earlier risk factors' (Loeber & Farrington, 2011, p. 163). Unsurprisingly, the majority of juvenile lifers in my research grew up in suburbs/towns 'known disproportionately to 'feed' the work of police, courts and prisons' (Halsey & Deegan, 2015, p. 212). While there were a few instances where participants enjoyed happy childhoods devoid of abuse and/or exposure to drug use and crime, the themes of dislocation, rejection, neglect, racism, and other markers of extreme community disorganization were recurring. In fact, the archetypal example of unresolved trauma – 'the sense of being born poor, of being beaten as a child, of not having a father-figure, of knowing, essentially, only milieus of violence and dysfunction' (Halsey & Deegan, 2015, p. 126) – was the landmark in their changing attitudes, leading participants to become mistrustful, frustrated, hot-headed, and angry during everyday interactions with people. Some were victims of horrendous bullying and ridicule that continued throughout their school life. What I am talking about is something a child actually experiences. They actually see it. They actually hear it, smell it, taste it, whatever. A set of impressions comes to them which, under the right circumstances, provokes an aggressive response – even before the individual is subject to any taunting or humiliating abuse. Added to this emotional background noise were anecdotes from others about their own violent acts, a mode of violent coaching Athens

(1992) and others call 'vain glorification'. The predictability of these narratives is also noted by Athens (1992, p. 48), who summarizes the script as follows: 'a "good" person becomes entangled in a physical altercation with an "evil" person; then the good person subjects the evil one to a decisive and humiliating, but well-deserved, defeat'. Against such a backdrop, the concept that a young person might think that they have to carry a weapon with them for self-protection – however frightening and inappropriate – was seen to arise. How certain of the participants happened to have a loaded firearm in their possession remains a particularly worrying aspect of their crimes. It allows questions to be asked of how different the situation could have been if these young men had not owned or had access to guns or taken matters into their own hands.

Instead of connecting children to a stable and safe community – a kind of social safety net – most of the juveniles in my research attended numerous schools. They left one school, went to another school, went to another school, went to another school and eventually dropped out. By and large, these were classrooms where aggressive behaviour and low academic proficiency were the norm: 'I had a few friends . . . guys who kind of had the same mindset and the same anger problems, yeah, so we kind of got along pretty well' (Will). In this light, many had 'developed a track record of negative behavior that conventional . . . programs [could not] contain or reverse' (Garbarino, 2000, p. 209). In these instances, attempts to foster a positive learning environment often devolved into classrooms with high levels of staff burnout and 'the harsh use of reprimands . . . related to the educator's emotional exhaustion' (O'Brennan, Bradshaw, & Furlong, 2014, p. 127). As Aaron commented:

> [The] teacher used to say, 'You won't amount to shit in life' 'cause I didn't do the work [and] I argued with him. He didn't understand I had fucking mental problems. I just didn't want to do school and . . . he was sitting there . . . like always running me down and shit.
>
> (Aaron)

Given the kinds of stories related by participants during interview, creating a trauma-informed school climate was an undertaking entirely lost on the educational system – that you can't just shorten a school day and expect a (troubled) young person to turn up ready to re-engage academically, socially, emotionally. Jake said as much in his first interview:

> There was a group of us at my school put on a slow program like flexi [i.e., alternative] classes and that to make it a bit easier . . . just to make the days a bit shorter for us . . . [but] I still didn't end up going to that really.
>
> (Jake)

Generally speaking, the day of the murder was often very similar to many other days of participants' lives, where they had been drinking alcohol, smoking cannabis, and/or taking other drugs with friends or similarly situated peers. Recall that several had been supported to live independently by various non-government organizations that appeared only to hasten their emerging criminal proclivities:

> [Lucy was] set adrift in a world where she had to rely on people like her co-offenders with no way of getting herself out. . . . [They] weren't going to look out for her in the way that we would have as her parents – the system who's hiding her – and how am I going to know if she gets in trouble? And sure enough, the police rang and yeah, *she's in trouble*.
>
> (Vanessa, mother)

Notwithstanding that, the majority of the participants (63%) had no prior criminal convictions *whatsoever* or had very little in the way of relevant criminal history (10%). To this extent, previous convictions remain a very weak predictor of future homicide offending. However, this has to be balanced against the fact that the homicides perpetrated by many of the participants did not represent the first time that juveniles had engaged in the types of behaviour that ultimately led to the deaths of the victims. There can be no doubt that several juveniles had engaged in serious and premeditated criminal behaviour before committing murder:

> Jake was no angel by that stage. He was selling – doing whatnot – and I was fully aware of that and I don't know if that's good or bad but as a mum, how do you draw the line? I remember he used to have those wads of money. *God, I wish I had that money*. . . . Then all of a sudden someone introduced him to Ice and then that's when he really went downhill.
>
> (Desiree, mother)

The tendency in these cases would be to think about parental responsibility in relation to children who exhibit antisocial behaviour and become involved in crime. If one subscribes fully to the stereotypical image of the murderer, one envisions him (or her) as a reclusive social misfit with a long history of setting fires, bedwetting, and mistreating animals. The perceived failure of relatives – particularly mothers – to respond to red flags at critical moments (Lickel, Schmader, & Hamilton, 2003; Melendez, Lichtenstein, & Dolliver, 2016) remains an issue of great significance within public discourse and debate when crimes like these occur. However, the narratives presented in this book indicate that self-laceration regarding what they did, did not do, or wished to have done in the lead-up to the crime is perhaps the most toxic and paralysing form of emotional abuse murderers' parents will confront. This, to be sure, entails that 'established social ritual and practice such as exist to help one cope with illness or death are not available for coping with the experience of one's child being accused of murder' (Macleod, 1982, p. 199). Lionel Dahmer, father of infamous American serial killer Jeffrey, provides a striking case in point. He has spoken extensively about coming to the gradual realization that 'following some unknowable process, his child had crossed the line that divides the human from the monstrous' (1994, p. 11). Looking back, Dahmer can see early warning signs in his son and – having regard to a wide range of problematic behaviours – takes upon himself much of the guilt for the horrors that eventually occurred.

> Now, many months after Jeff's trial and our ordeal, I remain a man in constant rumination, often tortured in my soul by the deeds of my offspring. I find I remain in the grip of a great unknowing, both in terms of Jeff himself, and my effect on him as a father, by omissions and commissions. Fatherhood remains, at last, a great enigma, and when I contemplate one day that my other son may one day become a father, I can only say to him, as I must to every father after me, 'Take care, take care, take care."
>
> (Dahmer, 1994, pp. 254–255)

While there is good evidence for the censure of some parents, I do not generally believe blaming them to be justified – or particularly helpful – when children kill. Let us remember that parents are people. They are not saints. Parents are human beings who make mistakes in bringing up their children as they do in other ways. One writer summed up my general feeling here:

> Lionel is haunted by the idea that had he been a better father, he might have averted Jeffrey's descent into evil. Yes, but. Maybe. The world is full of lousy dads, messed-up sons and sad, broken families. That is no sure-fire recipe for a serial killer.
>
> ('The man who sired a monster', 1994)

Having said as much, it would be absolutely remiss not to focus 'on making the social environment around [disadvantaged youth] – family, school, and community – more competent in meeting their special needs' (Garbarino, 2000, p. 238). My argument has been that young people will find a way to value themselves in the face of a socially unequal world in which their experience of care – being cared for and being given the opportunity to care for others – has been abusive, neglectful, indifferent, and/or inconsistent. In such circumstance, and in line with Agnew's (1992) general strain theory, it is little wonder that the young people in this book came to focus primarily on their own needs and valued these needs more highly than the needs of others around them. As Pras rhymed in the platinum hit song 'Ghetto Supastar (That Is What You Are)' (1998, Interscope), 'some got, hopes and dreams, we got, ways and means'. It is true, of course, that

> those who embrace [such music] as emblematic of [their] 'ghetto' reality have not only been desensitized to the faux violence and sexual objectification in hip-hop, but also, even more alarmingly, desensitized to the violence, injustice, and exploitation that mark the lives of so many of the genre's core constituency.
>
> (Neal, 2013, pp. 121–122)

As discussed in a previous chapter, 'rites of passage for teenage males in poor communities relate closely to the enculturation of "ghetto specific manhood roles", namely the tough guy, the hustler, and the player' (Warley, 2011, p. 137). This needs to change.

In past work, I have discussed in detail the need to 'invest as heavily as possible in the services and infrastructure known to enhance social inclusion and personal opportunity' (Halsey & Deegan, 2015, p. 212) as a means to address youth offending. I do not discount family-systems therapy as a means to draw young people and their significant others closer together while assisting them to develop satisfying relationships with other people. What I do discount are measures to assign offenders' families with 'responsibility for increasing the effectiveness of the criminal justice system' (Light & Campbell, 2006, p. 298) by positioning them as de facto treatment professionals, police, gaolers, and the like. Desiree, speaking in the context of trying to save her son from a raging addiction to crystal methamphetamine, aptly articulated the key problem with using 'significant others (and/or the family 'unit' more generally) . . . as proxies for chronically under-funded rehabilitation programmes' (Halsey & Deegan, 2014, p. 2). As is evident from the following excerpt, her son Jake had developed two distinct strategies that he employed to have his needs met, one of which was to present with charm and the other was to resort to tactics of violence and intimidation:

> Before the actual incident happened, [he'd] come around here, demanding to come in. His little ploy was, 'Oh, I just want to come in, grab a shower and I'll be gone'. That was his ploy: that Dad would let him in and . . . that's when he'd blow up 'cause he wanted money. . . . He was heavily into the Ice and he was desperate. Weighed about 40 odd kilos . . . and yeah, he smashed a window and smashed my wardrobe and so that was that. . . . [Another time] he just wanted money too so he took a laptop computer and when we wouldn't give it, he just chucked it onto the floor in one of his mad, mad, psychotic frenzies. . . . You hear a lot about domestic violence and women getting hurt but you don't often hear of domestic violence involving your children. And we went through a lot of shit. *A lot of shit.*
>
> (Desiree, mother)

The third thing that stands out is the counterproductive nature of prolonged punishment, particularly for young people (Ghandnoosh, 2017). I am especially concerned with the recent introduction of a 20-year mandatory minimum sentence, marking a 'transition from leniency to severity' (Griffin, 2018, p. 4) in relation to juveniles convicted of murder in South Australia. Realistically, while rejecting the deterrent value of harsh punishments, there is no running away from the fact that by committing such dreadful crimes, several of my participants have deprived themselves of the right to live in the outside community for a lengthy period of time. But as I have identified previously, 'the really challenging work arises in the context of trying to make sense of what happens to the young [lifers] as they age out their teens through their twenties [and beyond]' (Halsey & Deegan, 2015, p. 180) in prison. In this, a politically driven law-and-order model can claim no great success. Is it fair (and accurate) to condemn Eddie as a serious violent offender? At age 15, he threw a punch after finding himself in the midst of a violent affray. Is it fair to subject him to the same (life-long) consequences as Aaron? And what of Aaron? Will the label of 'dangerousness' successfully applied to him at the age of 14 become 'a way of stimulating, suggesting, emphasizing, and evoking the very traits that are complained of' (Tannenbaum, 1938, p. 19)? Back in 1938, Tannenbaum argued that 'the dramatization of the "evil" which separates the child out of his group for specialized treatment plays a greater role in making the criminal than perhaps any other experience' (p. 19). In more recent times, Griffin (2018, p. 152) has noted the way in which

> [j]ustifying the detention of a life sentence prisoner on the grounds of risk and public protection can belie the true purpose of detention: exclusion based on public disapprobation for the offence and the perception of dangerousness, rather than the reality presented in terms of likely recidivism.

It would be wrong to say that we as a community should not feel appalled and frightened by the offending behaviour of the young people in this book: behaviour that clearly has no place in society. The conduct of the offenders raises many questions and, indeed, many participants have asked some of these questions of themselves. To this extent, I fully agree with Kelly and Totten's (2002) observations regarding young people who have killed:

> Custody is, in part, an opportunity to pause and consider what they had done, where they had been, and where they would go in the future. Generally, they viewed incarceration as putting a brake on their out-of-control lives.
>
> (p. 249)

But – and harking back to my point about the politicization of the sentencing process – there is a significant difference between getting tough on young people who commit serious crimes (and actually rehabilitating them) and/or improving community safety. Because when I think of my participants, people such as Will and Sonny, I know that their potential status as non-violent and useful members of society is directly at odds with their placement, from the ages of 14 and 15, respectively, in prison environments where they remain, well into their 20s and 30s. Public opinion is a powerful factor in our lives and in our thinking. But it has consistently overemphasized the annual homicide rate and the proportion of juvenile crime that involves violence, while underestimating the severity of sentencing practices and the severity of prison life (Gelb, 2006, p. 13). To this, I would add that research routinely demonstrates 'that it is those who have the lowest levels of knowledge who also hold the most punitive views' (Gelb, 2006, p. 14). In this light, Contreras (2013, p. 237) has warned at length about the broader societal implications of 'doing something' – *or being seen to 'do something'* – in response to public outcry:

> The tragedy of ethnographic research is that policy makers rarely use it to shape their work. The problem is that policy makers are politically embedded,

> often matching their proposals with the current political and public mood. And more often than not, political or public opinion is not based on empirical research, but based on anger, fear, and frustration that have been stirred up for political ends.
>
> (Contreras, 2013, p. 237)

The sentencing remarks of the juveniles in my study provide some support for the view that the road to rehabilitation might be a long one. It is a sad paradox that the (mandatory) penalty of 'life' *guarantees* it will be. Contrary to rehabilitative ideals, the extent to which empathy, passivity, and social responsibility are fundamentally at odds with various custodial climates proved a real issue for lifers in my study:

> The last violence I had on my [prison] record I think was in 1996 – not that I ever went looking for trouble, but if you jumped on my toes, I'd defend myself. . . . Since then I've been turning the other cheek and believe me, that's a very hard thing to do in a place like this because other people see it and they want to go you, you know? It's a weakness.
>
> (Derek)

Looking more closely at the factors that contributed to the sense of hopelessness showed that a significant factor was the participants' difficulties understanding how a crushing sentence assisted them to eventually rejoin society in a mainstream way. Remember that Floyd (Chapter 6) was anxious to participate in programmes, access education, and maintain familial connections as a means to develop as a person and to offset the negative effects of incarceration. As long as imprisonment continues without hope for the future, he argued, it cannot help but to counteract any positive effects of various intervention strategies or natural development processes:

> I'm not saying that they owe me anything or I deserve this or I deserve that. Nah, I'm not saying that. I'm saying there's never been a pattern of anything good from these people [i.e., in authority]. So any time they've been involved in a conversation or involved in sitting on or determining how they're going to shape your life, they've never assisted it, they've never helped. They've only detrimented it more – worse, by separating you from your family, by making sure you're not getting visits, by making sure you're not getting the suitable courses you need to do, you know what I mean? Whether it's intentional or whether it's not intentional, that's not my point. But I'm saying, the way the system is, it doesn't help the young kid that's come in for a life-lagging. It doesn't help them. It doesn't better them unless they've got a real strong mind, unless they've got a real strong support network of family, unless they've got that love there, unless they have that determination, they've got that fortitude to keep battling on, and overcoming hurdles. Without that, if they don't have them elements, what have they got? They're going

> to be coming into the system, they don't know what methadone and Bupe[1] and other drugs were, they've never had it, and now they're going to have a full-blown habit and gaol's broken them. Or they're going to lose their mind and have a mental [breakdown]. And now they're damaged. What good are they in society? What can they contribute? What can they do for their own family? Or what can they do for themselves? What can they do for their neighbourhood?
>
> (Floyd)

As seen in Chapter 6, many young lifers present as biding their time in regard to their 'rehabilitation', as their current circumstances hamper their ability to access appropriate courses, educational facilities, or otherwise make headway in terms of planning a life outside of prison. Of course, while 'it is the length of time served in prison that captures the interest of most observers' (Griffin, 2018, pp. 223–224), Eddie's experiences remind us that a life sentence does not end at the prison gate. In no small way, learning to be an employee, a partner, a citizen, balanced against the demands of his parole, 'contributed to [Eddie's] extreme sense of feeling like an 'outsider' when he so very much wanted to be 'normal' (Halsey & Deegan, 2015, p. 172). Failures on parole, of which there were many, were seen as 'rooted in a complex mixture of individual, institutional, and community factors' (Kelly & Totten, 2002, p. 250). Writing in 2006, criminologist Mark Halsey (p. 362) put it this way:

> In no small way, young [people] subject to [significant] periods of incarceration carry this transgressional sense of self with them because custody confirms – in the most visceral of ways – that they *are* offenders first and foremost and only secondarily (and incidentally) people dealt a rough hand or start to life, or who made bad 'choices' at 'critical' moments, or who could indeed 'make good' given half a chance (given the kinds of support desired by each young person).

Serious young offenders do, undoubtedly, undergo processes of maturation and transformation that enable them to eventually rejoin society as valued workers, partners, parents, and the like. Eddie and (to some extent) Toby and James fall into this category. Others may not achieve this transformation. For Derek and Cody, being sentenced to life was like being Humpty Dumpty: they were never really able to put the pieces back together again. Only a longitudinal follow-up with these men will determine whether this is the end, or just the start, of the conversation. It was put to me, during my last interview with Derek, that the developmental path toward positive change might sometimes 'follow a zig-zag path . . . going from noncrime to crime to noncrime again' (Glaser, 1964, p. 85). Here, Garbarino's (2000) remarks regarding the management and guidance of violent boys speak to the redemptive value of equipping prisoners with hope for their futures. As he observed with young lifers he met in Pennsylvania, 'sometimes it had taken a decade of resistance and false starts to find that gateway [to transformation] and to gather up the courage to walk through it' (p. 238). Of my participants who were yet to achieve such redemptive transformation, all were firmly of the belief that they would work their way towards rehabilitation '*in spite* of prison, not because of it' (Unkovic & Albini, 1969, p. 160). In short, no one believed that the adult prison system remotely resembled a respectful and supportive family environment or put into effect the objects of the *Young Offenders Act*, dedicated towards the development and nurture of young people who infringe against the criminal law. Perhaps on this last count, I should leave the final word to Derek:

> It's education. It's work. It's a combination of a lot of things. People have to put their time into [prisoners] and if they're serious about doing things, well, you know, you've really got to . . . not give up the first time around. And just because a 20-minute course doesn't work, don't turn around, you know, and say to a person, well he's a waste of fucking space . . . because he's just had 15 years of having the shit kicked out of him.
>
> (Derek)

Note

1 Buprenorphine, aka 'Bupe', 'Subutex', or 'Suboxone' is a prescription opioid that is used to treat heroin and methadone dependence. Inexpensive, widely available, and relatively easy for prisoners to divert, it is the drug of choice in many Australian gaols.

References

Agnew, R. (1992). Foundation for a general strain theory of crime and delinquency. *Criminology, 30*(1), 47–88. DOI:10.1111/j.1745-9125.1992.tb01093.x

Athens, L. H. (1992). *The creation of dangerous violent criminals*. Champaign, IL: University of Illinois Press.

Bennett, T., & Brookman, F. (2008). Violent street crime: Making sense of seemingly senseless acts. *International Review of Law Computers and Technology, 22*(1–2), 171–180. DOI:10.1080/13600860801925128

Contreras, R. (2013). *The stickup kids: Race, drugs, violence, and the American dream.* Berkeley, CA: University of California Press.

Dahmer, L. (1994). *A father's story*. London: Warner Books.

Decker, S. H. (1993). Exploring victim-offender relationships in homicide: The role of individual and event characteristics. *Justice Quarterly, 10*(4), 585–612. DOI:10.1080/07418829300092031

Garbarino, J. (2000). *Lost boys: Why our sons turn violent and how we can save them.* New York: Anchor Books.

Gelb, K. (2006). *Myths and misconceptions: Public opinion versus public judgment about sentencing.* Sentencing Advisory Council, Melbourne Victoria Australia. Retrieved from https://www.sentencingcouncil.vic.gov.au/sites/default/files/2019-08/Myths_and_Misconceptions_Public_Opinion_versus_Public_Judgment_about_Sentencing.pdf

Ghandnoosh, N. (2017). *Delaying a second chance: The declining prospects for parole on life sentences.* Washington, DC: The Sentencing Project. Retrieved from www.

sentencingproject.org/publications/delaying-second-chance-declining-prospects-parole-life-sentences/

Glaser, D. (1964). *The effectiveness of a prison and parole system*. Indianapolis: Bobbs-Merrill.

Griffin, D. (2018). *Killing time: Life imprisonment and parole in Ireland*. Cham, Switzerland: Palgrave Macmillan.

Griffiths, E., Yule, C., & Gartner, R. (2011). Fighting over trivial things: Explaining the issue of contention in violent altercations. *Criminology, 49*(1), 61–94. DOI:10.1111/j.1745-9125.2010.00218.x

Halsey, M. (2006). Negotiating conditional release: Juvenile narratives of repeat incarceration. *Punishment and Society, 8*(2), 147–181. DOI:10.1177/1462474506062102

Halsey, M., & Deegan, S. (2014). "Picking up the pieces": Female significant others in the lives of young (ex) incarcerated males. *Criminology and Criminal Justice*. Retrieved from http://crj.sagepub.com/content/early/2014/03/12/1748895814526725.ref.html. DOI:10.1177/1748895814526725

Halsey, M., & Deegan, S. (2015). *Young offenders: Crime, prison and struggles for desistance*. UK: Palgrave Macmillan.

Kapardis, A. (1990). Stranger homicide in Victoria, January 1984–December 1989. *Australian and New Zealand Journal of Criminology, 23*(4), 241–258. DOI:10.1177/000486589002300404

Kelly, K., & Totten, M. (2002). *When children kill: A social-psychological study of youth homicide*. Ontario: University of Toronto Press.

Lickel, B., Schmader, T., & Hamilton, D. L. (2003). A case of collective responsibility: Who else was to blame for the Columbine High School shootings? *Personality and Social Psychology Bulletin, 29*, 194–204. DOI:10.1177/0146167202239045

Light, R., & Campbell, B. (2006). Prisoners' families: Still forgotten victims? *Journal of Social Welfare and Family Law, 28*(3), 297–308. DOI:10.1080/09649060601119524

Loeber, R., & Farrington, D. (2011). *Young homicide offenders and victims: Risk factors, prediction, and prevention from childhood*. New York: Springer.

Loftin, C., Kindley, K., Norris, S. L., & Wiersema, B. (1987). An attribute approach to relationships between offenders and victims in homicide. *The Journal of Criminal Law and Criminology, 78*(2), 259–271. DOI:10.2307/1143449

MacLeod, R. J. (1982). A child is charged with homicide. His family responds. *British Journal of Psychiatry, 141*(2), 199–201. Retrieved from www.cambridge.org/core/journals/the-british-journal-of-psychiatry

Melendez, M. S., Lichtenstein, B., & Dolliver, M. J. (2016). Mothers of mass murderers: Exploring public blame for the mothers of school shooters through an application of courtesy stigma to the Columbine and Newtown tragedies. *Deviant Behavior, 37*, 525–536. DOI:10.1080/01639625.2015.1060754

Michel, P. (1998). Ghetto Supastar (that is what you are). On *Ghetto Supastar*. Philadelphia: Ruffhouse Records.

Mouzos, J. (2002). *Homicide in Australia: 2000–2001 National Homicide Monitoring Program (NHMP) annual report*. Research and public policy series No. 40. Retrieved from https://aic.gov.au/publications/rpp/rpp40

Neal, M. A. (2013). *Songs in the key of black life: A rhythm and blues nation*. New York: Routledge.

O'Brennan, L. M., Bradshaw, C. P., & Furlong, M. (2014). Influence of classroom, and school climate on teacher perceptions of student problem behavior. *School Mental Health, 6*, 125–136. DOI:10.1007/s12310-014-9118-8

Pampel, F. C., & Williams, K. R. (2000). Intimacy and homicide: Compensating for missing data in the SHR. *Criminology*, *39*(2), 661–680. DOI:10.1111/j.1745-9125.2000.tb00902.x

Polk, K. (1994). *When men kill: Scenarios of masculine violence*. New York: Cambridge University Press.

Statutes Amendment (Youths Sentenced as Adults) Act 2017 (SA) (Austl.). (2017). Retrieved from https://www.legislation.sa.gov.au/LZ/V/A/2017/STATUTES%20AMENDMENT%20(YOUTHS%20SENTENCED%20AS%20ADULTS)%20ACT%202017_67/2017.67.UN.PDF

Tannenbaum, F. (1938). *Crime and the community*. New York: Columbia University Press.

Unkovic, C. M., & Albini, J. L. (1969). The lifer speaks for himself: An analysis of the assumed homogeneity of life-termers. *Crime and Delinquency*, *15*(1), 156–161. DOI:10.1177/001112876901500114

Warley, R. M. (2011). *Juvenile homicide: Fatal assault or lethal assault*? El Paso, TX: LFB Scholarly.

Wolfgang, M. E. (1958). *Patterns in criminal homicide*. New York, NY: John Wiley and Sons Inc.

Young Offenders Act 1993 (SA) (Austl.). Retrieved from www.legislation.sa.gov.au/LZ/C/A/YOUNG%20OFFENDERS%20ACT%201993/CURRENT/1993.57.AUTH.PDF

Index

For Product Safety Concerns and Information please contact our EU
representative GPSR@taylorandfrancis.com
Taylor & Francis Verlag GmbH, Kaufingerstraße 24, 80331 München, Germany

www.ingramcontent.com/pod-product-compliance
Lightning Source LLC
LaVergne TN
LVHW021126300926
849160LV00010B/886
* 9 7 8 0 3 6 7 6 7 7 0 2 2 *